The Common Agricultural Policy of the European Community

The Common Agricultural Policy of the European Community has generated an impressive amount of literature over the past twenty years or so. But despite the intense interest which it has aroused throughout its stormy life the actual operation of the CAP seems to remain one of the great mysteries of our day. It is not uncommon to find people holding forth on the real or imaginary iniquities of the policy without having the faintest idea of how it works. Why should this be so, since the policy is no secret? The explanation seems to be that despite the impressive literature on the subject it is actually very difficult to find a book which explains how the policy works, how it is administered, what aspects of agriculture it covers, and so forth. Too much of what is available has been written by those in the know for each other, using the special vocabulary that goes with the policy but providing little or no explanation of its meaning. Most people just do not know where to begin. It is to help them over the first hurdle in their search that this book has been written.

It should prove to be invaluable to academics and students in agriculture, economics, geography and political science; to businessmen in the agricultural sector and to farmers. Because the book is not biased towards the experience of any one country it should be useful to readers in every Member State of the existing Community; to those in countries currently negotiating to join, and to those in countries which trade with the Community and which are therefore affected by the operation of its agricultural policy.

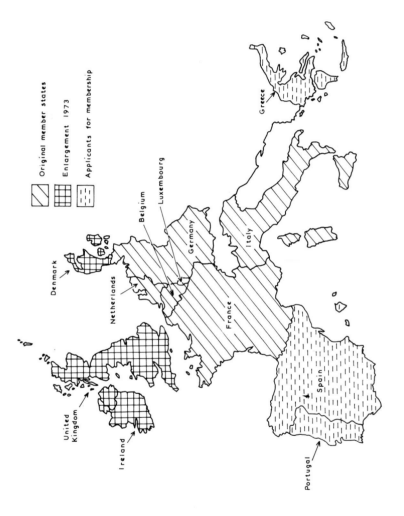

Original member states

Enlargement 1973

Applicants for membership

United Kingdom

Ireland

Denmark

Netherlands

Belgium

Luxembourg

Germany

France

Italy

Greece

Spain

Portugal

The Common Agricultural Policy of the European Community

Its institutional and administrative organisation

Rosemary Fennell
Institute of Agricultural Economics,
University of Oxford

GRANADA
London Toronto Sydney NewYork

ALLANHELD, OSMUN
Montclair

Granada Publishing Limited–Technical Books Division
Frogmore, St Albans, Herts AL2 2NF
and
3 Upper James Street, London W1R 4BP
117 York Street, Sydney, NSW 2000, Australia
100 Skyway Avenue, Rexdale, Ontario M9W 3A6, Canada
PO Box 84165, Greenside, 2034 Johannesburg, South Africa
CML Centre, Queen & Wyndham Streets, Auckland 1, New Zealand

ISBN 0 246 11197 6

First published in Great Britain by Granada Publishing Limited 1979

British Library Cataloguing in Publication Data
Fennell, Rosemary
The Common Agricultural Policy of the
European Community.
1. Agriculture – Economic aspects –
European Community countries
I. Title
338.1'81   HD1920.5.Z8   79-40915
ISBN 0 246 11197 6

Printed and bound in Great Britain by
William Clowes (Beccles) Limited, Beccles and London

Granada®
Granada Publishing®

Published in U.S.A. by
Allanheld, Osmun,
Montclair

Library of Congress Cataloguing in Publication Data
Fennell, Rosemary
The Common Agricultural Policy of the
European Community.
Includes index.
1. Agriculture and state – European
Economic Community countries
I. Title
HD1920.5.Z8   1979   382'.41'094
ISBN 0 916672 29 8

Contents

Preface

The Common Agricultural Policy (CAP) of the European Community
has generated an impressive amount of literature over the past twenty
years or so. But despite the intense interest which it has aroused
throughout its stormy life, the actual operation of the CAP seems to
remain one of the great mysteries of our day. It is not uncommon to find
people holding forth on the real or imaginary iniquities of the policy
without having the faintest idea of how it works.

Why should this be so; after all the policy is no secret? The explanation seems to be that despite the impressive literature on the subject, it is actually very difficult to find a book which explains how the
policy works, how it is administered, what aspects of agriculture it
covers, and so forth. Most people just do not know where to begin. It is
to help them over the first hurdle in their search that this book has been
written.

Perhaps I am particularly acutely aware of the existence of this void
in the literature because I lecture to students on various aspects of the
CAP and give talks to farmers' groups from time to time. Frequently, I
am asked to recommend an introductory book which will explain the
rudiments of the policy. When this happens I am faced with something
of a dilemma.

The explanatory material which does exist, although excellent in its
own way, is either very brief or deals with certain aspects of the policy
only, or at the other extreme is too detailed for any other than the
specialist. Unfortunately, too, much of what is available has been
written by the knowledgeable for the knowledgeable, using the special
vocabulary that goes with the policy but providing little or no explanation of its meaning.

Obviously in a work of this kind the aim must be to try to be comprehensive while recognising that it is impossible to be exhaustive. The
book is intended to be no more than a base on which greater and more
detailed knowledge can be built. In order to be as much use to as

many readers as possible–both within the Community and outside–I have deliberately refrained from giving the book a bias in favour of any particular country and its experience in operating the CAP. The only exception to this rule occurs in chapter 4 where, for the sake of convenience, I have relied rather heavily on British experience.

In writing any work on a living, evolving topic, the writer is faced with the problem of the material dating very rapidly. For that reason this book is not the place to seek information on institutional price levels or much physical data about Community agriculture. Fortunately, although minor changes are taking place all the time in the market and price regimes, and on the structural side, major changes are much less frequent. In terms of their framework, the regimes show a marked resilience, and if one grasps the essentials of the framework, then it is relatively easy to superimpose subsequent modifications.

Although the book is fundamentally about the CAP, it is impossible to explain it in a vacuum and therefore it seems important to set the policy in its Community context. The book starts with a brief scene-painting chapter outlining the state of agriculture in Western Europe leading up to the founding of the Economic Community, the reasons why a common agricultural policy was created and an analysis of the principles on which the policy was built.

The second and third chapters deal with the mechanics of administering the policy–the functions of each of the main Institutions of the Community and their relationship one with another–and the process by which legislation is passed. Chapter 4 complements these two chapters by describing the main national institutions which have links in some way with the organisation and implementation of the CAP.

Chapters 5 and 6 are concerned with money matters. They describe the financing of the annual budget of the Community and deal with the vexed and complicated topic of 'Green Money', i.e. the accounting device used in the setting of agricultural prices.

The next four chapters form a unit and comprise an analysis of the organisation of the market and price system which lies at the heart of the CAP. Sometimes people are surprised to find how many systems of support are in use under the policy; these and their implications are described in chapter 7 which acts as an introduction to chapters 8 to 10 in which the particular systems used for each commodity are outlined.

Chapters 11 and 12 move on to the much neglected social and structural measures under the CAP, while chapter 13 discusses the problems which may arise as a result of enlarging the Community further during the 1980s.

A few words should be said about the treatment of fisheries in this book. Fish are one of the commodities which come under the CAP, and the price and market regime and the structural measures for this sector are outlined. But there is no discussion of the much wider issues of fisheries policy which have come up in recent years and which are bound, when resolved, to have important implications for fish production and trade.

No work of this kind is possible without the help and advice of many people although, alas, in the usual manner I alone must remain responsible for the final outcome. I should like first of all to express my appreciation of the help which I received from Michael Tracy, of the Council of Ministers Secretariat. He commented on over half the chapters in the book, a service which I found particularly useful. I should also like to single out Marilyn Chamberlain, of the European Community's London office, who so often came to my rescue when I was seeking material, and who was invariably cheerful and helpful. Next my thanks must go to Martyn Ibbotson who made a very simple suggestion on the handling of the commodities, which I think has improved the presentation considerably.

So many people helped me with individual chapters or sections that I should like to acknowledge the assistance they gave chapter by chapter: Chapter 4: Bob Attwell, Ann Davison, Jean Edge, Michael Strauss, Rhodri Walters and David Williamson;
Chapter 5: Valerie Williams and Beth Woods;
Chapter 6: Howard Fearns and Peter Nash;
Chapter 8: Ray Anderson, Tony Elston, Hugh MacKinnon, Peter Reed, Bill Seccombe and Jim Wildgoose;
Chapter 9: Alison Blackburn, Jean Blake, Colin Bodrell, Leslie Mitchell, Jim Springate and John Vaughan;
Chapter 10: Peter Boyling, Ken Buckley, Peter Gething, Frank Parker and Geraldine Walsh;
Chapters 11 and 12: Frank Harrison;
Chapter 13: Cathal Cavanagh and Michael Ring.

I should not like to leave this list of people without recording my thanks to their many colleagues who also helped but who were unknown to me.

Finally, I come to the staff of the Institute of Agricultural Economics. My grateful thanks go to Ken Clark who prepared the diagrams, to Shirley Brown the Librarian, to Margaret Machin who typed much of the draft material, and to Hilda Riggs who typed the remainder and who gallantly came out of retirement to type the fair copy. My thanks also go to the remaining secretaries–Maureen Cousin, Freda Timms and Louise White–to whom fell the task of handling the voluminous correspondence which the writing of this book entailed.

To all these kind and helpful people my many thanks.

The citation of Community legislation

Because of the importance of Community legislation, some explanation should be given at this stage of the manner in which reference is made throughout the text to Regulations, Decisions and Directives.

Each Regulation/Decision/Directive has an official number and it is common practice to refer to this number rather than to the actual title of the piece of legislation concerned. Thus Regulation 17/64/EEC which is 'on the conditions for granting aid from the European Agricultural Guidance and Guarantee Fund' is usually referred to simply as Reg. 17/64. Throughout the text the colloquial usage is the more usual. The only exception to this occurs on the first occasion on which reference is made to the particular piece of legislation when it is given its correct title. On this occasion also it is followed by a reference indicating where it can be located.

In the example given above, we first meet Reg. 17/64 in chapter 5 where it is given its full title and is followed by (Sp. OJ 1963–1964). This indicates that the text can be found in the Special Edition of the *Official Journal* relating to 1963–1964. The significance of the Special Edition is that when the Community was enlarged in 1973 all earlier Regulations, Decisions and Directives *which were still operative* were gathered together in a series of reference volumes. Of course, it is still possible to go back to the original *Official Journal* source but it must be remembered that prior to 1973 no official English language texts existed.

All Regulations/Decisions/Directives passed subsequent to the 1973 Enlargement are referred to on first acquaintance with their full title followed by their *Official Journal* number and date thus: Directive 75/268/EEC *on mountain and hill farming in certain less-favoured areas* (OJ L128, 19 May 1975). On all subsequent occasions this Directive is simply referred to as Directive 75/268.

The only other point to note is that for Directives and Decisions the year of enactment is always the first number of the pair, whereas for Regulations the year comes second. The legislative measures cited above illustrate this point.

CHAPTER 1

Background and aims of the CAP

Because the Common Agricultural Policy (CAP) looms so large on the European Community scene, we are apt to forget how modest is the size of the agricultural sector today in terms of employment and its contribution to gross domestic product (GDP). For instance, in 1976 in the original six Member States—Belgium, Federal Republic of Germany, France, Italy, Luxembourg and the Netherlands—agriculture, forestry and fishing accounted for 10 per cent of total employment and probably about 5 per cent of GDP at factor cost (see table 1). These percentages contrast sharply with the late 1950s when, in the same six original Member States, agriculture, forestry and fishing represented over 20 per cent of the work force and contributed about 11 per cent of GDP. The addition of the three new Member States—Denmark, Ireland and the United Kingdom—has not materially affected the position except to

TABLE 1
Employment and GDP arising in the agricultural sector

Member States	Employment in agriculture, forestry and fishing				GDP at factor cost in agriculture, etc. as % of total GDP	
	Number '000		% of total employment			
	1959	1976	1959	1976	1959	1976
Belgium	423	128	12[a]	3	7	3
France	5213	2263	27[b]	11	12[c]	5[d]
Germany (FR)	3788	1714	15	7	8	3
Italy	6370	2929	30	15	19	9
Luxembourg	35	9	26[a]	6	9	4[e]
Netherlands	470	295	11	6	10	5
Community of Six	[16,000]	7338	[24]	10	[11]	[5]
Denmark	—	223	—	9	—	8
Ireland	—	243	—	24	—	18[f]
United Kingdom	—	660	—	3	—	3
Community of Nine	—	8464	—	8	—	[5]

Notes: (a) 1947; (b) 1954; (c) 1956; (d) at current market prices; (e) 1975; (f) 1972. Figures in brackets are rough estimates.

Source: [65 and 49]

reduce still further the importance of agriculture as a source of employment.

Given the relative importance of the agricultural sector in the 1950s, especially in terms of employment, it is hardly surprising that when plans were being drawn up with the aim of creating an economic union, the interests and needs of agriculture had to be considered. But more than that: the circumstances of the farming industry at the time were such that careful thought had to be given to its welfare. The rural exodus of labour was well under way; incomes were low; governmental policies were many and sometimes contradictory; in short, agriculture was a problem sector.

To understand what was wrong we must try to visualise the situation which had emerged over the previous couple of decades. In the early part of the century–certainly until the Depression of the 1930s–protection at the frontier and internal support measures for farming were limited both in scope and level. The 1930s presented the unfortunate coincidence of a considerable expansion in production with a shrinking of effective demand, as a result of which world market prices for food fell to very low levels. To try to counteract the worst effects of the slump West European governments, along with many others, began to strengthen the protection which they afforded to their farmers.

An ECE/FAO study [46] describes the 1930s thus: 'In the inter-war period, when the supply of agricultural products in the world tended to outrun demand and world market prices for food fell very low in terms of industrial manufactures, the protection of agriculture was strengthened and expanded in Western European countries as a means of shielding their domestic producers against the worst effects of the depression. In so doing, they not only reduced their dependence on the outside world, but also restricted inter-country specialisation within Europe.'

Usually this protection took the form of high tariffs and quantitative restrictions on imports, which helped to reserve the bulk of the home market for domestic producers. These frontier measures were combined with internal price supports and subsidies of various kinds either on farm inputs or at consumer level.

The onset of World War II brought a further extension of state intervention in farming, moving it from mere protection to much more positive measures of direct management, with the introduction of comprehensive systems of price controls and guarantees. This trend was continued in the immediate post-war period, partly as a result of the habits developed during the war and partly due to the continuing difficulties faced by farmers, not least of which was a series of poor harvests. The main objective of agricultural policy at that time was to ensure adequate supplies of food, but the disruptions suffered by agriculture during the war continued into the subsequent period. Indeed reconstruction in agriculture took much longer than in industry with the result that world demand for agricultural products outstripped supply for a number of years.

However, by the early 1950s things had begun to change with the more widespread application of technology to food production. While it is true that there was technical progress in West European farming during the inter-war period, it was largely limited to a few of the more advanced countries and to small numbers of farmers. The result was that, in general, the findings of scientists were considerably beyond the practical application on the farm. But as Coppock [45] has described: 'In the fifteen years following World War II European agriculture underwent greater changes in methods of production than it had experienced in the preceding century–and the end was not in sight. In a few short years much of Europe's farming was changed from a kind of handicraft to an industrial operation.'

While this technological revolution and its concomitant expansion in food production were getting under way, demand began to weaken somewhat and food prices tended downwards. This situation was exacerbated by the rapid growth of farm output and the build-up of huge stocks in the United States. It is hardly surprising that, in such a climate, international efforts to obtain liberalisation of trade in agricultural products met with little or no success.

Once the immediate post-war years of shortage were past, governments had become less concerned with ensuring higher food output and more concerned with supporting farmers' earnings. One of the main tools used was the limitation of imports and it was this policy which made the liberalisation of trade such an intractable problem. Various efforts were made to combat the trade restrictions, in particular within the framework of the General Agreement on Tariffs and Trade

(GATT), through the Organisation for European Economic Co-operation (OEEC), and in the discussions on the 'Green Pool' i.e. the attempted creation of a common West European market in agricultural products, negotiations on which began in 1951.

Success in these various efforts was restricted. Under GATT, for instance, while some tariffs were reduced, those on other products were actually raised when quantitative restrictions were lifted. The ECE/FAO report quoted above summed up the situation in 1954 as follows: 'The rigidity in the pattern of production and in the structure of costs in Western European agriculture, with its many small and poor producers, is one of the main hindrances to freer trade in agricultural products. Most Governments fear that to remove quantitative restrictions and to reduce tariffs on imports would depress farmers' incomes without inducing an increase in their productivity. Obviously, therefore, any major steps towards freer trade need to go hand-in-hand with internal measures in the importing (and in some cases also in the exporting) countries, aiming at facilitating the necessary adaptations in the production and cost structures.'

Herein lay the crucial problem: how to assist farmers to adapt to new economic circumstances at home and abroad without undue disruption. The structural circumstances were not favourable, as Coppock put it: 'Western Europe emerged from World War II with an agricultural industry which was fundamentally inefficient. It was under-equipped and overmanned.' The industry was composed of millions of farms which were too small to provide productive employment for a family unless they concentrated on some specialist crop or livestock product. Many farmers produced the bare necessities with only a small surplus for sale.

While Eastern Europe was experimenting with state farms, collectives and producer co-operatives, governments in Western Europe were agreed on the preservation of the family farm as the basis of production. In this connection some attempts were made to improve farm structure, but efforts were concentrated far more on price supports and import controls. The effect, not unnaturally, was for there to be a decline in trade, an increase in self-sufficiency and a curtailment of regional specialisation. But, despite all the government intervention on their behalf, farmers' incomes fell more and more behind those of other sectors. It was within such a context that Mansholt declared [60]: 'It is only in a wider setting than that of national frontiers that a solution can be found for the problems of agriculture.'

The impetus to set up the European Economic Community (EEC) came from the Benelux countries (i.e. Belgium, the Netherlands and Luxembourg) in the mid-1950s. Their proposals, made to their partners in the European Coal and Steel Community (ECSC), were contained in a memorandum dated 20 May 1955 and suggested the convening of an inter-governmental conference to draw-up treaties covering a general common market and action in the field of atomic energy.

This memorandum was discussed at a meeting of the ECSC foreign ministers held at Messina the following month. It was agreed that preparations should be made for the convening of an inter-governmental conference to prepare the texts of the necessary treaties. The United Kingdom was invited to participate in the preparatory work which it did–albeit reluctantly–for some months. A number of committees were set up to discuss the various issues involved and from their findings a report was drawn up early in 1956 which came to be known as the *Spaak Report*. This document formed the basis on which the treaty to establish the European Economic Community was built.

The Spaak Report [7] contained a chapter devoted to agriculture and its problems. It stated boldly that the creation of a general common market which excluded agriculture was inconceivable. The authors recognised the special circumstances of agriculture: its social structure based on the family farm; the need for stability of supply; the market difficulties stemming from weather conditions and demand inelasticity. Because agriculture had been subject to detailed governmental intervention, it was realised that the mere removal of quotas and tariffs would not be enough to ensure the free circulation of goods. The problems which had justified the regulation of certain markets would not disappear because of the creation of a common market but rather a common solution to these problems would have to be found.

The Spaak Report laid down a number of objectives for the future agricultural policy among which were: the stablisation of markets; security of supply; the maintenance of an adequate income level for normally productive enterprises; and a gradual adjustment of the structure of the industry. The objectives of the CAP as subsequently set out in Article 39 of the Treaty of Rome[1] are a faithful reflection of the aims spelled out in the Spaak Report.

It is clear that to those who conceived the idea of an Economic Community the inclusion of agriculture was an obvious necessity. Firstly, it was a major employer; secondly, there was a great need to improve incomes in the sector; and thirdly, the extent of government interference in agriculture made the goal of a common market particularly difficult to achieve by conventional means. The authors of the Spaak Report recognised that the new policy could not be a mere collation of the divergent policies of the countries concerned. Andrews [3] states that when the CAP was being devised it was necessary to reconcile about 30,000 different rules and regulations relating to agriculture. He goes on to comment: 'It was naïve to assume, as some did, that a few strokes of the pen and the announcement of a few general principles could wipe away the highly protective system built into the economic system of each country over the years. The agricultural sector could not be subjected overnight to the "discipline of international competition".'

There were other reasons as well why agriculture received special attention. The whole concept of the Economic Community is built on four freedoms: the free movement of goods; free movement of workers; freedom to exercise a trade or profession; and the free movement of payments and capital. If agricultural policy had remained in the hands of the individual Member States with all the restrictions, limitations and interventions accumulated over the years, the result would have been to undermine, in part at least, the common policies being pursued in other spheres. As Swann has put it [66]: 'If trade was not free, and national price levels could differ, then countries with low price levels would enjoy a competitive advantage in so far as low food prices give rise to low industrial wages.'

Swann also refers to the other widely held belief as to why agriculture was included within the framework of the Rome Treaty namely, the trade-off between Federal Germany and France. The argument is that for Federal Germany one of the great advantages of the proposed Community was the prospect of free access to the French industrial market. For France, as the largest agricultural producer among the Six, free trade in agricultural products would provide her with greater opportunities in the German market.

It is quite true that in the early 1950s the French decided to expand their exports of farm produce in order to help pay for the importation of industrial raw materials and in the hope of achieving equilibrium in the balance of payments. However, it is interesting to note that Camps maintains [5] that during the run-up to the signing of the Rome Treaty the main debate as far as agriculture was concerned was between France and the Netherlands. 'The principal differences of view were over the extent to which the development of agricultural trade within the Community should be controlled or should be left free, with the Dutch favouring as free a system as possible and the French arguing for specific measures both to guard against disruption of the internal market by imports and to stimulate intra-Community trade.' It was only after the currency realignments of 1957–1961 that agriculture became an issue between France and Federal Germany.

The Treaty of Rome as it applies to agriculture

The Treaty establishing the EEC contains 248 Articles, of which ten apply directly to agriculture (Articles 38–47), but it would be quite wrong to believe that the remainder of the Treaty is irrelevant. The motives underlying the establishment of the Economic Community are set out in the Preamble to the Treaty [67] and the tasks facing the Community are enumerated in Art. 2 as follows: 'To promote ... a harmonious development of economic activities, a continuous and balanced expansion, an increase in stability, an accelerated raising of the standard of living and closer relations between the States belonging to it.'

The means by which these tasks are to be achieved are outlined in Art. 3 and include the elimination of customs duties, quotas and similar measures; the establishment of a common customs tariff and of a common commercial policy in relation to non-member countries; the abolition of obstacles to free movement of persons, services and capital throughout the Community; the adoption of common policies in agriculture and transport; the institution of a system to prevent distortion of competition; the coordination of economic policies; the approximation of laws in the Member States so as to achieve the common market; the creation of a European Social Fund and the establishment of a European Investment Bank; and the association of overseas dependencies of Member States with the Community in order to increase trade and to promote economic and social development.

Clearly the agricultural sector is affected by the creation and operation of all these instruments and not merely by those directly related to itself.

As for the Articles on agriculture, we must see them as a framework around which the actual policy was to be erected later. Art. 38 defines the overall scope of the common market as it applies to agriculture. It covers 'the products of the soil, of stock farming and of fisheries and products of first-stage processing directly related to these products'. The actual commodities included within this broad definition are listed in detail in Annex II of the Treaty. Art. 38 also provides that the common market in agricultural products was to be accompanied by a common agricultural policy among the Member States.

The objectives of this policy are set out in Art. 39.1 as follows:

(a) to increase agricultural productivity by promoting technical progress and by ensuring the rational development of agricultural production and the optimum utilisation of the factors of production, in particular labour;

(b) thus to ensure a fair standard of living for the agricultural community, in particular by increasing the individual earnings of persons engaged in agriculture:

(c) to stabilise markets;

(d) to assure the availability of supplies;

(e) to ensure that supplies reach consumers at reasonable prices.

In Art. 39.2 the Treaty stipulates that in working out the CAP, account was to be taken of the social structures of agriculture and of the disparities between the various farming regions. It reminds policy makers of the need to make the necessary adjustments to agriculture by degrees and of the close ties binding agriculture with the economy as a whole.

Art. 39 must be one of the most frequently quoted Articles in the whole Treaty but Art. 40–although just as significant–rarely gets a mention. It is under Art. 40 that provision is made for the creation of the various instruments by which the goals set out in Art. 39.1 are to be achieved.

Firstly, the Treaty stipulates that there was to be a transition period during which the CAP should gradually come into operation. Secondly, that a market organisation should be set up. The actual form which this would take was left open within certain guide-lines. Thirdly, the scope of the proposed common organisation was spelled out. It was free to include 'regulation of prices, aids for the production and marketing of the various products, storage and carry-over arrangements and common machinery for stabilising imports or exports.' Fourthly, the Treaty stipulates that the common organisation 'shall exclude any discrimination between producers or consumers within the Community' and fifthly, in the same spirit, that 'any common price policy shall be based on common criteria and uniform methods of calculation'. Finally, Art. 40 provides for the establishment of one or more funds to finance the common organisation of markets.

It is worth remembering that it is to the edifice erected on this slim base that so much of the remainder of this book is devoted and about which so much heat has been generated since the early 1960s.

Provision was made under Art. 41 for measures to be taken in the fields of vocational training, research and the dissemination of agricultural knowledge. Provision was also made under the same Article for the totally unrelated activity of promoting consumption of certain products.

It was mentioned above that the Rome Treaty as a whole is relevant to agriculture and not merely the ten Articles specifically related to this sector. While this is true, certain exceptions are laid down. Art. 42 provides for a derogation in the case of production and trade in agricultural commodities from the rules on competition laid down in Arts. 85–94. This was done so that the Community could introduce and operate the common organisation of markets provided for under Art. 40. Also, the Council of Ministers was given specific freedom under Art. 42 to grant aid: '(a) for the protection of enterprises handicapped by structural or natural conditions; (b) within the framework of economic development programmes.'

Art. 43 sets out the procedure which was to be adopted in the drawing-up of the CAP. The first action to be taken was the convening by the Commission of a conference of the Member States to compare their existing agricultural policies and to formulate a statement of their resources and needs. This conference was held in Stresa, Italy in July 1959 and its conclusions are discussed in the next section of this chapter.

Art. 43 goes on to outline the subsequent sequence of events in establishing the CAP: the consultations with the Economic and Social Committee, whose role is outlined in chapter 2, and the submission of proposals on the CAP to the Council of Ministers within two years of the coming into operation of the Treaty. It then lays down the procedure to be adopted by the Council in implementing the CAP: specifically that, on a proposal from the Commission and after consulting the European Parliament, the Council is required 'to make regulations, issue directives or take decisions.'

Attention should be drawn to one feature of this Council procedure because of the problems which arose subsequently over it and which have not yet been satisfactorily resolved. It was laid down that for a period of time the regulations, decisions and directives passed by the Council should be made unanimously but that thereafter they should be made by qualified majority. This latter mechanism is described further in chapter 2 but the point to be made here is that the Council has not moved on to the use of the qualified majority as a matter of course as laid down in Art. 43.

Articles 44–46 need not detain us as they are concerned with procedures which were available to the Community to regulate its agricultural affairs during the transition period during which the common market organisation came fully into operation. When we read these Articles setting out transitional procedures in such detail, we can sense the nervousness of the Member States surrounding themselves with safety devices when embarking on a voyage in uncharted waters. We know from the history of the CAP how tough in fact were the negotiations to set it up and to carry it forward through its various stages. While we may legitimately criticise certain features of the policy as it operates, we must never forget the immense political achievement which it represents.

The final Article dealing specifically with agriculture–Art. 47–is concerned with the functions of the Economic and Social Committee in the agricultural sphere and these are touched on more fully in chapter 2.

The Conference at Stresa

As we have seen, the objectives of the CAP are set out in Art. 39 of the Rome Treaty and they resemble the typical aims of agricultural policy in developed countries the world over. However, it would be wrong to believe that Art. 39 represents the only considerations involved in the devising and implementation of the policy. For instance, the conference convened at Stresa by the Commission in accordance with Art. 43 discussed many of the broad issues facing agriculture at the time–issues which were to be taken into account in drawing up the CAP and many of which are still very relevant today.

The conference ended with a general resolution [44] which highlighted those aspects of the agricultural scene that the delegates regarded as important. The main points of that final resolution are that:

1. Agriculture should be considered as an integral part of the economy and as an essential factor in social life.
2. There should be progressive development of trade within the Community, taking account of the need to maintain commercial trade, and the contractual, political and economic ties with third countries, and to maintain the possibility of protection against dumping.
3. There should be a close correlation between the policies for structural adaptation and the market: the former should contribute to an evening out of production costs and to the rational orientation of production, while the latter should be managed in a manner which would stimulate the improvement of productivity.
4. An equilibrium should be found between production and market outlets, taking possible trade into account, so that specialisation would conform to the economic structure and natural conditions of production within the Community.
5. Efforts made to raise productivity should permit the application of a price policy which simultaneously avoided overproduction, while allowing farmers to remain or to become competitive. At the same time a policy of aid to disadvantaged regions or farms would make the necessary adaptations possible.

6. The elimination of aids contrary to the spirit of the Treaty should be considered as essential.

7. The development of production and of demand in the associated countries and territories (colonial and ex-colonial countries brought into association with the Community) should be taken into consideration during the elaboration of the CAP.

8. An improved structure should permit the capital and labour used in European agriculture to receive remuneration comparable with that which they would obtain in other sectors of the economy.

9. Given the importance of the familial structure of European agriculture and the unanimous wish to safeguard this character, every effort should be made to raise the economic and competitive capacity of such enterprises.

10. The retraining of the agricultural labour force and the industrialisation of the rural regions under the greatest pressure would allow for a gradual settlement of the problems posed for marginal farms which were economically incapable of being made viable.

The Commission's proposals on the CAP

It will be remembered that the Commission was required under Art. 43 to submit proposals for the working out and implementing of the CAP to the Council within two years of the entry into force of the Treaty. The Commission's final proposals appear in a document [12] with the call number COM(60)105.[2] There the Commission set out in detail its proposals on the market and price policies to be introduced. Understandably modifications were made to these proposals during negotiations, and adjustments have also been made in the intervening years to the mechanisms set up, but in essence the systems described later in chapters 7–10 are those which were put forward in 1960.

The Commission was much more reticent in its handling of the structural and social aspects of the new CAP. It is true that it devoted many pages to a discussion of the structural shortcomings of the agricultural sector, which follows closely the views expressed at the Stresa conference, but concrete proposals to improve the situation were few and weak, nor were they set out in the detailed manner adopted for all the main commodities. The approach was even more cautious where the social aspects of policy were concerned–indeed the Commission only included a discussion of social aspects as a result of criticism made by the Economic and Social Committee on an earlier draft. In effect, the Commission limited itself to an outline of social policy aims within agriculture, without making any provision for the translation of these aims into practical measures. Nevertheless, despite the perfunctory treatment, the objectives should be listed along with the principles enunciated at Stresa as they do represent a broadening and deepening of the bare statement contained in Art. 39 of the Treaty. They are as follows:

1. To ensure social protection for agricultural wage-earners and their dependents equivalent to that enjoyed by other categories of workers.
2. To encourage the adaptation of contractual relations within agriculture to accord more with modern conditions.
3. To narrow the gap between agricultural wage earners and those in comparable branches of activity with regard to remuneration, social security and working conditions.
4. To ensure that rural children have the same opportunities for general and vocational education as those elsewhere.
5. To aid young country dwellers wishing to set up as independent farmers or who wish to change to other types of farm work.
6. To ensure that the best conditions for success are available to those leaving agriculture for other employment.
7. To facilitate the retirement on pension of farmers and farm workers at the normal retirement age.
8. To improve rural housing.
9. To improve the social and cultural infrastructure of rural areas.

Other principles

In order to round off our discussion of the basic objectives of the CAP, we should consider four further principles. The first three form a trilogy originally enunciated in the early 1960s but often repeated subsequently. They are: market unity, Community preference, and financial solidarity.

The first—market unity—signifies that there should be a single market for any commodity coming under the CAP, and that there should be a common system of marketing and common pricing throughout the Community. While this may be universally accepted in theory, the use of monetary compensatory amounts and floating exchange rates in practice have seriously undermined this principle. This is a topic to which we shall have to return in chapter 6.

The second principle—Community preference—means in effect that producers inside the Community should always be more favourably placed than competing overseas suppliers. Or, to put it another way, that trade concessions granted to third countries should not be at such a level that Community producers would have difficulty competing with them on the Community's own markets.

Financial solidarity refers to the commitment of the Community to finance jointly the operation of the CAP. This is obviously of great importance to the weaker Community members and to those with large farm sectors. In the early days of the Community a belief did exist in some quarters that the Member States should get out of the Community Budget roughly the same proportion as they put in. From time to time this belief re-emerges, although there is a no basis in fact for it. Indeed, a moment's consideration should be sufficient to show that such a concept could have no place in a Community which is committed to a narrowing of the economic gap between regions and Member States. This must of necessity involve the richer countries contributing a disproportionate amount for the benefit of the less fortunate parts of the Community.

It is interesting to note in passing that these three principles, though often quoted and held to be sacrosanct, have somewhat vague origins. They represent a gloss on—or an extension of—the Treaty provisions. They seem to have originated in 1960 in a Resolution of the Council which arose out of its discussions on the Commission proposals contained in COM(60)109. Later they were enshrined in some of the early Community legislation on agriculture, in particular in 1962 in Regulation No. 19 on cereals and No. 25 on financing the CAP.[3]

The final principle to be added to the list is that of 'comparable earned income'—although it is possible that this concept should not be elevated to the level of a principle, as it is clear that some confusion exists in the doctrine and practice of the Community. The Treaty refers to ensuring 'a fair standard of living for the agricultural community' without defining the exact meaning of the term. However, the Stresa resolution—point (8)—refers to the attainment of comparable remuneration for capital and labour in agriculture as in other sectors, and in COM(60)105 the Commission in its social objectives refers to narrowing the gap between agricultural wage earners and those in comparable activities (point (3)). In its annual calculations on agricultural prices (discussed in chapter 7), the Commission uses the concept of modern or efficient farms as its base. The belief is that such farms should be able to provide an income comparable with that of non-agricultural employment in the same region. A similar concept is used in the structural policy on modernisation (see chapter 11).

Thus, it would seem that, little by little, common consent and usage has led 'a fair standard of living' to mean an income comparable with that earned in other sectors of the economy. However, it is important to stress that this is clearly intended to apply only to efficient farms.

Notes to Chapter 1

1. The term 'Treaty of Rome' is used throughout to denote the Treaty under which the European Economic Community was established. It is sometimes forgotten that there are in fact two Rome Treaties signed on the same day—25 March 1957—one for the EEC and the other for the European Atomic Energy Community (Euratom).
2. In some of the early literature on the CAP this document is referred to as the *Mansholt Plan*. This term should be avoided, as in 1968 another document was issued which also came to be known as the *Mansholt Plan*.
3. I am indebted to Michael Tracy and his colleagues in the Council Secretariat for having tracked down this information.

CHAPTER 2

Institutions of the Community

There are four major Institutions within the administrative framework of the European Community[4] and a number of lesser bodies. The major Institutions are the Commission, the Council, the Parliament and the Court of Justice. The most important lesser bodies are the Economic and Social Committee (ESC), the European Investment Bank (EIB); the various types of consultative committees attached to the Commission; the Committee of Permanent Representatives and the Special Committee on Agriculture, both attached to the Council.

Surprising as it may seem, the Institutions as yet have no permanent base. Brussels is the most important of the temporary locations as this is where the Council has its secretariat and the Commission its main office. It is also the home of the ESC. Luxembourg is the seat of the Court of Justice, the EIB and the secretariat of the Parliament. The Commission has a subsidiary office there also.

The Community has a presence of one kind or another in many other locations. For instance, there are the various centres where research is carried out under the auspices of Euratom; the information offices in cities both inside and outside the Community; the European schools and university; and many more.

The situation with regard to the regular meeting places of the main Institutions is even more complicated than the location of their offices. The Council meets in Brussels except in April, June and October when it meets in Luxembourg. The Parliament meets in Luxembourg for about half its sittings, the remainder being held in Strasbourg. The meetings of parliamentary committees are held in Brussels.

The peripatetic nature of these Institutions has arisen through historical accident combined with intense political resistance to settle on a permanent headquarters. The present situation is cumbersome and expensive to operate. For instance, when the Council meets in Luxembourg not only do large numbers of its staff and their attendant documents have to move, but the Commission similarly has to move personnel and material. The parliamentary sessions in Strasbourg equally require an upheaval. The sensible solution would be to have all major Institutions located permanently in one place. Brussels is the most obvious choice as it is the most important centre, but it must be recognised that any move to a permanent headquarters would mean a loss of status and business for the cities that would lose their present offices.

The Commission

If one thinks of the Institutions of the European Community in terms of their national equivalents, then the Commission can be seen as the equivalent on a Community level of a national civil service. However, this is a very partial analogy and certain of its functions make the Commission quite distinctive as will become clear below.

The present Commission came into being in 1967 as a consequence of the provisions of the Brussels Treaty of 1965 [67] which merged the three existing administrations, namely, the High Authority of the ECSC, the Commission of the EEC and the Euratom Commission. The Commission staff–excluding those engaged on research into atomic energy–numbers about 9,000, well over one-third of whom are involved in the translation of documents and interpreting at meetings. The reason why such a large army of people is necessary for basic communications is because the Community has six official working languages. In practice, much of the work among the officials is carried out in either French or English. Further Enlargement of the Community will add greatly to the problems of communications unless a decision is taken to reduce the number of languages used.

The Commission is divided into twenty directorates-general, each of which deals with one or more topic areas. Agricultural matters are handled by DG VI, fisheries by DG XIV, regional policy by DG XVI and so forth. Besides the directorates-general, there are other departments within the Commission such as the legal service, the statistical office, the environment and consumer protection service, the official publications office, etc.

The Commission is presided over currently by thirteen Commissioners–two from each of the large Member States (France,

Italy, Federal Germany and the UK) and one from each of the small Member States (Belgium, Denmark, Ireland, Luxembourg and the Netherlands). Each Commissioner presides over one or more topic areas. The appointments are for four years renewable and are made by agreement between the governments of the Member States. A President and five Vice-Presidents are appointed from within the group of thirteen and they hold office for two years renewable.

Suggestions have been made in recent years–by Tindemans [20] for example–that this system should be altered and that only the President of the Commission should be appointed by the Member States and that, once appointed, the President should then be free to select the remaining Commissioners. These suggestions have met with little enthusiasm among the governments, although it is true that they did discuss their proposed nominees for the Commission which took up office in January 1977 with the new President. This is not to say that he received the colleagues he would have chosen if free to do so.

Only nationals of the Member States may become Commissioners and while there must be at least one national from each Member State among the Commissioners, there may not be more than two from any Member State (Art. 10 Merger Treaty [67]).

It is possible that with the further Enlargement of the Community, these rules will have to be altered on the grounds that the group of Commissioners is already very large and that it would be impossible to find substantive portfolios for any greater number of Commissioners than at present. The Commission has suggested [35] that the number of Commissioners should be limited to one from each Member State irrespective of size.

Although the Commissioners are appointed by the governments of the Member States they are expected to be completely independent in the performance of their duties. In the words of Art. 10 of the Merger Treaty: 'They shall neither seek nor take instructions from any Government or from any other body. They shall refrain from any action incompatible with their duties. Each Member State undertakes to respect this principle and not to seek to influence the members of the Commission in the performance of their tasks.'

Under Art. 155 of the Rome Treaty four areas of responsibility are set out as being the particular province of the Commission. Firstly, it must ensure that the provisions of the Treaty are applied; secondly, it is to make recommendations or give opinions on matters arising out of the Treaty; thirdly, it has its own power of decision and must participate in the formulation of measures taken by the Council and Parliament; and fourthly, it exercises the powers conferred on it by the Council.

The Commission is the watchdog of all the Treaties. It has the power to take to the Court of Justice any organisation or individual infringing a Treaty provision or the legislation which flows from the Treaties. The Commission is also the motor driving the Community forward and it alone has the power to initiate proposals for legislation. In both these roles it acts differently from a national civil service. Only in its role of administrator of legislation passed by the Council does it act in a manner closely analogous to a national civil service.

The Council

As with the Commission, the present Council of Ministers was established under the 1965 Merger Treaty to take the place of the Special Council of the ECSC and the Councils of the EEC and Euratom. According to Art. 145 of the Rome Treaty, the Council has two functions: to 'ensure coordination of the general economic policies of the Member States' and to take decisions. It is in fact the primary legislative organ of the Community and cannot be compared with a national government or cabinet.

Normally, each Member State is represented on the Council by a government minister, although on occasion a junior minister or high-ranking civil servant can take the minister's place. The personnel attending a Council meeting vary with the topic under discussion, thus when agriculture is being discussed it is the ministers for agriculture who form the Council; when it is foreign affairs, the foreign affairs ministers; transport the transport ministers and so forth.

The Council is presided over by a President who holds office for six months at a time. This post rotates among the Member States in the alphabetical order of the countries' names in their own language which gives: Belgium, Denmark, Federal Germany, France, Ireland, Italy, Luxembourg, Netherlands, UK. This rotation of the Presidency involves the rotation of the chairmanship of all committees and working parties convened under the auspices of the Council.

The Council meets when convened by the President on his own initiative or when a request is made for a meeting by a Council Member or by the Commission. The voting procedure at meetings was laid down in the Rome Treaty (Art. 148) as follows: 'Save as otherwise provided in this Treaty, the Council shall act by a majority of its members.' This simple provision has not been followed nor has the Council made much use of the provision for decision by qualified majority, i.e. by a weighted vote.

This weighted vote is so constructed that it prevents the larger Member States as a group being able to outvote the smaller Member States. At present the weighting is as follows: ten votes each for Federal Germany, France, Italy and the UK; five each for Belgium and the Netherlands; three each for Denmark and Ireland; and two for Luxembourg. A qualified majority requires at least forty-one votes out of fifty-eight.

Controversy over majority voting reached a head in 1965 when the French withdrew from Community activities for six months.[5] The quarrel was patched up in a makeshift way during a meeting of the Council in January 1960 at which a statement known as 'the Luxembourg compromise' or 'the Luxembourg accords' was agreed [67]. The effect of this rather unsatisfactory compromise is that, in discussions of an issue on which majority voting is allowed under the Treaty, a Member State is free to declare that its vital interests are at stake and, as a result, agreement can only be reached unanimously.

Obviously in certain circumstances it can be extremely difficult to achieve unanimity, and the temptation is to try to reach a compromise solution which may well prove to be unsatisfactory. It is true that since 1975 majority voting in the Council has been extended gradually but there is need to encourage this trend further, particularly when the Community is once more enlarged. It must be recognised that major issues would be involved in any such change and that certain Member States would view this development with suspicion and alarm. The Commission has analysed the voting problem in some detail in its opinion on the institutional implications of Enlargement [35] and its solution is a matter of vital importance to the smooth running and future development of the Community.

COREPER and SCA

The Council is not permanently in session but meets from time to time as the pressure of business warrants. However, it has its own back-up administrative staff permanently at work in Brussels and it also has the services of a Committee known as COREPER (*Comité des Representants Permanents*) which prepares the agenda for each Council session.

This Committee, which was not referred to in any of the early Treaties, nevertheless dates from 1958. It received specific recognition under Art. 4 of the Merger Treaty where it is given responsibility 'for preparing the work of the Council and for carrying out the tasks assigned to it by the Council.' Each Member State has a permanent representative accredited to the Community in much the same way that they have ambassadors accredited to each other's capitals. It is these permanent representatives or their deputies who sit on COREPER.

COREPER has become increasingly important in the affairs of the Council as the work of the Community has become more extensive. The members of COREPER are at the centre of all negotiations between the Member States on Community matters, and between the Member States and the Commission. They are the guardians of the interests of the Member States, they coordinate the work of special committees and working parties which aid in the preparation of material for Council meetings.

One of the most important functions of COREPER is the preparation of the Council agendas. If matters arise on which the members of COREPER can agree among themselves, such topics appear on the Council agenda for ratification only and the issues are not re-opened. These previously agreed measures are contained in the 'A' section of the agenda. The Council of Ministers only actually discusses items which appear in the 'B' section of the agenda, i.e. those matters on which COREPER could find no agreement or only partial agreement.

It is this feature of the organisation of the work of the Council which gives its meetings the constant appearance of argument, heated discussion and frequent deadlock. The general public is unaware of the many decisions reached much more quickly within the realms of COREPER. The members of COREPER sit in at Council meetings as advisers to the Ministers, and frequently when the latter cannot reach agreement they refer the subject back to COREPER for further discussion and presentation at a later Council meeting.

As so often occurs, agriculture is treated slightly differently from other issues. Because of the great volume of decision-making involved in the management of the CAP, a separate body handles most of the preparation of the agenda for the agricultural Council meetings. This body is called the Special Committee for Agriculture (*Comité Spécial Agriculture*). Its membership is composed of high-ranking officials of the Member States within the permanent representation teams working in Brussels. SCA operates in the same way as COREPER.

Despite the existence of SCA, four broad areas of work in the agricultural sphere remain the preserve of COREPER. These are proposals for harmonisation of legislation; financial matters; commercial questions concerning third countries; and fisheries. It is quite feasible for both SCA and COREPER to present papers to the Council covering different aspects of the same question. For instance, there could be discussions on a proposal concerning agricultural structure on which SCA would prepare a report dealing with the policy implications, and another report prepared by COREPER dealing with the financial implications of the same proposal.

The European Council

Some brief reference should be made to the activities of the European Council, i.e. the Council of Ministers when it is composed of the heads of state or government of Member States. The European Council has no constitutional basis in any of the Treaties. Its origins lie in the Summit meetings which were held from time to time to find solutions to serious issues of contention or to move the Community forward to a new point on its path towards integration. Gradually these meetings became institutionalised and the term 'Summit' was dropped. In recent years the meetings have been held three times per year.

Although it is true that the European Council does discuss broad issues of interest to the Member States, nevertheless the agendas are full of lesser problems to which the relevant Council of Ministers could find no solution. Obviously it is a good idea to have some means whereby deadlock can be resolved but there are dangers. By making the meetings of the European Council a regular feature of the Community decision-making process, the ordinary Councils may strive less diligently to find solutions to the problems which confront them because they know that the matter can be referred up to the European Council. In turn this runs the risk of trivialising the meetings of the latter body.

A further drawback to these meetings is that, while the European Council can reach agreement on any issue, such an agreement has no legal validity. This means that the topic has to be referred down to the appropriate Council of Ministers, where it is discussed in the ordinary way on the basis of a proposal from the Commission. It is often difficult in practice for the Council to reach agreement on the details of such an issue, even when a broad brush solution has been adopted at the highest level.

The European Parliament

Of all the Institutions of the Community, probably the one with the greatest potential for change and development currently is the Parliament.[6] As from June 1979 its members are to be directly elected by the electors in each of the Member States rather than being appointed from the ranks of the national parliamentarians as was the case previously. The change over to direct elections is in accordance with Art. 138 of the Rome Treaty under which the Parliament was given the task of drawing up 'proposals for elections by direct universal suffrage in accordance with a uniform procedure in all Member States.' This event—so long in coming—can be seen not so much as a climax in the history of the Parliament but rather as the beginning of a new phase of development.

The new Parliament is considerably increased in size from the old: a total of 410 members compared with 198. The composition is that there are eighty-one members each from Federal Germany, France, Italy and the UK; twenty-five from the Netherlands; twenty-four from Belgium;

sixteen from Denmark; fifteen from Ireland; and six from Luxembourg. The Commission has suggested [35] that on accession Greece should have twenty-four members, and that subsequent Enlargement of the Community to include Spain and Portugal could add a further eighty-two members (fifty-eight for Spain, twenty-four for Portugal). Although members are elected nationally, they do not sit by country but rather by political groups which span national boundaries.

The term of office is five years and members of the European Parliament may also be members of their own national parliament. For the first election each Member State was allowed to choose the particular system of voting it wished, but the intention is that a uniform system should be worked out for future elections. While allowing variations in the system of voting for the first election helped to ensure that the arrangements for the new Parliament were accepted, it may prove very difficult to achieve a common system at a later date.

The Parliament is presided over by a President assisted by twelve vice-presidents (at the time of writing it was not known whether this number would be increased) and together they form what is known as the Bureau, which is responsible for the day-to-day running of the Parliament. The Bureau's members are elected annually.

The parliamentary year starts in March and plenary meetings are held on average once a month and last for a week at a time. These sessions are open to the public, but committee meetings usually are not. The Parliament has twelve specialised committees, each of which deals with one or more particular topics. As might be suspected, agriculture has a committee to itself. All the preparatory work on any topic coming before the Parliament is carried out in one or more of the committees. The exact procedure followed by the Parliament is set out in chapter 3 in discussing the Community's legislative process.

We have already seen that the Council is the primary legislative organ in the Community and that the Commission has derived legislative powers. What then, one might well ask, are the powers and function of the European Parliament? In the broadest terms as set down in Art. 137 of the Rome Treaty it is to 'exercise the advisory and supervisory powers which are conferred upon it by this Treaty.'

In practice the roles of the Parliament can be defined as fivefold:

(1) by a two-thirds majority of the votes cast to pass a motion of censure requiring the Commission to resign as a body (i.e. the Commissioners, not the permanent staff of the Commission); (2) to ask questions—written and oral—and to call the Commission to account in plenary or in committee debates. (Parliament's rights over the Council are far less, as the latter can decide for itself the conditions under which it will be heard by the former); (3) to pass resolutions; (4) to be consulted as laid down in the Treaties and as further extended in practice by the Council; and (5) to exercise control over parts of the Budget and to adopt the Budget as a whole (to be discussed further in chapter 5).

This list may look impressive but the drawback to the effectiveness of the Parliament is that, apart from its ability to dismiss the Commission, it lacks powers of compulsion. Of its present powers, in practice the two most important are those listed as (4) and (5) above. But even with these, theory is stronger than reality. For instance, under Art. 43.2 of the Rome Treaty, the Council must consult the Parliament before passing legislative Acts in the field of agriculture (and similar requirements to consult the Parliament are imposed on the Council in other spheres also) but, although the Council abides by these requirements, it may if it thinks fit ignore the formal Opinion of the Parliament expressed on any particular proposed measure. Similarly, if the Commission decides to revise a draft proposal submitted to the Council, it may do so without incorporating the Parliament's views in the new draft.

The Parliament's greatest hope for raising the level of its significance lies in the increased powers over the Budget which it has obtained and the advent of direct elections. These two factors may provide the necessary impetus for the development of greater democratic control over the activities of the Council and the Commission.

The Court of Justice

The Court of Justice has the task of ensuring that Community law is observed in the interpretation and application of the various Treaties. The Court consists of nine judges assisted by four advocates-general. Enlargement of the Community would mean an increase in these numbers. The judges and advocates-general are appointed 'by common accord of the Governments of the Member States for a term of six years' (Art. 167 Rome Treaty). Curiously, there is no provision that members of the Court should be drawn from each of the Member States, nor is there any provision that they must be nationals of the Member States. In practice, however, it is hard to imagine a Member State foregoing the nomination of a judge or nominating someone from outside the Community. Usually the advocates-general come from the larger Member States.

Unlike the appointment of Commissioners, the Court appointments are staggered so that part of the Court comes up for renewal at three-yearly intervals. Although it is renewable, Brown and Jacobs [4] and Kapteyn and Verloren van Themaat [59] criticise the shortness of the six-year term of appointment in view of the fact that the appointments are made by the governments of the Member States. As the latter authors express it: 'Too small an institutional guarantee of their [i.e. the judges and advocates-general] independence is given. Very great confidence indeed is thus placed in the disinterestedness of the governments with respect to their appointment and in the moral qualities of the persons appointed, a confidence which fortunately has so far been justified.'

The Court can sit either in plenary session or divided into two chambers. Usually it sits as a full court and must contain an uneven number of judges so that a majority decision can be reached. Only one judgement is given, no separate or dissenting judgements being allowed. The judges elect one of their number to serve as President of the Court for a term of three years renewable. The President's functions are to direct the business and administration of the Court and to preside at hearings and deliberations.

Once a case has been heard the task of the advocate-general is to make a reasoned submission in open court to the judges on the facts as presented, the submissions made, the relevant law, and an expression of his own opinion as to how the judges should decide the case. The purpose of this statement is to assist the Court to reach a decision, although the Court does not have to follow the recommendation of the advocate-general and indeed frequently does not.

The Court has power to hear cases brought before it by a Member State, by one of the Institutions of the Community or, in certain circumstances, by an individual. Its competence is very wide: it exercises judicial control over the other Community Institutions, not only in relation to their administrative actions but also over Community legislation. The Court may also rule on the conformity with the Treaties of any international agreement entered into by the Community. It can hear cases brought against a Member State for alleged violations of the Treaties. The Court can be the forum for an action for damages against an Institution of the Community and it acts as an appeals tribunal in disputes concerning the terms of employment of Community officials.

The Court may also give a preliminary ruling on questions submitted to it by a Court of a Member State in accordance with Art. 177 of the Rome Treaty. These rulings concern the interpretation of Community law or the validity of Community legislation. Such interlocutory referrals to the Court are becoming much more common as national and Community legislation become increasingly interwoven and are an important means of developing Community law.

The Economic and Social Committee (ESC)

When the Treaties establishing the EEC and Euratom were drawn up, they provided for a new body–the Economic and Social Committee (ESC)–which was intended to play an advisory role in the work of the Council and Commission. It is not an Institution on a par with the European Parliament as it is clearly under the control of the Council.

The ESC consists of 'representatives of the various categories of economic and social activity, in particular, representatives of producers, farmers, carriers, workers, dealers, craftsmen, professional occupations and representatives of the general public' (Art. 193 Rome Treaty). In practice, the members are grouped into three broad categories–employers, trade unions and independants. Members are appointed by the Council from lists supplied by the Member States and serve for a term of four years renewable. Although they are nominated by their Member States, the members are appointed in their personal capacity 'and may not be bound by any mandatory instructions' (Art. 194).

The ESC consists of 144 members divided as follows: twenty-four each from Federal Germany, France, Italy and the UK; twelve each from Belgium and the Netherlands; nine each from Denmark and Ireland; and six from Luxembourg. It has been suggested [35] that on further Enlargement of the Community there should be an additional eighteen members from Spain, and twelve each from Greece and Portugal.

Most of the work is carried out in sections reminiscent of the organisation of the European Parliament into committees. Each section deals with one or more specialised field: agriculture has a section to itself, something specifically required under the Rome Treaty (Art. 197). Each of the three broad interest groups decides how to allocate its members between sections and, as a general rule, no one person may belong to more than three sections.

As with the European Parliament, the ESC has a Bureau which is responsible for preparing and organising the proceedings of the Committee and for co-ordinating all Committee activities. The Bureau consists of a chairman, two vice-chairmen and eighteen members elected for a two-year term. Apart from the many section meetings, the full ESC meets in plenary session about nine times per year.

According to the Rome Treaty the ESC must be consulted on certain subjects by the Council or the Commission and, over and above that, it may be consulted 'by these institutions in all cases in which they consider it appropriate' (Art. 198). Mandatory consultation is specified on matters concerning free movement of workers, freedom of establishment and the provision of services, the approximation of laws, the European Social Fund, and policy issues involving transport, social affairs and common vocational training. While Art. 43.2 required that the ESC was consulted on the establishment of the CAP, consultation on its operation and development is purely optional. In fact, when its opinion is sought, little attention is paid to it by the Council. This is regrettable as its views are often well thought out.

Right from the start of its activities the ESC felt hampered by its subordinate relationship *vis-à-vis* the Commission and Council and it has made a number of attempts to widen the scope of its activities. In particular, it sought the right to put forward on its own initiative its views on any issue within its competence without having to wait for a request from the Commission or Council. The ESC felt especially that it suffered from being asked for its opinion very late in the consultative process and it wished to be in the position of being able to undertake studies when draft documents were being drawn up by the Commission.

Its years of patient knocking at the door paid off when, at the European Council meeting in Paris in 1972, the participants invited 'the Community institutions to recognise the right of the Economic and Social Committee in future to advise on its own initiative on all questions affecting the Community' [47]. In 1974 the Council officially recognised the Committee's right of initiative but, despite this advance, it must be stated that the role and influence of the ESC remain very limited.

Other Statutory Committees

The ESC and COREPER are not the only committees specifically provided for under the Treaties. There are, for instance, the Monetary Committee (Art. 105 Rome Treaty); the Transport Committee (Art. 83); the Committee of the European Social Fund (Art. 124); and a number of others.

However, by no means is this all. Many committees have been created under various Regulations with the task of assisting in the decision-making process. There are a number of ways in which these consultative committees can be classified. For instance, they can be classified according to the composition of their relationship. Some are composed entirely of officials from the Member States, chaired by a representative of the Council or Commission; others are composed entirely of representatives of vocational interests, usually such committees are chaired by the Commission; and finally there are joint committees which include members representing vocational interests, officials of Member States, and officials from Community Institutions.

Another—perhaps more meaningful—classification is found by dividing the committees according to whether consultation with them is mandatory or not. Within the mandatory group we find that a high proportion are concerned with agricultural matters. Of these, undoubtedly the most important and the most active are the

Management Committees (which are described further below). The mandatory group also includes such committees as the:

Committee of the European Agricultural Guidance and Guarantee Fund;

Joint Committee on the system of agricultural accounting information;

Standing Committee on agricultural structures;

Committee of the European Development Fund;

Committee on the Nomenclature of the Common Customs Tariff; and many more.

Turning to the non-mandatory consultative committees, we can distinguish three rough sub-groups:

(a) Committees which foster the co-ordination of Member States' policies and cooperation between Member States and Community Institutions in areas in which it is not always easy to define clearly their respective jurisdiction.

Examples: Short-term policy committee;

Medium-term economic policy committee;

Budget committee.

(b) Committees which foster close collaboration between the Commission and the Member States in the application of Community law.

Examples: Technical committee on the freedom of movement of workers within the Community;

Advisory committee on own resources;

Advisory committee concerning a common system for imports from non-member countries.

(c) Committees to achieve co-operation between the Community and vocational and economic interests.

Examples: Advisory agricultural committees on the organisation of markets (described more fully below);

Joint advisory committee on social questions relating to paid agricultural workers;

Joint advisory committee on social questions relating to farmers;

Joint advisory committee on agricultural structure policy;

Joint advisory committee on social questions in the sea fishing industry.

Management Committees. The day-to-day operation of the CAP in the commodity field requires considerable work of a technical nature within the Commission. In this it is aided by the Management Committees (*Comités de gestion*) which have been set up for each of the commodities (or groups of commodities) for which a market regime is in force. These Committees provide a forum for discussion of the viewpoints of the Member States, both in the operation of existing Regulations and on proposals being worked out by the Commission for amended or new Regulations. The committees also fix, where necessary, the levels of levies and export restitutions on particular commodities.

The Management Committees are composed of up to five representatives from each Member State, drawn from the national ministries of agriculture and related bodies, presided over by a representative of the Commission who has no vote. The Commission also provides the secretariat. Voting on the Committees is by qualified majority on lines similar to those described above for the Council.

Each Management Committee has its legal basis in an article of the basic Regulation setting up the organisation of the market regime for the commodity concerned. Rules of procedure are identical for each Committee, and meetings can be convened either by the Commission or by request of one of the Member States. Some of the Management Committees meet quite frequently—perhaps twenty times in a year—and the relative importance of the commodity is reflected in the work load of its particular Management Committee.

When the Commission wishes to issue a Regulation of a technical or managerial nature to help ensure the smooth functioning of a commodity regime, the procedure is for the draft measure to be submitted to the relevant Management Committee for its opinion. This opinion is not directly binding on the Commission which can, if it wishes, go against the Committee's advice and proceed to promulgate the original draft as the definitive Regulation. In the event of a conflict of this kind the matter goes before the Council which may within one month reverse the Commission's decision. In practice disputes of this nature are very rare.

A number of other committees operate in exactly the same way as Management Committees. In agriculture these include the Standing

Committee on agricultural structures, and the Committee of the European Agricultural Guidance and Guarantee Fund.

Advisory Agricultural Committees. These Committees are the foremost among the group established to foster links between the Commission and the various vocational and economic interests in the Community. There is one Advisory Committee for each commodity (or group of commodities) paralleling the Management Committee for the same commodity. Besides these, in the agricultural sphere, there are also Advisory Committees on social matters and structure, as referred to in (c) above.

The legal basis for these Committees usually is to be found in a statement in the preamble to the basic Regulation covering the particular commodity or subject matter concerned. The members are nominated by the Commission on the proposal of the relevant vocational organisations at Community level. The Commission provides the secretariat and takes the chair. The number of meetings varies but is up to six per year. The Advisory Committees are consulted on early drafts of proposals but the opinions expressed do not bind the Commission.

The European Investment Bank

The last of the Community Institutions to be outlined here is the European Investment Bank (EIB) and it is a very different type of Institution to those already described. The Bank was established under Art. 129 of the Rome Treaty and its tasks are set out in Art. 130. It is intended to contribute 'to the balanced and steady development of the common market in the interest of the Community'. The Bank operates on a non-profit-making basis and grants loans or gives guarantees to facilitate projects falling within three broad fields. These projects must be (a) for developing less developed regions; (b) for the modernisation or conversion of existing undertakings, or for the development of fresh activities called for by the progressive establishment of the common market; and (c) of common interest to several Member States. The second and third types of project must be of such a size or nature that they cannot be completely financed by the conventional means available in the individual Member States.

In practice, this means that the Bank finances investment in less developed regions (many of which are highly dependent on agriculture); in industrial regions with structural difficulties or which need to convert to other forms of activity; in high-technology projects; and in such things as cross-border infrastructural developments.

The EIB is governed by a Board of nine Governors who are government ministers in each of the Member States. Under this Board is a Board of Directors on which there are currently eighteen seats, one for the Commission and the remainder for the Member States. Below that again is a Management Committee which is responsible for the day-to-day running of the Bank, and an Audit Committee which verifies the operations and accounts of the Bank.

The Bank can lend to private and public enterprises, to public authorities and to other financial institutions. The loans are usually large, with a preferred minimum of at least one million units of account (the unit of account is described in chapter 5), and are for long duration—about 7–12 years for industrial projects and up to 20 years for infrastructure projects. As the Bank is a non-profit making institution, the interest rates are kept low and higher rates are not charged for more risky projects or for borrowers with a low credit rating, although sureties are required. The Bank's capital comes from the Member States and from the Bank's own borrowings on international capital markets. It is willing to lend up to 50 per cent of the fixed capital cost of a project or up to a ceiling of 80 million units of account.

Although Art. 130 of the Rome Treaty indicates that EIB activities are to be concerned with projects on the territory of the Member States, under Art. 18 of the Statute of the EIB, signed at the same time, provision was made for the Bank to extend its activities further afield [67]. This derogation had to be authorised by the Board of Governors acting unanimously on a proposal from the Board of Directors. In fact, in 1963 the Bank commenced lending money overseas to countries which had cooperation agreements with the Community, and these activities have become more important over the years. Many of these loans go to some of the poorest countries in the world.

Notes to Chapter 2

4. It will be noted that throughout this book the term 'European

Community' is used. Strictly speaking this is incorrect; the plural should be used as there are three Communities–ECSC, EEC and Euratom. However, the term 'European Community' is widely used and is much less pedantic.

5. The issue of majority voting was bound up with a desire to alter (and much reduce) the role of the Commission. A very interesting account of this major crisis in the life of the Community can be found in Camps [6].

6. On reading the Treaties it will be noticed that reference is made throughout to the Assembly whereas the term used here is Parliament. This latter is in accord with the Parliament's own policy since 1962 and common usage.

CHAPTER 3

Legislative process of the Community

Types of legislation

There are two broad categories of legislation at Community level. The first comprises all the founding Treaties and their accompanying documentation, together with international treaties, agreements and similar transactions entered into by the Community. The second is made up of acts carried out by the Council and the Commission under Art. 189 of the Rome Treaty, the first part of which states: 'In order to carry out their task the Council and the Commission shall, in accordance with the provisions of this Treaty, make regulations, issue directives, take decisions, make recommendations or deliver opinions.'

Brown and Jacobs [4] point out that the legislation created under Art. 189 is often referred to as 'secondary legislation' in contrast with the Treaty provisions which in some sense are regarded as 'primary'. They regard this classification as misleading as 'there is nothing secondary, in character or in scope, about the basic regulations of the Council in such fields as agriculture, the free movement of workers, social security and competition. This legislation is both as fundamental in character and as broad in scope as any national legislation, and its relationship to the founding Treaties is comparable to that which national legislation has to a national constitution.'

As far as Council regulations, decisions and directives are concerned, Brown and Jacobs prefer the term 'Community legislation'. They do acknowledge that the implementing legislation enacted by the Commission is 'often akin to subordinate or delegated legislation' and therefore presumably they would not object to it being regarded as secondary in some sense.

Of the five activities referred to in the quotation from Art. 189 above, three have legislative force–the making of regulations, the issuing of directives and the taking of decisions. A *Regulation* is of general application; it is binding in its entirety and it is directly applicable in all the Member States (Art. 189). It becomes law automatically without the need for ratification by the national parliaments of the Member States. It binds not only national governments and organs of the State, but also all persons and institutions as well. Under Art. 191 of the Rome Treaty all Regulations must be published in the *Official Journal* of the Community (see below). They enter into force on the date specified within the Regulation or, if no date is specified, then on the twentieth day following their publication.

A *Directive* is binding 'as to the results to be achieved upon each Member State to which it is addressed but shall leave to the national authorities the choice of form and methods' (Art. 189). Directives are not binding on individuals but rather on the national administrations, which must enact the appropriate legislation necessary to give the Directives legal effect. There is no obligation to publish Directives in the *Official Journal* though in practice most are. The only obligation is to notify the parties to whom Directives are addressed.

One may wonder at the practical considerations which prompt the Community to use these two types of legislative instrument. Regulations are precise and rigid. Kapteyn and Verloren van Themaat [59] refer to the 'impersonal non-individualised character of the situations' to which Regulations apply. Regulations indicate that the same policy and practice should prevail throughout the Community and that it is the Community and not the individual Member States which is competent to regulate the issue involved. For this reason they are used in the organisation of the various commodity regimes for agricultural products—it will be remembered from chapter 1 that under Art. 40 all producers must be treated alike in the setting up of the common organisation of agricultural markets.

Directives are more flexible in that, providing the national measures which are taken in accordance with the Directives are acceptable, variations between countries or between regions can occur which help to tailor the measures involved to the particular needs of the situation. This is the reason why, for instance, Directives are favoured in combating agricultural structural problems which differ in scope and intensity in different parts of the Community.

A *Decision* is in the nature of a limited Regulation. It is binding in its entirety on those to whom it is addressed (Art. 189). Decisions can be addressed to one or more Member States, to private individuals, and to firms. Like Regulations, Decisions operate automatically without the intervention of national parliaments and they must be communicated to the person or organisation to whom they are directed. In practice, like Directives, they also appear in the *Official Journal*.

Article 189 also refers to the power to issue *Recommendations* and *Opinions*. These are just what the words suggest and have no binding force. The Council also issues *Resolutions*. These have no basis in the Treaties but are broad policy statements by the Council of its intention to take action in a particular field. The Council uses yet another device—the *Declaration*—which has no binding force and no basis in the Treaties. A Declaration is a statement in the Council minutes relating to the adoption of a Regulation or Directive. In the Declaration the Council or a Member State or indeed the Commission states its position on the subject concerned. Declarations can be of political importance: for instance, say a Member State has opposed a particular piece of legislation, through a Council declaration it may make its position formally known which could be of later significance.

The Official Journal

Before outlining the legislative process, a brief explanation of the function of the *Official Journal* may be helpful. A Journal was called for in Art. 191 of the Rome Treaty when, as we saw above, it was stipulated that Regulations had to be published in it. The ECSC had its own *Journal*, but in September 1958 the Council issued a Decision creating the *Official Journal of the European Communities* in which legislative acts for the ECSC, EEC and Euratom were all to be published.

Since the beginning of 1968 the *Official Journal* has been divided into two separate series. The 'L' series contains legislation, i.e. Regulations, Directives and Decisions. The titles of legislative Acts published in the 'L' series are printed in bold type and are preceded by an asterisk when they relate to matters other than the day-to-day management of the agricultural sector. The titles of Acts relating to the latter are printed in light type. The 'L' series is published on every working day of the year and on some days more than one issue is published. To give some idea of the operation of the 'L' series during the month of April 1978 (taken at random as an example) there were thirty-three issues containing:

	Regulations	Directives	Decisions	Recommendations
No. by Council	23	1	6	—
No. by Commission	244	4	78	10

The 'C' series contains communications and information. Although published less frequently than the 'L' series, the range of material is considerable. There are judgments of the Court of Justice; draft proposals submitted to the European Parliament and the ESC; the Opinions of these bodies on such drafts; discussion documents of various kinds prepared by the Commission; Recommendations and Opinions of the Council and the Commission; Resolutions of the Council, housekeeping matters such as tenders and notifications of employment vacancies in the Institutions of the Community.

The legislative process for Council Regulations and Directives

We come now to a description of the stages through which a proposal must pass before it emerges as a Council Regulation or Directive. Decisions are excluded because they are much fewer in number and the procedure much less elaborate. Figs. 1 and 2 may help to make the steps clearer but it should be realised that both they and the verbal explanation can only hope to give a broad outline of the sequence of events and obviously variations can take place. For the purposes of illustration it is assumed throughout that the proposal concerns some aspect of agriculture.

The legislative process can be divided into three stages:

(a) elaboration within the Commission;

(b) discussion within other Institutions of the Community, and

(c) action by the Council.

(A) WITHIN THE COMMISSION

As we have seen, the power to initiate legislation lies with the Commission. This power of initiative relates to the formulation of proposals, the preparation of drafts and their supervision as they go through the consultative process towards final adoption by the Council.

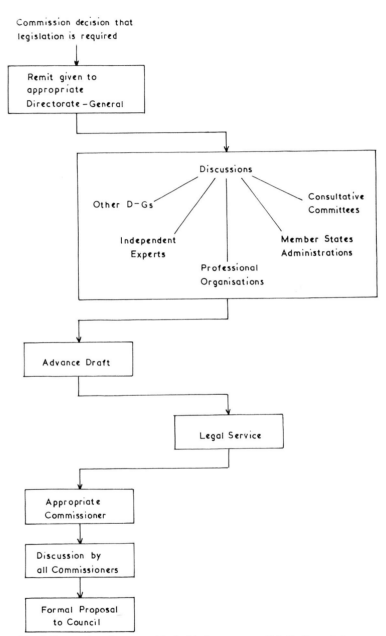

Fig. 1: Preparation of a proposal for legislation: process within the Commission.

The *origin* of the idea in any proposal does not necessarily lie with the Commission. It may have arisen in the Council, the European Parliament, a Member State, the ESC, trade interests, etc. As Noël [61] has described, the Commission has the duty 'to assemble vast amounts of information and to seek the widest advice in order to establish what is in the general interest of the Community. The Commission has therefore to carry out an open-door policy, keeping itself informed of points of view, and pre-occupations, both of Governments and their administrations, of political circles, and trade unions and professional organisations.'

Irrespective of where the basic idea comes from, the Commission (in the person of the Commissioners) decides that legislation in a particular field is necessary and the Commissioner within whose competence the matter comes (in this case agriculture) is requested to set the procedure in motion. The preparatory work is organised by the Commissioner and a small group of staff from the relevant Directorate-General, i.e. D-G VI.

The D-G consults widely at this early stage with trade and professional bodies, with technical experts, with national civil services and, internally, with other directorates-general which have an interest in the topic area concerned. In many cases these initial contacts are very informal but *ad hoc* working parties may be set up or existing working groups asked to consider the suggested legislation as part of their general activities. The opinion of one or more of the various consultative committees, referred to in chapter 2, may be sought and the D-G may also consult relevant special interest groups (see chapter 4), many of which keep offices in Brussels.

On completion of these preliminary consultations the D-G has the advance draft put into the correct legal form with the help of the Commission's legal staff. When ready the draft proposal is submitted to the Commissioner who may have it examined by his own *cabinet* (i.e. his personal staff). When the draft has been approved by the Commissioner, he presents it to his fellow Commissioners who, in their turn, must approve it by a simple majority decision.

Two procedures are available to ascertain the Commissioners' views on a draft proposal: either it can be discussed at one of their weekly meetings or it can be handled according to the written circulation procedure. Owing to the tremendous volume of work involved, this latter procedure has become more common, especially for agriculture and in particular for topics on which it is not expected that there will be much controversy. The Secretariat-General of the Commission circulates the draft to each of the Commissioners who are allowed to make comments or raise objections within a set period of time. If there are no objections, the draft is automatically adopted.

(B) DISCUSSION WITHIN OTHER COMMUNITY INSTITUTIONS

We now come to the second stage in the legislative process. The Commission, having approved the proposal, submits it formally to the Council. The Council Secretariat puts it on the agenda of COREPER or SCA for preliminary consideration. These two committees may in turn delegate their examination of the proposal to working parties composed of government experts. Once the proposal has had its preliminary consideration by COREPER or SCA, it is forwarded to the European Parliament and–if relevant–to the ESC for their Opinions. The Parliament refers the proposal to its agricultural committee and the ESC refers it to its specialised section dealing with agriculture. While the proposal is under consideration by all these various bodies, D-G VI is represented at their meetings and the Commission has the opportunity to explain and defend its proposal, and to work out a compromise if needed.

The agricultural committee of the Parliament appoints a *rapporteur* and commences discussion of the proposal which is introduced to the committee by a representative of D-G VI. The *rapporteur* draws up a report in the form of a motion and an explanatory statement which the committee discusses. Minority opinions may be added to the report, as may be the opinions of other interested committees. When the report is adopted it is sent forward to a plenary session of the Parliament. If the topic is a purely technical one the committee may recommend that the motion be adopted without a debate. If, however, the topic is of political interest the report is presented to the full Parliament by the *rapporteur* and a debate follows. A vote is taken on the motion and on any amendments to it. If the motion is agreed it then becomes a Resolution

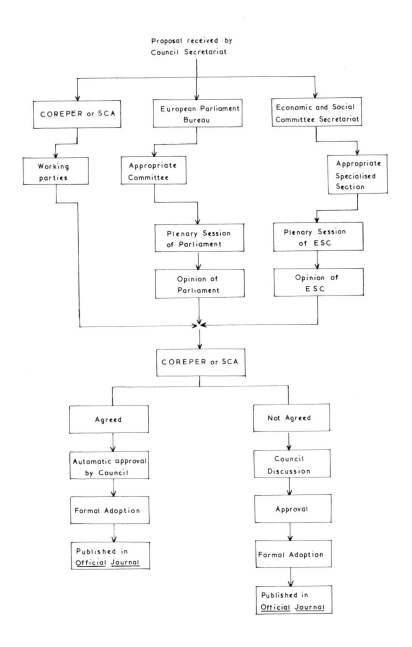

Fig. 2: Legislative Process at the Council stage.

or opinion (as the case warrants) of the Parliament which is then forwarded to the Council.

The procedure adopted in the ESC is somewhat similar. A *rapporteur* is appointed from the members of the specialised section on agriculture. The proposal is introduced by a representative of D-G VI and a general discussion follows. After this initial discussion the *rapporteur* draws up a working document which, in the course of later discussions, becomes the section's draft opinion. When the section has adopted the opinion, the *rapporteur* draws up a final report which must be an objective account of the views expressed during discussions. The opinion, the final report and any other relevant documentation (including the opinions of other specialised sections) are forwarded for consideration at a plenary session of the ESC. If the opinion of the specialised section is adopted by the full ESC, it and all the accompanying documents are forwarded to the Council as the official Opinion of the ESC.

(C) ACTION BY THE COUNCIL

Having received the views of the European Parliament and the ESC, the Council must decide whether to accept or to reject them. Let us assume the Council agrees to modify its views (which only happens in a minority of cases), then the new version will be considered in the Council's name by COREPER or SCA. As described in chapter 2, if agreement can be reached in these Committees, no further discussion is necessary at Council level. The item will be placed in the 'A' section of the agenda and passed by the Council on the nod. If, however, a discussion is required then the matter can be dealt with verbally at a meeting of the Council. When a proposal has been approved by the Council the text of the new Regulation or Directive must be verified in all the official Community languages. It is then formally adopted by the Council and is published in the 'L' series of the *Official Journal*.

Legislative process by the Commission

Council Regulations and Directives frequently delegate certain powers of implementation to the Commission. This is in accordance with

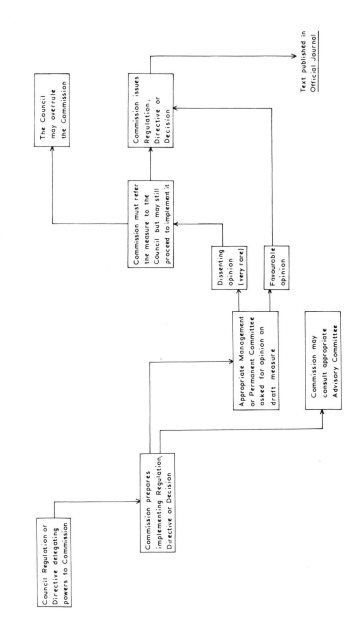

Fig. 3: Legislative process by the Commission.

Art. 155 of the Rome Treaty which states that the Commission should 'exercise the powers conferred on it by the Council for the implementation of the rules laid down by the latter.' The subject matter of these delegated powers is usually technical or administrative. Although the powers of the Commission in the legislative field are circumscribed, they are not any the less important because of that. Commission Regulations are frequently more immediately relevant to large numbers of persons than the original Council Regulations on which they are based, in that it is the Commission legislation which controls the day-to-day operations of the CAP.

The procedure–illustrated in fig. 3–is for the Commission to prepare a draft Regulation or Directive, often in consultation with the appropriate Advisory Committee. The draft is then transmitted to the relevant Management Committee if it concerns a commodity coming within the scope of the CAP, or to the other relevant committees such as the Standing Committee on agricultural structures or the European Agricultural Guidance and Guarantee Fund Committee.

In the event of a favourable opinion from the Management (or similar) Committee, the draft is approved by the Commission–usually according to the written procedure–and the Regulation or Directive is published in the *Official Journal* 'L' series, after the necessary verification of the text in the official languages of the Community. In the event of an unfavourable opinion, the Commission must refer the measure to the Council for its adjudication. However, while awaiting the Council's ruling the Commission can, if it wishes, proceed with the implementation of the disputed measure on a temporary basis. As pointed out in chapter 2, disputes between the Commission and these committees are very rare. In cases of extreme urgency the Commission can decide to act alone without having first consulted the Management or other Committees. Such measures are usually of short duration or are subject to subsequent endorsement by the relevant Committee.

CHAPTER 4

National links with the CAP

The Common Agricultural Policy is often depicted as something remote, administered from afar by a bureaucracy in Brussels with which people in the individual Member States have very little contact. In reality this is far from the truth. Some indication has already been given in chapter 2 of the extensive network of committees–some statutory, some not–which play an important role in the consultative and decision-making process. In this present chapter some further insights are given into the links which exist between institutions and interests in the Member States and the Community Institutions, particularly the Commission.

The examples chosen are very different one from another: they operate at different levels and defend very diverse interests. The discussion starts with a description of the links between the Ministry of Agriculture (it could be in any Member State but for convenience the UK has been chosen) and the Commission and Council in the legislative process. It then turns to the subject of the scrutiny of Community legislation by national parliaments. The third institution is the intervention agency or agencies set up by each Member State to carry out the domestic market intervention measures required under the CAP. Finally, there is an examination of the links which exist between special interest groups and the Commission, focussing particularly on producers and consumers.

Ministries

The links between the various national government departments and the Commission are many: some formal, some very informal. The closest links and most frequent contacts undoubtedly occur in the agricultural sphere. The role of the Management Committees has been discussed already in chapter 2, and the reader will recall that national civil servants sit on these committees and help the Commission to administer the day-to-day operations of the various commodity regimes.

Our present concern is with the procedure adopted when a government department is considering a proposal for legislation by the Council. Throughout it is assumed that it concerns agriculture. The model is the Ministry of Agriculture, Fisheries and Food (MAFF) in the UK. Obviously Ministries in other Member States may operate somewhat differently but, however they proceed in detail, basically they are performing the same function. Indeed procedure within MAFF is not always the same: some proposed legislation involves a far wider range of interested parties inside and outside the Ministry than others, and some proposals are far more important than others from a UK point of view.

MAFF usually knows well in advance that a particular piece of legislation is being drafted in the Commission–indeed members of the Ministry staff may have been consulted about it or may have sat on working parties discussing it, or it may have come up in the course of the activities of a Management Committee. Once the proposal has been formally adopted by the Commission (i.e. by the Commissioners at one of their regular meetings) and is submitted to the Council for its consideration, it becomes quite widely available and is often loosely referred to as a 'COM document'. This is a reference to its call number which always starts with the initials COM: so, for instance, we have COM(78)81 final, adopted by the Commissioners on 29 March 1978, entitled 'Proposals for a Council Regulation on the common organisation of the market in sheepmeat'. Frequently, these COM documents are published a little later in the 'C' series of the *Official Journal.* In the present example it appeared in C 93, 18 April 1978.

Once the Commission has formally adopted a proposal, it is sent to the Council Secretariat which distributes it under a Council reference number to the relevant government departments in the Member States. In the UK all agricultural proposals come in the first instance to EEC Division I in MAFF. This Division has a coordinating role in all matters to do with the European Community. It retains a master copy of the proposal and decides on the distribution of the remainder within MAFF. Obviously the Division or Divisions most closely involved with the subject matter of the proposal have priority. One copy is also sent to

EEC Division II, which acts as the Ministry's liaison point with the Parliamentary Scrutiny Committees, discussed below.

The Division most directly involved with the topic—let us assume it is a commodity—must develop the Ministry's view on the proposal. It will examine the implications of the proposal from the point of view of its effect on various national interests—producers, consumers, traders, manufacturers, etc.—and may well consult with some or all of these interests to hear their views. The Commodity Division must then write the brief to be used by the UK representative at the meeting of the SCA or the Council. When ready this brief is forwarded to EEC Division I. Often the Divisions involved have to work extremely quickly as there may not be much time between the Commission submitting the proposal to the Council and the first discussions in the SCA. The task is made more difficult if other ministries have to be consulted—for example, the Department of Agriculture and Fisheries in Scotland (DAFS) or the Department of Agriculture in Northern Ireland (DANI), or the Treasury.

Every week during which there is a meeting of the SCA or Council scheduled at which agricultural matters are to be discussed, a previous meeting takes place in MAFF of the Departmental Committee on Europe. At this meeting the agenda of the forthcoming SCA or Council meeting is discussed and the UK policy line on each item is agreed. To this meeting come representatives of the Divisions which are preparing briefs on topics appearing on the SCA or Council agenda. The Departmental Committee is usually chaired by the EEC Group Under Secretary and often is also attended by the Minister from the Permanent Representative's Office in Brussels who will actually attend the meeting of the SCA in Brussels. Some matters which are of particular importance may also be discussed in one of the Inter-departmental Committees in Whitehall which deal with Community affairs, and which are co-ordinated by the Cabinet Office.

While all the above activity is taking place, EEC Division II will have been pursuing its role as liaison point with the Parliamentary Scrutiny Committees. Its first task is to request the Commodity Division to prepare an explanatory memorandum on the proposal. This memorandum summarises the proposal, indicating its legal and policy implications and gives an estimate of the likely timetable of its consideration by the Council. Usually the Division has a week in which to write this memorandum. It is then edited, submitted to a Minister for signature, reproduced and sent down to the Houses of Parliament. To give some idea of the volume of work involved in this operation: in 1977 over 200 explanatory memoranda were forwarded to the Scrutiny Committees and the figure is rising all the time. Of course, it must be emphasised that the work-load on the agricultural side is by far the heaviest: other Ministries do not have nearly so much draft legislation to handle.

Parliamentary scrutiny

It will be recalled from chapter 3 that Council and Commission Regulations have the force of law without any intervention by the parliaments of the various Member States. We saw how the European Parliament is given an opportunity to express its views on proposed Council legislation but that such views do not have to be accepted by the Council. Where then does this leave the national parliaments? There is no formal link between them and the Community Institutions[7] and any influence which they wish to exert must be indirect either through the government of their own country or through making their views known to the Commission. As we have seen Commission Regulations are adopted very quickly—usually after consultation with the Management (or similar) Committee—and frequently these Regulations are of limited duration. Clearly the national parliamentarian's role in this process is nil. However, the national parliaments can and do play a part in the legislative process as it applies to Council Regulations and Directives. This they do by discussing the draft legislation as proposed to the Council by the Commission.

Not all Member State parliaments are equally involved nor are they all equally interested in making their voice heard. The least involved are probably those of France, Belgium and the Netherlands; the most involved are those of the new Member States; and the remaining countries somewhere in between.[8] Neither the French Assembly nor the Senate has a committee on European affairs and there is no detailed scrutiny of Community legislation. In Belgium there is a European Affairs Committee in the House of Representatives but its responsibilities lie in the field of information and liaison and it does not take part in the scrutiny of proposed or enacted Community legislation. The Dutch First Chamber (Upper House) has a Committee of European Affairs but scrutiny of Community legislation is not one of its functions. This is carried out by the various specialist Committees of the Second Chamber (Lower House).

In Federal Germany the *Bundesrat* (Upper House) has a Committee for European Community matters which coordinates the examination of draft Community legislation carried out in the various specialist committees of both the *Bundesrat* and *Bundestag* (Lower House). The examination is carried out in the *Bundesrat* as soon as possible after publication of the proposal. The *Bundestag* committees follow on somewhat later so as to be able to take account of changes agreed during the early negotiations in the Council. The committees in both Houses report to their respective House whose final opinions are forwarded to the Federal Government.

The Italian Senate has a Committee for European Affairs which, on its own initiative, can express an opinion on Community legislation—draft or enacted. Legislation is also examined and reported on by the appropriate specialist committee. In the Chamber of Deputies discussion of draft Community legislation generally takes place in the Foreign Affairs Committee or in its permanent Sub-Committee for Community Affairs.

In Ireland, the Oireachtas (Parliament) has a Committee on the Secondary Legislation of the European Communities, with members drawn from both the Senate and *Dáil*. This Committee examines and reports on Commission proposals. It meets once a month in public and evidence is heard by sub-committees in private. The Committee's reports are made to both Houses.

In Denmark, the *Folketing* (Parliament) has a Market Relations Committee which must be informed about any proposals coming before the Community Council of Ministers which have a direct bearing on Danish law. Great importance is attached to the Committee's opinion which can set the limits on the Danish position in Council negotiations. It can happen that the Danish Minister attending a Council meeting has to ask for an adjournment while he consults the Committee further.

The UK has two parliamentary committees: the House of Lords Select Committee on the European Communities, and the House of Commons Select Committee on European Legislation. Both these Committees scrutinise proposals for Council legislation. A Ministry works on the assumption that if it hears nothing from the Lords it can go ahead and reach an agreement in Brussels but it looks for positive clearance by the Commons, i.e. that the proposal is not considered to be of legal or political importance. Should a proposal be recommended for debate, this debate will normally be held before agreement is reached in Brussels as the UK Government gave an undertaking to Parliament that, except in special circumstances, it would not agree to any decision in the Council of Ministers if one or other of the Scrutiny Committees had recommended a debate on the issue but that debate had not yet taken place.

The mode of operation and the terms of reference of the two Committees are not the same. To take the House of Lords first; once the Ministry's explanatory memorandum has been received by the Chairman of the Committee, he sifts the proposals into A-type (thought not to require any special attention) and B-type (requiring further consideration or containing important information). B-type proposals are then forwarded to whichever of the seven sub-committees is the most relevant: one of the sub-committees deals with agriculture, fisheries and consumer affairs. Some proposals are considered by more than one sub-committee. About one-third of all proposals are classified as B-type, although the proportion is probably lower in agricultural matters. If the sub-committee decides to examine the proposal further, it is free to take written and oral evidence from interested parties, including Ministries and to make a report to the House for debate or information. In the majority of cases the sub-committee reports to the House without recommending a debate, although again this is less likely to be true in the case of agriculture.

The House of Commons Select Committee on European legislation normally meets every week while the House is in session and its agenda is available a few days in advance. Government departments may request extra items to be put on the agenda in the light of the likely developments in the Council of Ministers in the near future. Usually all matters are discussed in full committee rather than in sub-committee as in the Lords.

When the explanatory memorandum comes over from the Ministry, one of the clerks to the Committee draws up a brief on the topic for the Committee members. If the Committee decides to investigate a proposal further, it may take written and oral evidence in much the same way as the Lords. One important difference is that if oral evidence is required from the Government, the House of Commons Committee will expect a Minister to appear before it, while in the Lords evidence is usually taken from senior civil servants, except on very political matters where Ministerial evidence has to be taken. Sometimes the Lords and Commons Committees hear evidence concurrently in order to avoid duplication but their reports are not joint and can differ in approach.[9]

Intervention agencies

Chapters 7 to 10 are devoted to a discussion of the operation of the market and price support systems for agricultural products. All the methods employed find their legal base primarily in Council Regulations but much of the detail is left to later Commission Regulations. While these two Institutions pass Regulations to fix prices, set up systems and to devise frameworks within which trade can take place, they are not–and could not be–responsible for the detailed administration of the policies in the individual Member States. This is left to a group of organisations known collectively as 'intervention agencies'. Each Member State has devised its own system for handling the work involved within the framework set out in Art. 4 of Reg. 729/70 (*On the financing of the common agricultural policy* (Sp. OJ 1965–1966)). This Article defines the procedure under which Member States designate the various agencies; it specifies the information which has to be supplied to the Commission about these agencies; and it details the arrangements made to provide the agencies with the finances needed to carry out their tasks.

In some Member States existing bodies were pressed into service when the new responsibilities arose, in others, new bodies were set up especially to carry out the tasks. The Member States also differ in their approach as to whether the responsibilities of the various intervention agencies are divided according to the commodities which they handle or according to the tasks which they perform. What follows is a brief account of the arrangements in the Member States.

In *Belgium* three bodies are involved:

OCCL (*Office Central des Contingents et Licences*) which is responsible for the payment of export refunds;

OBEA (*Office Belge de l'Economie et de l'Agriculture*) which is responsible for domestic market intervention measures, with the exception of certain matters in the dairy sector which are handled by:

ONL (*Office National du Lait et de ses dérivés*).

In *Germany* all export refunds are paid by the *Oberfinanzdirektion*–Hamburg; intervention is carried out by the *Bundesanstalt für landwirtschaftliche Marktordnung* in Frankfurt.

France is the prime example of a country which pressed into service a variety of previously existing bodies and which, when the need arose, did not hesitate to create new ones. They are organised along commodity rather than functional lines, each body handling (where relevant) both intervention and export restitutions for the commodities for which it is responsible.

The French agencies are:

ONIC (*Office National Interprofessionel des Céréales*) which, as its name suggests, deals with cereals;

FORMA (*Fonds d'Orientation et de Régularisation des Marchés Agricoles*) which deals with a wide variety of products not dealt with by the other more specific commodity agencies;

FIRS (*Fonds d'Intervention et de Régularisation du Marché du Sucre*) which deals with sugar;

SIDO (*Société Interprofessionnelle des Oléagineux*) which deals with oil seeds;

ONIBEV (*Office National Interprofessionnel du Bétail et des Viandes*) which deals with livestock and meat;

ONIVIT (*Office National Interprofessionnel des Vins de Tables*) which deals with wine;

FIOX (*Fonds d'Intervention et d'Organisation des Marchés des produits de la pêche maritime et de la Conchyculture*) which deals with fisheries; and *Services des Alcools* which deals with distillation.

In *Italy* all export restitutions and production payments are handled by the *Intendenza Finanza di Roma* while all remaining domestic market measures are handled by:

CCZ (*Cassa Conguaglio Zucchero*)–sugar;

ENR (*Ente Nazionale Risi*)–rice; and

AIMA (*Azienda di Stato per gli Interventi nel Mercato Agricolo*)–all other commodities.

The *Netherlands* is rather like France in having a considerable number of commodity centred bodies, each of which handles both domestic intervention measures and export refunds, but not buying-in operations.

These agencies are:

Hoofdproduktschap voor Akkerbouprodukten (arable crops);

Produktschap voor Zuivel (dairy products);

Produktschap voor Vee en Vlees (beef and veal);

Produktschap voor Groenten en Fruit (vegetables and fruit);

Produktschap voor Pluimvee en Eieren (poultry and eggs);

Produktschap voor Vis en Visprodukten (fish and fish products);

Produktschap voor Margarine, Vetten en Olien (fats and oils); and

VIB (*Voedselvoorzieningsin–en Verkoopbureau*) which is responsible for buying-in operations in all sectors.

Denmark, Ireland, Luxembourg and the *UK* all have the neatest systems, i.e. one organisation in each handling both domestic intervention and export restitutions. In the first three countries it is the Ministry of Agriculture which handles these matters; in the UK it is the Intervention Board for Agricultural Produce (IBAP).

Intervention agencies are umbrella organisations which can and often do delegate functions to other bodies which act on their behalf. However, the intervention agencies remain responsible for seeing that the Regulations are implemented correctly and that the funds involved are properly used.

The intervention agencies work very independently and have relatively few contacts with similar bodies in other Member States. This may seem strange at first sight but it must be remembered that, while each agency is applying Community law, each is also working within its own national context and national law. Contacts with the Commission are more frequent and can be important. The main opportunity for contact comes through attendance at the relevant Management

Committee meetings as members of the delegation from individual Member States. This can be very helpful to the Committee because the intervention agencies have practical experience of administering the commodity regimes and are better placed to judge the feasibility of carrying out particular practices.

Expenditure incurred in the course of the operations of the agencies is borne partly by the Community and partly by the Member State. For example, the national exchequer bears the cost of administering the agencies; technical costs of support buying (i.e. handling, storage and insurance costs) and the cost of purchasing intervention stocks are funded in the first instance by the national exchequer, but the technical costs are reimbursed later by the Community at standard rates. If intervention stocks are subsequently sold at a loss, this is borne by the Community; if they are sold at a profit, it is the Community which benefits. Some operations are jointly funded: for instance, the beef premium and the general butter subsidy. Other operations are directly paid for by the Community, such as the expenditure on monetary compensatory amounts necessitated by currency fluctuations.

If we look at the activities of one intervention agency, we can perhaps get a better idea of the range of its activities. The example chosen is that of IBAP in the UK. In one sense this is not a very good choice because it deals with the whole range of commodities and therefore is quite unlike, say, the French or Dutch systems, but in another sense the fact that it deals with all the UK commodities makes its operations easier to follow. It should be remembered that there are various support arrangements which do not come within IBAP's range of activities because of the northerly location of Britain.

The first thing to note about IBAP is that it does not physically handle any commodities itself; it sets up the framework, and then uses other bodies to carry out the work, overseeing their operations. IBAP is responsible for virtually every operation which is funded from the Guarantee Section of FEOGA (outlined in chapter 5). This means that it supervises not only the withdrawal of produce from the domestic market in times of over-supply, but it is also responsible for the payment of production subsidies and payments on the area of certain crops. The only responsibility which it has handed over to another government agency is the Community subsidy on school milk which (although financed through IBAP) is administered by the Education Departments.

When IBAP receives offers of commodities from over-supplied markets, it uses various public agencies and other bodies to undertake the physical arrangements. For example, it uses the Home Grown Cereals Authority (HGCA) for all matters relating to cereals intervention; the Meat and Livestock Commission (MLC) for the market support arrangements for beef; when butter is sold into intervention, IBAP stores it under contract in commercially-operated cold stores.

IBAP uses the Agricultural Departments (MAFF, DAFS and DANI) as its agents for checking many physical and technical matters related to the Board's activities. For instance, they check the actual quantities of dairy products in intervention store and verify that the quality of the produce is up to the minimum standards laid down.

Each year IBAP produces a report on its activities in which it gives details of operations within each commodity area: the quantities of butter, skimmed milk powder, cereals and beef sold into intervention; the tonnage of fish withdrawn from the market; the quantity of seeds (herbage, field beans and peas) and dehydrated fodder on which subsidy was paid; the area of hops on which subsidy was paid and so forth. Table 2, which is taken from IBAP's report for the calendar year 1977 [57], summarises by type of scheme the expenditure in the UK borne by FEOGA Guarantee Section. It is somewhat misleading to take one year in isolation as is done here, because the amounts paid out under the various schemes can fluctuate appreciably from one year to another. The only merit of the table is that it illustrates the range of activities. The same strictures apply to table 3 which summarises expenditure by IBAP borne by the UK exchequer in the same year.

The Brussels lobbies

When the ECSC Treaty was drawn up in 1951 provision was made (under Art. 46) for the High Authority (i.e. the equivalent of the Commission) to consult 'Governments, the various parties concerned (undertakings, workers, consumers and dealers) and their associations, and any experts.' The Article went on to state that 'undertakings,

TABLE 2

Summary by scheme of UK expenditure borne by FEOGA Guarantee Section, 1977

	1977 *£'000*
Aids to private storage:	
butter	4218.3
sugar	6649.6
beef	7779.2
pigmeat	131.0
Compensation for withdrawn produce:	
fish	792.9
fruit and vegetables	13.6
Aids to animal feed:	
skimmed milk and skimmed milk powder	11673.3
denaturing of sugar	2.3
Third Country Trade:	
export refunds	28258.9
import refunds	79622.1
Intra-Community Trade:	
import refunds	3617.0
export refunds	48.4
export levies	(57697.6)[a]
Production subsidies:	
cereals for starch manufacture, etc	1850.0
casein and caseinates	1715.3
dehydrated fodder	459.3
oilseeds	6478.4
herbage seeds	1055.2
flax	222.8
hops	625.7
Beef premiums	2571.2
Meat promotion scheme	58.4
Social beef subsidy	0.2
Non-marketing of milk and conversion premium	499.9
Co-responsibility levy on milk	(2546.2)[a]
General butter subsidy	38198.0
Selective butter subsidy	0.8
Sugar–DOM refining	1431.1
Intervention buying of beef, butter, oilseeds and skimmed milk powder, losses and costs for reimbursement by FEOGA	8681.6
TOTAL	146410.8

(a) figures in brackets represent amounts credited to FEOGA

Source: [57]

TABLE 3

Summary of IBAP expenditure borne by the UK exchequer, 1977

	1977 £'000
Intervention buying:	
skimmed milk powder	42714.4
butter	20553.1
beef	13269.3
oilseeds	0.8
Incidental expenses: (expenditure on insurance, transport, handling, drying and storage (including reservation of storage space) and revaluation of stocks	7153.8
General butter subsidy	13967.2
Beef premiums	7991.5
Social beef scheme	0.4
TOTAL	105650.5
Receipts from sales of intervention stocks	20144.2
Net expenditure	85506.3

Source: [57]

workers, consumers and dealers, and their associations, shall be entitled to present any suggestions or comments to the High Authority on questions affecting them.'

Thus, a two-way channel of communication between the High Authority and sectional interests was established and organisations representing economic and professional activities began to open offices in Brussels, so as to keep in touch more easily with the activities of the new Community. Although the Rome Treaty establishing the Economic Community is silent on this consultation process, the habit had been formed, and an even wider range of interests came together to form umbrella organisations to represent them at Community level. A special impetus was given to this development on the agricultural front by a declaration by the Commission at the Stresa Conference that it wished to cooperate closely with the various groups and institutions concerned in the formulation of the CAP.

Collectively these various organisations have come to be known as 'Special Interest Groups'. Some have what amounts to a semi-official status: for example, we saw in chapters 2 and 3 how the Commission consults with outside bodies to quite a considerable degree, and it prefers to deal with Community-wide organisations rather than with national ones. The links are fostered in a number of ways. Firstly, the Commission consults with bodies such as the Advisory Agricultural Committees for the various commodities. The membership of these Advisory Committees is made up of 50 per cent farmers and 50 per cent food manufacturers, consumers and trade unions combined.

Secondly, there are many informal meetings between Commission staff and representatives of the various Special Interest Groups. Thirdly, there are the consultations with the ESC whose members are drawn from vocational interests. Fourthly, in the case of agriculture, there are regular meetings between the Commissioner for Agriculture and COPA–the farmers' professional organisation, referred to below.

From time to time the Commission publishes two *repertoires* or directories which list the hundreds of non-governmental organisations at Community level. Not all have offices in Brussels, but a very high proportion have. One of these directories deals with non-agricultural special interest groups [22] (though curiously it does include information on the food and drink industries); the other deals exclusively with agricultural organisations [11]. If we examine the latter directory we find that it lists 152 organisations representing agricultural interests subdivided as follows:

A. Agricultural producers	15
B. Agricultural and food products processing industries	66
C. Agricultural and food trading	42
D. Agricultural cooperatives	9
E. Agricultural and food industry workers	2
F. Consumers	3
G. Miscellaneous	15
TOTAL	152

COPA

Among the agricultural producers' organisations the most influential is undoubtedly COPA (*Comité des Organisations Professionelles Agricoles*). Its membership is composed of the major agricultural organisations in each of the Member States of the Community. At the moment there are twenty-two member organisations: one each from Federal Germany, Ireland and Luxembourg; three each from Belgium, Denmark, Italy, the Netherlands and the UK; and four from France. The Praesidium of COPA decides on the admission of new member organisations. Considerations taken into account in making such a decision are whether the applicant body represents genuine farmers or not, what its political persuasion is (Communist organisations so far have not been admitted), the type of producers represented (smallholders' organisations would not be admitted).

COPA has an Assembly which meets at least once a year and which lays down the general guidelines of policy on the basis of a proposal put forward by the Praesidium. This latter body is composed of one or two permanent representatives from each member organisation (usually the presidents of the member organisations fulfil this function). It meets on a regular basis and represents COPA at discussions with the Commissioner for Agriculture. It takes all decisions within the framework of the Assembly's general guidelines.

The Praesidium is assisted by two levels of officials. Firstly, there is the General Experts Group: its functions are to carry out studies of an economic or policy nature for the Praesidium and to coordinate the positions and recommendations of the various working groups referred to below. Its membership is usually composed of the senior staff of the member organisations, or the permanent representatives of the member organisations in Brussels. Secondly, there are the various working groups which examine current policy in their respective sectors and make recommendations to the Praesidium. These working groups cover all the major and some of the minor commodities, as well as social matters and farm accounts. Their membership is drawn from the relevant sections of the national organisations.

COPA exists to put forward a unified producer view to the Community Institutions and in particular to the Commission. The question naturally arises as to how COPA can do this when its membership is composed of organisations which, although they all represent farmers, do not always have the same interests on a specific issue. Occasions have arisen in the past in which COPA was deadlocked internally but such strong differences are tending to become infrequent. It is usually possible to reach a compromise on the basis of common interest. If such a compromise is impossible, then all points of view are presented to the Commission. It is no mean feat that COPA is as effective as it is considering that it must resolve within itself conflicts which are based on national or sectoral divergences of interest, and also conflicts which arise between the organisations which make up its membership from those countries where more than one producers' organisation is represented.

The survival of COPA is dependent on its effectiveness and credibility and, while its contacts with the Commission are many and are at every level from the most formal to the most informal, its contacts with the Council and the Parliament are less well developed. Indeed particularly as far as the Council is concerned, the national producers' organisations are more important than COPA in terms of lobbying power. The reason is that as the Council is composed of government ministers from the Member States, it is inevitable that the individual national farmers' organisations make representations direct to the relevant minister in the national capitals. He then comes to Council meetings briefed by his own farmers and not by COPA.

Besides its involvement with the Commission, COPA shares with COGECA (*Comité général de la co-opération agricole*) the functions of providing personnel to fill the agricultural posts on the various Advisory Agricultural Committees on commodities, structure and other matters. The Commission tends to give greater weight to the opinions of–above all–the Management Committees, but also of the European Parliament and ESC than it does to the deliberations of the Advisory Committees. Whether this is a reflection of the quality of the views of the respective organisations or not it is difficult to tell, but it suggests that COPA's main lobbying role lies elsewhere.

It should not be thought for one moment that any appreciable number of the Special Interest Groups are in as influential a position *vis-à-vis* the Commission as COPA. The contacts between the Commission and agricultural interests are closer and more constant than in other areas of economic life. However, as the Community develops in other directions it is likely that contacts with other sectional interests will grow *pari passu*. One interest group which undoubtedly has strengthened its position in recent years is that of consumers, and to this we now turn.

Consumer interests

There are a number of ways in which the consumer voice is heard at Community level. The oldest are to be found in the consumer representation on the ESC and on the Advisory Agricultural Committees. Consumers do not have a place as of right on the ESC: it is dependent on the governments of the individual Member States putting forward the names of people who will represent the consumer interest on the Committee among the one-third of its membership which is reserved for 'independants'. The position of consumers' representatives on the Advisory Agricultural Committees is more formal. As we have seen above, half the membership of each Committee must be drawn from the ranks of food manufacturers, consumers and trade unions.

In 1973, steps were taken by the Commission to strengthen the position of the consumer at Community level. Firstly, it established as a separate department within its organisation the Environment and Consumer Protection Service. In 1975, the Council followed up this initiative by adopting an action programme for a consumer protection and information policy. Secondly, also back in 1973 the Commission set up a Consumers' Consultative Committee (CCC). This Committee has twenty-five members: of these, fifteen are appointed by the Commission from organisations representing consumer interests; there are four experts appointed by the consumer organisations; and six independent experts.

The consumer representatives on the CCC are drawn from four organisations functioning on a Community-wide basis. These are:

BEUC (*Bureau Européen des Unions de Consommateurs*);

ETUC (*European Trade Union Confederation*);

COFACE (*Comités des organisations familiales auprès des Communautés Européennes*); and

EURO-COOP (*European Community of Consumer Cooperatives*)

The function of CCC is to examine draft legislation on such things as consumer credit, labelling of foodstuffs, textiles, etc., doorstep selling and so forth. It meets once every three months and its steering committee holds periodic additional meetings. CCC also nominates representatives to the Advisory Committees on Agriculture and Foodstuffs.

In terms of its functions, BEUC is to the national consumers' organisations what COPA is to the farmers' organisations, i.e. it is the Community-wide umbrella body which represents consumers' interests. In some ways its task is easier than that of COPA because its member organisations tend to have very similar interests and opinions on consumer issues. However, it is handicapped by not having COPA's standing in terms of both its formal and informal contacts with the Commission, nor does it have the same kind of financial backing. For instance, while BEUC has existed since 1962, it was only in 1973 with the Enlargement of the Community that it felt able to open its office in Brussels.

At the moment BEUC has twelve full member organisations–two each from Belgium, France and the UK, and one each from the other Member States. It also has a number of associate member organisations. In order to qualify for full membership a national organisation must serve the interests of consumers alone and must not have other wider objectives. The member organisations in each country are responsible for the task of putting pressure on governments to nominate consumers' representatives to the ESC. They are also expected to brief members of the ESC on consumer matters.

Apart from having three permanent seats on the CCC, BEUC also seeks to influence Community policy by giving evidence before a number of committees of the European Parliament–in particular those which deal with the environment, consumer protection and public health; and agriculture.

One of the most important opportunities which BEUC has to put forward its views is during the discussions on the annual price proposals for agriculture. In recent years BEUC has had meetings with the Commissioner for Agriculture and with the President of the Council of Agricultural Ministers concerning these price proposals. It will be recalled that Art. 39 of the Rome Treaty has as one of its aims 'to ensure that supplies reach consumers at reasonable prices'. BEUC believes that this aim cannot be properly fulfilled unless the Community moves away from a purely agricultural policy for farmers towards a food policy for both farmers and consumers.

Notes to Chapter 4

7. Except in so far as some members of national parliaments are also members of the European Parliament, although this practice is likely to become exceptional once the latter is directly elected.
8. The summary of practices in the various parliaments (with the exception of the UK Parliament) is taken from an account of scrutiny procedures prepared by the House of Lords Select Committee on the European Communities [56].
9. It is interesting to contrast how the two Committees handle the same topic: an example is the reports on the draft proposal on sheepmeat; see House of Lords [55] and House of Commons [53].

CHAPTER 5

Financing the Community

The European Community has long been groping its way towards some form of economic and monetary union and has been seeking the most suitable means by which such a union might be achieved. Given that from its inception the Community has perceived itself as much more than a customs union, it may seem illogical that it did not start out by creating an economic and monetary union. Such a beginning would have led naturally to the development of many policies in individual fields which the Community is still struggling to achieve. But that is not how things evolved: one must appreciate that the steps taken in the 1950s to create an Economic Community were sufficiently bold in themselves in the context of their time without contemplating the ultimate achievement of an economic and monetary union.

Indeed, when reading the Treaty of Rome one cannot help being struck by the tentative way in which the Treaty designers approached monetary and economic matters (see especially Arts. 103–109). For instance, there is the polite sentiment expressed in Art. 104 that 'Each Member State shall pursue the economic policy needed to ensure the equilibrium of its overall balance of payments and to maintain confidence in its currency, while taking care to ensure a high level of employment and a stable level of prices.' This is followed by one of the great understatements of the Treaty: 'In order to facilitate attainment of the objectives set out in Art. 104, Member States shall coordinate their economic policies . . . .' Note that this does not call for a *common* economic policy but only for coordinated *national* policies. This may appear a limited goal but even its achievement has proved very difficult in practice.

As the Community progressed in the attainment of its more mechanical objectives–such as the elimination of barriers to trade–the realisation grew that there were certain things which it could not achieve in the absence of economic and monetary union. In a sense, the Community is confronted by a vicious circle: the greater the integration, the greater the need for a more highly developed economic and monetary union, but at the same time in the absence of such a policy the greater the hindrance to integration.

The Community has faced a second puzzle in this regard: during the 1960s when the economies of its Member States were buoyant, the achievement of economic and monetary union seemed an attractive–but perhaps not an essential–goal. In the 1970s when the Community has suffered along with the rest of the Western World the problems of fluctuating exchange rates, high unemployment, high inflation, stagnating trade, and widening income gaps between rich and poor regions, the achievement of economic and monetary union seems an urgent necessity but, because of the economic climate, it is very much harder to reach. Many ideas and plans have been put forward to enable the Community to move at least some of the way towards economic and monetary union, but success has been exceedingly limited. The latest move is the development of the European Monetary System (EMS) which, although a long way from the ultimate goal, is an attempt to lay a stepping stone along the route.

The design, management and control of the Community Budget is but a small part of the wider economic and monetary issues and of necessity this chapter is confined to the narrower field. It is concerned with five topics: the development of the Community's own resources; the choice of the unit of account used in budgetary calculations; the exercise of control over the Budget; the size and composition of the Budget; and the position of FEOGA *vis-à-vis* the rest of the Budget. Although we are not concerned with plotting developments on the wider economic and monetary front, nevertheless we must keep them in the backs of our minds because of their importance. Evolution on the more limited budgetary stage is not unconnected with the wider issues.

The development of the Community's own resources

Prior to 1971 the activities of the Economic Community were financed from three sources: the proceeds of a levy on certain agricultural products imported from third countries; the proceeds of an internal levy paid on sugar production in the Community; and, most important of all, payments made by the Member States from their own budgeted funds and based on a series of fixed keys or percentages. The Treaty of Rome made provision for the replacement of the fixed key contributions by the development of the Community's own resources. One source of revenue which it singled out in particular, which should accrue to the Community as of right, was the proceeds of the proposed common customs tariff (Art. 201).

This is not the place to record the vicissitudes which surrounded the attempts to introduce own resources: it is sufficient to record that under Council Decision 70/243 (ECSC, EEC, Euratom) *on the replacement of financial contributions from Member States by the Communities' own resources* (Sp. OJ 1970 (I)) agreement was reached that as from 1971 the Community would move to a new financial basis. The new system was to be introduced gradually over a period of years and not become fully operative until 1978. In the event this deadline was not met.

Decision 70/243 provided for three main sources of revenue: the levies and other similar charges arising from the trade with non-member countries within the framework of the CAP, together with the internal sugar levy (collectively known as 'agricultural levies'); the proceeds of the common customs duties; and a given percentage of the VAT revenue in the Member States, calculated on a uniform assessment base for each country.

It should be noted that in discussing sources of revenue it is customary to ignore the many minor sources such as the proceeds from income tax on staff salaries in the various Institutions, sales of publications, income from investments, sales of property, etc. Needless to state all these lesser items are recorded in the Community Budget.

The agricultural levies accrued to the Community as from the start of 1971. A proportion of the customs duties accrued to the Community the same year and the remainder was added gradually over the following four years. Because the Member States act as agents of the Community in collecting the levies and duties, they receive a payment to cover their expenses equal to 10 per cent of the amount collected. During the period 1971–1975 the revenue from levies and duties was inadequate to finance all the operations of the Community, so provision was made under Art. 3.2 for the Member States to top up the Community's own resources, by making a financial contribution to the

Budget based on yet another fixed percentage key. As from 1975 this key was to be replaced by the third element of own resources namely, the VAT contribution. The Community foresaw the possibility that some Member States might not have adopted the necessary legislation enabling the uniform basis for assessing VAT to be introduced and it arranged that in such circumstances the contribution of the Member States concerned should be based on the relationship of their GNP to the GNP of the whole Community.

While the agricultural levies and customs duties accrued to the Community in the manner envisaged under Decision 70/243, the Member States failed to meet the 1975 deadline on VAT. Indeed, the Council did not adopt the necessary Directive until 1977[10] and a sufficient number of Member States did not enact the required legislation in time for the 1978 Budget. Thus 1979 became the first year in which the VAT contribution was operative and the system of the Community's own resources was to all intents and purposes complete, although some Member States were still contributing on the basis of their relative GNP shares of total Community GNP. They had until the end of 1979 to pass the required national legislation to bring them into line.

Some brief explanation of Directive 77/388 (commonly referred to as the 6th Directive on VAT) seems appropriate. It is important to be clear that it does not harmonise the rates of VAT throughout the Community but rather that it harmonises the *basis on which VAT is assessed*. The Directive lays down common rules on liability to the tax, the circumstances in which VAT becomes chargeable, exemptions to the tax, and so forth. It also lays down (under Title XIV) special schemes to apply to certain sectors, including farming. The aim of these schemes is to operate a simplified procedure—such as a flat rate system of charging and collecting the tax—in those circumstances in which the Member States would have difficulties in applying the normal VAT regimes.

Actual rates of VAT differ considerably, not only between Member States but also within Member States, depending on the type of goods concerned. There is no obligation on Member States to harmonise their rates in any way but they must harmonise the basis on which the rates are assessed. Let us take the draft 1979 Budget by way of illustration.

The Commission estimated that in order to balance the Budget the Community would require a VAT element in its revenue equal to 0.75 per cent of the harmonised VAT base. If, in a particular Member State, VAT was levied on a good or service at say, 10 per cent, it would mean that the national exchequer would retain 9.25 per cent of the revenue collected and would hand over 0.75 per cent to the Community. If the rate of VAT were 16 per cent, it would retain 15.25 per cent and still hand over 0.75 per cent as before–and so on.

The achievement of the system of own resources by the Community has a number of implications. Firstly, it gives the Community–as an entity in itself–greater independence. Secondly, it is claimed that the own resources system is economically more neutral in its effects on the Member States than the fixed key contributions. This is because the keys were based on relative GNP shares,[11] whereas the new system is based on the levels of economic activity in each Member State. This cuts both ways: a reduction in imports of dutiable or leviable goods or a fall in the level of internal business transactions means a decline in the funds available to the Community; an increase in trade means more revenue to the Community. This leads to the third point: should the Budget remain as it is–little more than a glorified trading account–or should it be used as an instrument of economic management? If the Community opts for the latter, then it plunges into much wider issues of economic management, but logically such a development would seem almost inevitable, as there is little point in going to considerable trouble to ensure that the Community is financially independent if it is then expected to do little more than act as an agency working on behalf of the Member States in a very limited manner.

The budgetary unit of account

The Treaty of Rome called for the drawing up of the Budget in units of account (Art. 207). This is a device whereby monetary values can be expressed in a manner independent from that of national currencies but linked to these through fixed conversion rates.

The unit of account was established in 1960[12] and its value was fixed at 1UA=0.88867088 grammes of fine gold. As it so happened, this too was the value *at that time* of one US dollar in terms of gold, so that in effect 1UA=1$ US. The advantage of this arrangement was that it linked the new unit of account directly into the world financial system as it then existed.

Like most of the world's major trading countries, the Member States operated a system of fixed exchange rates. They declared a parity rate of their currencies to the International Monetary Fund (IMF), expressing the rate in terms of fine gold, and they were obliged to limit the degree of fluctuation between their currencies and the US dollar to plus or minus 1 per cent of the par value. Their currencies were not directly convertible into gold but they were convertible into the US dollar which was convertible into gold. Thus to all intents and purposes each currency bore a fixed relationship to all other currencies in the network. It was a simple matter to slip the unit of account into this system: because of its fixed relationship to gold and thence to the US dollar it also bore a fixed relationship to each of the currencies of the Community.

Despite the obvious advantages of the system adopted, the Community was conscious of the possible complications which could arise: for instance, through a revaluation of the price of gold or a change in the value of a Member State's currency. In the event, the instability of international exchange relationships in the late 1960s and early 1970s overtook the Community's deliberations.

The first upsets came with the devaluation of the French franc in 1969 and the revaluation of the German mark later the same year. While these events created problems on the agricultural front (to which we shall return in chapter 6) they did not result in budgetary difficulties because, although parities were changed, they were changed to a new fixed position in relation to gold, the US dollar and therefore to the unit of account.

A more serious occurrence was the abandonment in 1971 of the system of relating exchange rates to parity levels declared to the IMF. It was replaced by a system whereby exchange rates were related to central rates. This was a much looser arrangement in which countries agreed to limit fluctuations of their currencies to plus or minus 2.25 per cent of a declared central rate (the so-called Smithsonian Agreement). Earlier in 1971 the US dollar had been devalued and was no longer convertible into gold. This left the unit of account in a highly anomalous situation, still defined in terms of gold at the original level but no longer convertible into it via the US dollar, and no longer equal to one US dollar.

The market rates of the various Community currencies began to diverge noticeably from the old fixed parity rates and the trend was intensified in 1973 with the floating of Community currencies. The majority of the currencies floated together, i.e. they agreed to retain fixed limits between each other but to float against the rest of the world. The British and Irish pounds and the Italian lire were outside this system and floating independently. The French franc oscillated between being a party to the joint float and floating independently.

While these currency movements and realignments were taking place the Member States were still making their contributions to the Community Budget in terms of the old pre-Smithsonian fixed parity system. The effect was to introduce ever increasing distortions into these payments. Thus a country whose currency had appreciated against the old parity rate was now paying more of its currency into the Budget, and a country whose currency had depreciated was now paying less.

In the early 1970s it became increasingly apparent that the international monetary system had changed fundamentally and that the parity concept was out of date. The first move to a new system was made by the Community in 1973 when it introduced a new type of unit of account in the financial transactions of the EIB. This unit was based on a basket of currencies. It was followed shortly after by the introduction of Special Drawing Rights (SDR) on the IMF, also based on a basket of currencies. This basket is constructed from those currencies whose issuing countries have a share of more than 1 per cent of the world trade, weighted in relation to their share of that trade (except for the US dollar which was given a higher weighting). The IMF publishes the value of this unit every day.

Late in 1974 the Commission proposed that the Community should gradually introduce a new unit of account based on a basket of all the Member States' currencies. The new unit—called the European Unit of Account (EUA)—was adopted for the transactions of the European Development Fund (EDF) and the ECSC in 1975.[13]

The EUA basket—which is linked to the SDR basket—is arrived at by weighting the currencies of the Member States in relation to their GNP and to their share of intra-European trade. It is intended to reflect the productive and trading capacities of the economies which comprise the Community. The EUA is calculated daily and fluctuates in sympathy with the fluctuations of the currencies which comprise it.

While this new system was being introduced for the EDF and the ECSC, the Budget was struggling along with its old gold-based fixed parity unit of account. Under the Financial Regulation of 21 December 1977 *applicable to the general budget of the European Communities* (OJ L356, 31 December 1977), it was agreed that as from 1978 the Budget would be drawn up in EUA. The use of the new unit has also been extended to other Community activities such as the Statistical Office and for the purposes of the common customs tariff (CCT).

Control over the Budget

In 1975 certain changes were made in the organisation and control of the Budget under the Budgetary Treaty (not to be confused with an earlier Budgetary Treaty in 1970). Article 203 of the Rome Treaty was amended so that the financial year should correspond to the calendar year. This change necessitated alterations in the timetable required for the preparation of the draft Budget and its discussion by the various Institutions. These must now draw up estimates of their expenditure before 1 July each year and the Commission is charged with the task of consolidating these estimates into a preliminary draft Budget which it must present to the Council before 1 September. The Council may change the preliminary draft at this stage, but once it has adopted the text (voting by qualified majority), the draft Budget is forwarded to the Parliament which must receive it before 5 October.

Influence and control over the Budget is shared by the Commission, Council and Parliament. In recent years these three Institutions have held discussions in the spring to review budgetary problems in the light of Community policy. To facilitate these discussions, the Commission prepares a paper setting out its own thinking on current budgetary issues (see, for instance [33]). Subsequently, when consolidating the various estimates for the preliminary draft Budget, the Commission is empowered to attach an opinion to the preliminary draft in which it puts forward different estimates. The Council shares with the Parliament the final say over different elements in the Budget. The Parliament alone adopts the final Budget and has the power to reject the draft as a whole if there are important reasons for so doing. The vote on rejection must be by a majority of its members and two-thirds of the votes cast.

If the Council modifies a parliamentary amendment or rejects or modifies a parliamentary proposal, the draft Budget so altered must be re-submitted to the Parliament. Within fifteen days the latter may amend or reject the modifications made by the Council and it must adopt the Budget accordingly. If it fails to act within the time limit, the Budget is deemed to have been adopted. When these procedures are completed the President of the Parliament declares that the Budget is finally adopted.

The divided powers of control exercised by Council and Parliament are highly technical and have been the subject of considerable controversy. They are governed by Art. 203 of the Rome Treaty, as amended by the Budgetary Treaty, and hinge on whether the particular item of expenditure is compulsory or non-compulsory, i.e. on whether the expenditure is 'necessarily resulting from this Treaty or from acts adopted in accordance therewith', or not.

In the case of compulsory expenditure, the Treaty lays down that Parliament has the right only to *propose* modifications of the draft Budget to the Council; the latter then has the power (acting by qualified majority) to accept or to reject the Parliament's proposals.

Parliamentary proposals to modify compulsory expenditure are of two kinds and the Council's response to them differs depending on which is involved. If the proposal does not have the effect of increasing the total amount of expenditure of the particular Institution (for instance, if it merely suggests that the existing level of expenditure be allocated differently as between objectives), the Council may *reject* the proposed modification. In other words, the Parliament's proposal stands unless the Council takes specific action against it.

If the Parliament's proposal has the effect of increasing the total expenditure of a particular Institution, the Council may *accept* the proposal. In other words, the proposal falls unless the Council takes specific action in its favour.

In the case of non-compulsory expenditure, the Commission

declares each year a maximum rate of increase in such expenditure which is allowable over what was incurred the previous year. This maximum rate is determined by reference to the trend in volume terms of the Community's GNP; the average variation in Member States' budgets; and the trend in the cost of living in the preceding financial year. The Commission must inform all the Institutions of the maximum rate before 1 May.

If the actual rate of increase of non-compulsory expenditure in the draft Budget is equal to more than half the maximum rate laid down, the Parliament may *amend* the level of expenditure so as to bring the total up to the maximum rate. If the Parliament, Council or Commission considers that the activities of the Community require the maximum rate to be exceeded, a new rate may be fixed by agreement between the Council and the Parliament.

Considering that the Community went to the trouble of sub-dividing expenditure into compulsory and non-compulsory, and devised an elaborate procedure for handling deliberations on them, one might be forgiven for assuming that the distinction between the two was of some importance and that there would be clear-cut rules as to which items fall into which category. While the distinction is important in the sense that it has generated much argument, by and large the division between compulsory and non-compulsory expenditure has differed over time and the issue has been resolved on the basis of horse trading between Parliament and Council. As things stand, agricultural expenditure arising from the Guarantee Section of FEOGA is now the only item regarded as compulsory. The explanation of this distinction is that expenditure on the various measures of price and market support is open-ended, i.e. it arises directly from the annual price adjustments for farm products and is thus not subject to annual or multi-annual decisions on the level of expenditure as is the case with, for instance, the Regional Fund or the Social Fund.

The fact that agricultural market and price supports are regarded as being in a category by themselves is of some practical significance because of the high proportion of the Budget which is still devoted to this one aspect of Community activity (this is illustrated below). It is also of significance in a political sense because it is an element in the tussle between Council and Parliament over which Institution has ultimate control. Naturally the Parliament would like to see the distinction between compulsory and non-compulsory expenditure abolished, and the added weight which direct elections give to this body must in the long run strengthen its hand.

Before leaving the subject of control over the Budget, a brief description should be given of the control exercised over the day-to-day handling of the Community's revenue and expenditure. Prior to the Budgetary Treaty of 1975 the task of examining Community accounts was entrusted to an Audit Board, but the 1975 Treaty revised Art. 206 of the Rome Treaty and established a separate Court of Auditors with much wider powers. This is not a court in the normal sense of that word[14] but an independent body which not only audits the books of Community Institutions and subsidiary organisations—as any auditor would do—but also has powers to investigate Community spending at any point and in any institution—Community or national if the latter is operating on behalf of the former. It is also empowered to conduct investigations and to make reports on matters within its competence at the request of one of the Community Institutions.

The size and content of the Budget

The general Budget of the European Community is the subject of a number of misconceptions as to its size and content. As to its size: it is in fact very small when compared with the Community GDP or the size of budgets of the central administrations of the Member States. It is true that the Budget is growing but even so it still equals less than 1 per cent of Community GDP and less than 3 per cent of the national budgets of the Member States. In this context, however, it should be remembered that it does not cover nearly so many types of expenditure as the normal national budget. Equally, one should not overlook that the Member States incur budgetary cost because of their membership of the Community.

As yet, the Community Budget is a very much simpler device than national budgets: it is not an instrument of economic management and has very little redistributive effect overall. It must be balanced, unlike national budgets which can be—deliberately or otherwise—in surplus or in deficit. It does not reflect Community activities very accurately.

There are two reasons for this:

Firstly, despite the fact that it is called the 'general' Budget it does not include all Community financial activities. For instance, it does not cover expenditure financed from the ECSC levies on coal and steel, expenditure on the EDF, or on the activities of the EIB, nor does it cover the administrative costs of various Community organisations. Attempts are being made to include at least some of these items in the general Budget–for instance, the EDF.

Secondly, many Community policies cost comparatively small sums of money–little more than their administrative expenses–yet they have an influence which far outstrips their expenditure. Examples are the free movement of goods and persons between Member States, the existence of the CCT, trade agreements with the third countries and so forth. The economic effects of such policies cannot be measured in terms of their budgetary costs.

What then does the general Budget include? It covers the cost of administering the various Institutions of the Community and the various common policies such as those on agriculture, regional and social matters, nuclear research, etc. The format of the Budget has changed over the years and the description given here relates to the latest Budget to hand at the time of writing (European Parliament 79/81/ECSC, EEC, Euratom *Final adoption of the general budget of the European Communities for the financial year 1979* (OJ L23, 31 January 1979)). Not surprisingly, the Budget is a large tome and it takes a little time to find one's way around.

It begins with four relatively brief parts which summarise revenue; the shares of the Community's own resources which originate in each Member State; expenditure by each of the Institutions (Parliament, Council, Commission, Court of Justice and Court of Auditors); and a numerical list of staff classified by Institution and grade. This summary is followed by five sections which give a much more detailed breakdown of revenue and expenditure. Itemising expenditure takes up by far the greater part of the volume as it is divided into titles, chapters, articles and items, each sub-division being narrower than the one which precedes it. The left-hand page shows appropriations for the Budget year and the previous year (in this case 1979 and 1978), and the actual expenditure for the year preceding that (in this case 1977). The right-hand page is used for notes and explanations.

The Commission is by far the biggest spender of Community resources: over 98 per cent of the Budget is appropriated for its use. There are ten broad titles of expenditure which relate to the Commission and they are subdivided as follows:

		% of Commission appropriations 1979
Title 1	Expenditure relating to persons working within the Institution	3.2
Title 2	Buildings, equipment and miscellaneous operating expenditure	1.3
Title 3	Community policies relating in particular to research, technology, industry, the social sector, the environment and the supply of energy and raw materials	2.4
Title 4	Repayments and aid to Member States and other aid	5.2
Title 5	Social and Regional Funds	8.0
Titles 6 & 7	European Agricultural Guidance and Guarantee Fund–Guarantee Section	72.4
Title 8	European Agricultural Guidance and Guarantee Fund–Guidance Section and Fisheries Policy	3.3
Title 9	Co-operation with the developing countries and non-member States	3.7
Title 10	Other expenditure	0.8
	Total 13,494,353,875 EUA =	100.0

The extraordinary imbalance in the distribution of appropriations is obvious at a glance. The dominant position of agriculture (Titles 6–8) is even greater than this summary suggests because certain appropriations directly related to agriculture are included in Titles 2, 3, 5 and 9, as will become clear below. Appropriations under Titles 6 and

7 are inflated by the inclusion there of the cost of monetary compensatory amounts (MCAs) collected or granted in respect of trade in agricultural products. In 1979, appropriations for MCAs amounted to just over 6 per cent of the total general Budget. Title 4 contains the appropriations for payments (referred to earlier in this chapter) made to Member States to reimburse them for the cost of collecting the Community's own resources.

The first title under which we find specifically agricultural appropriations is Title 2, Chapter 29. Here are listed the contributions made by the Community to the administrative expenses incurred in the operation of various international agreements including those on wheat, olive oil and coffee, together with token entries for those on sugar, cocoa and fisheries. Under Title 3, Chapter 31 we find entries for Community financial assistance towards campaigns inside and outside the Community for the eradication of livestock epidemics; costs of veterinary inspection; participation in measures concerning the marketing of seedlings and seeds; the cost of the Farm Accountancy Data Network (FADN);[15] contributions to the cost of agricultural research projects; the training of national officials responsible for monitoring FEOGA expenditure; and the cost of financing the operation of the European Training and Promotion Centre for Farming and Rural Life (CEPFAR–*Centre Européan pour la Promotion et la Formation en milieu Agricole et Rural*).

Under Title 5, Chapter 50 of the Community assists in the cost of training people who are leaving agriculture to take up non-agricultural employment. These appropriations come under the Social Fund. Title 9, Chaper 92 covers Community appropriations on food aid. This is subdivided by commodity: cereals, milk, sugar, and other products particularly those with a high protein content.

It should be pointed out that the various subventions outlined above are small in total compared with the appropriations listed under Titles 6–8. It is to these Titles which cover the needs of FEOGA to which we now turn.

FEOGA

FEOGA (*Fonds européen d'orientation et de garantie agricole*)[16] is the mechanism through which the CAP is financed. It was set up in 1962 under Regulation No. 25 *on the financing of the common agricultural policy* (Sp. OJ 1959–1962), although it was not until 1964 that detailed rules were laid down concerning its structure and the manner in which assistance is made available from it.[17] Regulation 25 is concerned with such issues as the sources of revenue and the broad types of expenditure coming under the new Fund, as well as detailed provisions on the transitional stage during which the CAP was gradually introduced. Although many of its provisions are no longer operative, it remains a very important Regulation. Under it three types of expenditure were defined: refunds on exports to third countries; intervention aimed at stabilising markets; and the financing of 'common measures adopted in order to attain the objectives set out in Article 39(1)(a) of the Treaty', i.e. structural measures.

These provisions are amplified in Regulation 17/64 which lays down that expenditure on export refunds and domestic market intervention[18] is to be financed from the Guarantee Section of FEOGA. This corresponds to Titles 6 and 7 of the Commission appropriations in the Budget. The entries in the budget are in considerable detail, broken down by product and type of expenditure, i.e. export refund or domestic intervention. Table 4 is a much condensed version of the entries under Titles 6 and 7 in the 1979 Budget and is intended as an illustration only of the range and scale of Community activities in the support of agricultural markets. It is important to remember that appropriations are not necessarily actually spent: market, weather and harvest conditions may alter the picture quite radically. This makes it extremely difficult to budget accurately.

Another point to bear in mind is that the sums appropriated for refunds and intervention for those commodities which benefit from both support systems can differ relatively from year to year. For instance, if the Commission in making its estimates anticipates a large surplus of soft wheat, it has to take market prospects into account in deciding whether storage (i.e. domestic intervention) will be the most heavily used support mechanism or whether export restitutions[19] will be more appropriate.

Although variations do occur between the relative amounts of support for different commodities, some aspects remain constant: in particular the lion's share of support which goes annually on milk and

TABLE 4

FEOGA Guarantee Section Appropriations: 1979 Budget '000 EUA

Commodity Group	Export Refunds	All Domestic Intervention	Total
Cereals	1,439,400	434,800	1,874,200
Rice	38,500	2,900	41,400
Milk and milk products	1,572,900	2,144,700[a]	3,717,600
Oils and fats	7,100	515,800	522,900
Sugar	751,800	252,800	1,004,600
Beef and veal	122,700	365,600	488,300
Pigmeat	68,600	16,300	84,900
Eggs and poultry	41,200	—	41,200
Fruit and vegetables	35,600	290,900	326,500
Wine	5,600	113,800	119,400
Tobacco	5,400	256,600	262,000
Fisheries[b]	6,500	13,500	20,000
Flax and hemp	—	17,500	17,500
Seeds	—	27,200	27,200
Hops	—	11,000	11,000
Silkworms		1,200	1,200
Dried fodder	—	49,300	49,300
Peas, broad and field beans	—	6,300	6,300
Processed agricultural products	176,200	—	176,200
Total Guarantee[c]	4,271,500	4,520,200	8,791,700

(a) net of producer contributions under the co-responsibility levy
(b) included from Title 8
(c) excluding accession compensatory amounts and monetary compensatory amounts

Source: OJ L23, 31 January, 1979.

support for different commodities, some aspects remain constant: in particular the lion's share of support which goes annually on milk and milk products, and cereals. Other commodities which represent a major call on the Guarantee Section are sugar, beef and veal, olive oil and oilseeds. Some years ago beef and veal would not have featured in this list, but support expenditure has increased considerably with the rise in the level of Community self-sufficiency. Support for wine, tobacco and fruit and vegetables is also of significance.

Finally, we turn to Title 8 of the Commission Budget appropriations. Article 1 of Reg. 17/64 provides that expenditure on structural improvement measures should be financed from the Guidance Section of FEOGA and it is this expenditure which is covered by Title 8, together with fisheries which were included under this title for the first time in 1979. Under Reg. 25 it was established that expenditure from the Guidance Section should correspond–as far as possible–to one-third of expenditure on the Guarantee Section. In practice this level was never reached. Not only that, but in 1966 under Regulation No. 130/66/EEC *on the financing of the common agricultural policy* (Sp. OJ 1965–1966) a new and more stringent limitation was placed on the level of expenditure. From the accounting period 1967/68 expenditure on the Guidance Section was limited to 285 million units of account. This ceiling remained in force until the Community was enlarged in 1973 when it was raised to 325 million, now changed to 325 million EUA and from 1980 it will be raised to 720 million EUA.

In fact, in recent years the Community has allocated more than the maximum allowed to the Guidance Section. It has been able to do this because, since 1969, the Community has appropriated sums of money each year to cover the financing of common measures coming within the meaning of Art. 6 of Regulation (EEC) No. 729/70. This is a technical way of referring to what is known as the 'Mansholt Reserve'. In 1970 the Commission proposed certain common structural measures and started to allocate budgetary funds for them, but it was not until 1972 that some of these measures were passed by the Council and it was 1973 before the first Member States started to put them into operation (see chapter 11). The funds allocated before these measures were applied, and while they were being applied only partially, built up into a reserve which was subsequently released as the need arose. However, it is expected that this reserve will shortly be used up and that from 1980 onwards the Guidance allocation will be inadequate. In view of this, and in view of the many new structural measures enacted in 1978 and early in 1979 to aid the Mediterranean areas of the Community (outlined in chapters 11 and 12), the Commission proposed to the Council that there should be a substantial increase in the ceiling on the Guidance Section [38].

The proposal was that from the beginning of 1980 there should be a total allocation over five years of 4200 million EUA or an annual average allocation of 840 million EUA. The Council passed the necessary legislation in May 1979 (Reg. 929/79, OJ L117, 12 May 1979) except that the total allocation for 1980–84 is limited to 3600 million EUA or 720 million per year.

TABLE 5

FEOGA Guidance Section Appropriations: 1979 Budget '000 EUA

Type of project	Appropriations
Those coming under Art. 13 of Reg. 17/64	40,000
Modernisation of farms	64,000
Cessation of farming	1,300
Vocational guidance and training	2,500
Disadvantaged areas	78,600
Producer groups–general	3,700
Hop producer groups	400
Fruit and vegetable producer groups	3,500
Fisheries producer groups	100
Marketing and processing aids–general	12,000
Marketing and processing aids in Mediterranean regions	2,000
Premiums to encourage beef and veal	4,500
Premium for non-marketing of milk and conversion of dairy herds	73,400
Eradication of diseases in cattle	20,000
Reorganisation of fruit production	4,000
Convertion premium for wine	31,500
Restructuring of vineyards	17,000
Collective irrigation works in the Mezzogiorno	20,000
Improvements of public services in certain regions	15,000
Land drainage operations in Ireland	28,000
Total Guidance Section	396,300

Source: OJ L23, 31 January 1979

Although the sums involved in the Guidance Section are small in comparison with the appropriations for the Guarantee Section they are spread over a wide range of activity, as table 5 indicates. One of the features of Guidance Section expenditure is that it is incurred over a period of years, so that funds are still being allocated for projects which were undertaken, or at least started, some years ago. Indeed, some of the items in table 5 relate to schemes which are no longer operative but for which payment must still be made.

Notes to Chapter 5

10. Directive 77/388/EEC *on the harmonisation of the laws of the Member States relating to turnover taxes – common system of value added tax: uniform basis of assessment* (OJ L145, 13 June 1977).

11. The keys in operation prior to 1971 were even more arbitrary and bore only a faint resemblance to GNP shares.

12. Règlement Financier *relatif à l'establissment et à l'exécution du Budget de la C.E.E. et à la responsibilité des ordonnateurs et comptables (Art. 209, (a) et (c) du traité)*, JO 83, 29 décembre 1960.

13. Decision 75/250/EEC *on the definition and conversion of the European unit of account used for expressing the amounts of aid mentioned in Article 42 of the ACP–EEC Conversion of Lomé*, OJ L104, 24 April 1975; and Decision No. 3289/75/ECSC *on the definition and conversion of the unit of account to be used in decisions, recommendations, opinions and communications for the purposes of the Treaty establishing the European Coal and Steel Community*, OJ L327, 19 December 1975.

14. It is a translation of *cour des comptes*: in terms of function, the nearest equivalent in English is Comptroller and Auditor General.

15. In French: RICA (*Reseau d'Information Comptable Agricole*). FADN provides information of a farm management nature from typical farms which are representative of the various regions of the Community. The data collected are used to assist in the decision-making process under the CAP, especially in the setting of prices.

16. In English: European Agricultural Guidance and Guarantee Fund. As this translation yields the highly inelegant and totally unpronouncable set of initials—EAGGF, the fund is normally referred to by its French (and Italian) initials.

17. Regulation No. 17/64/EEC *on the conditions for granting aid from the European Agricultural Guidance and Guarantee Fund* (Sp. OJ 1963–1964). This is a Regulation which we shall meet again in chapter 12.

18. The use of the word 'intervention' is unfortunately very confusing. The Community uses it in two senses: withdrawal of produce from an over-supplied market, and other methods of domestic support. In common usage it has come to mean the withdrawal of produce but technically its meaning is much wider.

19. The term 'export restitutions' is frequently used instead of 'export refunds'.

CHAPTER 6

Green money

In 1962, when the first commodity Regulations under the CAP were passed, they were based on the principle of uniformity of institutional prices throughout the Community. This necessitated the choice of a common denominator in which to express the price levels chosen and this denominator was called the Agricultural Unit of Account (AUA). It was defined in Regulation No 129 of 1962[20] in terms of gold and had the same value at that time as one US dollar, and therefore had the same value as the budgetary unit of account. The effect was that when common prices were expressed in national currencies the exchange rate applied was that which corresponded 'to the par values communicated to and recognised by the International Monetary Fund' (Art. 2.1). In other words, the original green rate equalled the market rate of exchange.

Strictly speaking, this Regulation set up a separate unit of account for use under the CAP–the 'green money' of the title of this chapter–but because the conversion rate used in agriculture was the par value with the US dollar, the existence of a separate AUA was not something to which much attention was given. Since, at that time, market exchange rates were kept very close to the par value, agricultural market prices under the CAP were more or less equal in external value in the different Member States. The simplicity of the system was not to last for long. We have already seen how international exchange relationships came under increasing pressure in the late 1960s and, in August 1969, the French franc was devalued by 11.11 per cent, followed in October by a 9.29 per cent revaluation of the German mark.

The effect of the devaluation of the French franc was to lower its gold content and therefore its value against other currencies and against the unit of account. Because, under Reg. 129 of 1962, the exchange rate used for agricultural purposes had to be the par value of the currency as notified to the IMF, so the green rate of exchange of the franc was devalued in exactly the same way as the market rate. The effect of this should have been that when common prices expressed in AUA were converted into francs, prices were immediately higher than previously. As the French devaluation had taken place in a time of rising inflation, such price increases on farm products were unacceptable to the French government. They succeeded in persuading the Council of Ministers to agree to a phased introduction of the new prices over a two-year period. In fact, the French realigned some prices immediately to the new exchange rate, but for those commodities for which a phased price change was made a completely new situation arose.

MCA system

Let us pause for a moment to examine the situation concerning intervention prices (about which more will be said in chapters 7–10). These are the floor prices which underpin the market for some of the major commodities—cereals, dairy products, beef, olive oil, etc. When market prices are weak, traders are able to offer produce to an intervention agency in the knowledge that they will receive the floor price (adjusted if necessary to take account of differences in quality).

Intervention prices are set in AUA and, as we have already seen, their external value was originally the same throughout the Community. But, in 1969, for those commodities for which the French did not immediately realign the prices, while the intervention prices remained the same in AUA, they became lower in France than elsewhere in the Community when converted at market exchange rates. This meant that 'had no action been taken it would have been possible for traders to buy produce in France and sell it into intervention in other member states, making a profit by selling the foreign currency received at the market exchange rate for francs, thus receiving a price in francs above that offered by the Intervention Agency in France.'[50]

To remove the incentive from French traders to sell produce into intervention abroad, an export levy was imposed at the French frontier which neutralised the effects of maintaining the old pre-devaluation price. Similarly, a subsidy was paid on imports to France on commodities for which the old green exchange rate was being used. This subsidy restored the competitiveness of the import on the French market. These border levies and subsidies were equal to the percentage difference between the old green rate of exchange and the new market rate of exchange multiplied by the intervention price of the commodity in question. These border adjustments were the original monetary compensatory amounts (MCAs).

It is important to be clear that in adopting MCAs the Community's main concern was not to facilitate trade but rather to protect the intervention system. When later in 1969 the German mark was revalued, the arrangements which had been made for France were once more brought into play but this time in reverse, i.e. the Germans were allowed to reduce internal farm prices gradually and MCAs took the form of levies on imports and subsidies on exports.

The arrangements made for France and Federal Germany were of a temporary nature but complications arose when, in 1971, a number of countries broke away from the fixed parity system and allowed their currencies to float. The Community responded to this development by reintroducing MCAs on a generalised and continuing basis. They were made applicable to any Member State so long as there was a divergence between market rates of exchange with the US dollar and the conversion rates used for agricultural purposes. These latter were still (for many commodities) the fixed parities declared to the IMF in terms of gold. The Regulation governing this system is (EEC) No. 974/71[21] and it has remained the basis of the MCA system since then, although with a number of amendments.

At the time Reg. 974/71 came into force MCAs were variable because they represented the difference between the parity rate of a currency as declared to the IMF and the spot market rate of the same currency against the dollar which was liable to considerable fluctuation. Once the Smithsonian Agreement on currency fluctuations (see chapter 5) was adopted, the variations in MCAs lessened appreciably because the countries involved in the Agreement undertook to maintain the value of their currencies at a level reasonably close to that of the US dollar.

The next development of long-term importance was the introduction of the concept of the 'representative rate' used first for the UK and Irish pounds but later extended to all Community currencies. When these two countries joined the Community in 1973 it was decided that instead of using the last declared IMF parity rate for converting pounds into

AUA, they should use the average exchange rate between the pound and the US dollar as it was in early 1973. It was this ratio which was called the 'representative rate' and it was introduced under Regulation (EEC) No. 222/73.[22] This was extended to all Member States' currencies under Regulation (EEC) 1123/73.[23]

During the same year, with increasing pressure on exchange rates, the majority of the Member States informed the IMF that they would cease to operate the Smithsonian Agreement on currency fluctuations and would allow their currencies to float on the money markets. However, as described in chapter 5, they agreed to maintain a narrow margin of fluctuation between each other's currencies. This became known as the 'joint float'. It meant that for the countries concerned (all the Member States other than the UK, Ireland and Italy),[24] while their currencies were free to fluctuate against other currencies outside the joint float, they were locked closely to all the currencies within the joint float. From 1973 onwards the central rates of the currencies participating in the joint float were no longer defined in terms of their relationship with the current value of the US dollar but rather in terms of the IMF Special Drawing Rights (SDR), which were equal in gold value to the unit of account and to the value of the pre-Smithsonian US dollar.

By 1973 the MCA system had become intolerably complex and the coming together of the majority of Community currencies in the joint float presented a golden opportunity to simplify the system. Under the revised arrangements the market rates of exchange between the Member States' currencies and the unit of account were no longer defined in terms of the US dollar but rather in terms of the collective value of the joint float currencies. In effect the unit of account now floated in sympathy with these currencies. As we have seen the central rates of the joint float currencies were expressed in terms of SDRs which in turn had the same gold content as the unit of account so, in a roundabout way, the market rates of exchange of the joint float currencies and the unit of account were fixed in relation to each other. Because the green (or representative) rates of exchange were also fixed for these currencies, so too were the MCAs fixed. The percentage MCA to be applied to agricultural commodities whose value is expressed in a joint float currency is simply the percentage difference between the central rate and the green rate of exchange. Table 6 demonstrates the relationship.

TABLE 6

Calculation of fixed MCA percentages for joint float currencies applicable from 22 January 1979

	Belgium	Denmark	FR Germany	Netherlands
Central rate 1 UA=	47.703095	8.566577	3.035242	3.289278
Green rate 1 UA=	49.348598	8.566577	3.402378	3.402703
Monetary coefficient[a]	0.967	0.0	0.892	0.967
Fixed MCA percentage[b]	3.3	0	10.8	3.3

(a) central rate ÷ green rate
(b) subtract monetary coefficient from 1, × 100

Despite the improvement in the operation of the MCA system brought about by the joint float, two problems remained: how to deal with those currencies which were not party to the joint float and how to deal with third country trade. Let us take the internal situation first, i.e. the calculation of MCAs for an independently floating currency. The MCA percentage in effect represents the amount by which CAP prices, when expressed in a floating currency, would have to increase if the green rate were to be aligned with the market rate of exchange. The calculation is complicated, but table 7 expressed in terms of sterling should make it easier to follow. Irving and Fearn [58] have described the MCA percentage calculation for an independently floating currency as representing 'the unweighted average of the variable percentage difference between [the green rate]–expressed in terms of each of the central rates of the joint float currencies–and the average of the weekly market rates in terms of the joint float currencies.'

The actual level of MCA charged is obtained by multiplying the MCA percentage by the intervention price for the commodity in the Member States concerned. When goods subject to MCAs are traded between two Member States, two MCAs are applied to the transaction: one imposed by the exporter and one by the importer. The only exception to this is Denmark which does not apply any MCAs.

TABLE 7

Calculation of UK MCA percentage applicable from 22 January, 1979

	Belgium	*Denmark*	*FR Germany*	*Netherlands*
1. Central rate joint float currencies 1 UA=	47.703095	8.566557	3.035242	3.289278
2. UK green rate UA/£		1.57678		
3. Central rate joint float expressed against £ at green rate, i.e. $(1) \times (2)$	75.21729	13.5076	4.78591	5.18647
4. Average of noon spot rates for sterling in previous Wednesday–Tuesday period (10–16 January)	58.46	10.2892	3.7051	3.9999
5. % depreciation of £ against its green rate in terms of joint float currencies, i.e. $\dfrac{(3) \times 100}{(4)} - 10$	28.6645	31.2794	29.1709	29.6650
6. Mean % depreciation of £		29.7		
7. Franchise or deduction for depreciating currencies[a]		1.5		
8. Net MCA percentage, i.e. $(6) - (7)$		28.2		

(a) an adjustment made to reduce the chance that the MCA percentage as applied to trade will over-compensate for currency fluctuations.

On third country trade, the Commission has to calculate the difference between the market rate of exchange of the third country currency and the unit of account in order to determine the 'offer' or 'world' price used in fixing the size of the import levy (see chapter 7). The system used is analogous to that employed in calculating MCAs for the independently floating currencies. In trade with third countries, MCAs are added to or subtracted from third country import levies and export refunds depending on whether the MCA is a charge or a payment.

Implications of green money system

Having outlined very briefly this highly complex topic, the question must arise: what are the implications of green money and what is its future? The system has been analysed many times, notably by Irving and Fearn [58] and on a number of occasions by the Commission, in particular in a report in 1978 [32]. The first observation that should be made is that the green money system has succeeded in fulfilling its original task, namely, the protection of the intervention mechanism and through this the operation of the CAP itself. It has allowed a market and price policy based on fixed exchange rates to survive in a world of fluctuating exchange rates.

But within this success there lies a fatal flaw. When introduced, MCAs seemed a clever device by which, over a limited time period, agriculture was given the means of adjusting gradually to a new exchange situation. MCAs were not intended to provide for the long-term insulation of farming from the realities of economic life. Their use over a period of a decade has brought with it a variety of distortions within agriculture itself, between Member States, and between farmers and consumers. It has also placed an extra financial burden on FEOGA which has helped to perpetuate its disproportionate claims on the Community Budget.

The most fundamental distortion brought about by the green money system lies in what has happened to the concept of common pricing. Instead of one common price operating throughout the Community, there are now seven separate price zones (Benelux is treated as one zone). Each zone (with the exception of Denmark) is protected by an MCA system which in effect means that each country has an individual set of farm prices. Denmark is unique in that it maintains its green rate of exchange in line with its central rate, thereby avoiding the necessity of applying MCAs. Thus it is the only country operating the pricing system as it was originally intended.

The existence of the green money system as it operates at present introduces a distortion into the manner in which producers are treated. This is due to the fact that the MCA system is operated for certain commodities only. We saw earlier in this chapter how the system was introduced to preserve the intervention support mechanism. Thus, in general, there are no MCAs on commodities for which no intervention price mechanism exists. The only exception to this rule is for those commodities which are directly dependent on other commodities for which an intervention mechanism does exist: the best examples are poultry and eggs with no intervention prices of their own but which are included under the MCA system because of their direct dependence on cereals for which there is intervention.

To add a further complication, MCAs do not operate for all commodities with an intervention price mechanism but only on those for which there is considerable international trade. Thus, at the time of writing, MCAs existed on trade in cereals (excluding rice), milk, sugar, beef and veal, pigmeat, eggs and poultry, and certain major processed products not coming under Annex II of the Rome Treaty (in particular sugar and chocolate confectionery, cakes and biscuits). The effect of this difference in treatment is that certain agricultural products are subject immediately to changes in the market values of currencies in the normal manner while others are not.

The operation of the green money system has had a profound effect on production, consumption and the free flow of goods throughout the Community. To take production first: an important outcome of the operation of a common market is that the theory of comparative advantage is allowed to function. This means that production should move to those areas displaying such an advantage leading to greater regional specialisation and higher productivity. When, however, through the upward valuation of a currency the price of farm output is artificially raised, exports are subsidised and imports of agricultural inputs are obtained at lower prices, distortions must result. Resources are retained in agriculture which otherwise would move to other sectors, and farmers who have no claim to comparative advantage are enabled not only to stay in production but actually to increase it.

The converse is to be found in a country with a devaluing currency. Here the existence of a separate green rate of exchange has the effect of depressing end prices, exports are subject to levies and inputs imported from abroad are more expensive because, unlike the end prices, they are paid for at market rates of exchange. Not unnaturally these anomalies have implications for food prices. In the revalued currency country because end prices are higher consumers have to pay more for food, while in the devaluing country food is cheaper. If the gap between the two types of country is sufficiently great, it could have implications in a much wider sense in that the cheap food country has a lower cost of living and therefore lower wage and salary needs. This should give it a competitive edge in production costs in those manufacturing and processing industries highly dependent on indigenous raw materials.

Trade distortions are not confined to comparisons between revaluing and devaluing currency countries but they also affect individual countries differently within each of these broad groups, depending on whether they are net importers or net exporters of agricultural produce. Take the case of the UK as an example of a country with a weak currency which is also a net importer of food: as Irving and Fearn point out, the maintenance of an overvalued green pound (i.e. the maintenance of an unduly large gap between the market rate and the green rate of exchange) results in massive transfers from FEOGA to the UK through the operation of the MCA system. These subsidies are required to bring the price of food items from stronger currency zones down to the UK level. They greatly outweigh in value the MCAs levied on UK exports of agricultural goods.

Contrast this with the fate of a net agricultural exporting country such as France or Ireland which finds that because of the weakness of its currency the costs of its exports must be raised through levies. This is done to prevent them undercutting home-produced commodities when they export to countries with revalued currencies. It is difficult for the theory of comparative advantage to operate in such circumstances.

It will be recalled from chapter 5 that MCAs represent a large item in the Community's Budget. There is no doubt that this burden is considerable. In the 1978 Commission report referred to above [32] it is stated that expenditure on MCAs in 1976 accounted for 9 per cent of total Guarantee expenditure and in 1977 as much as 14 per cent. The Commission also points out that this expenditure is not only the result of legitimate trade, but also contains elements of fraud. It is very understandable that a system of the complexity of green money must encourage fraudulent activities. It is almost inevitable as well that the system raises the cost of trade because it introduces additional administrative procedures into the already complicated world of international trade.

If green money has all the disadvantages listed here—and there are indeed others—why is it retained? There are two answers: one economic and one political. While MCAs would find very few champions to defend their existence, except on the most pragmatic of grounds that they actually work, everyone would agree that their abrupt removal would be economically impossible. The gap between the MCAs applied to the highest and lowest valued currencies is so great that the only hope is to bridge it in stages.

A good illustration of the problem is to be found in fig. 4 which demonstrates for one commodity—common wheat—the difference in target price, expressed in national currencies, between the country with the highest price and that with the lowest. The figure includes the early years of the Community when Member States were transitting to common prices, but since 1969/70 the cause of the difference is solely the existence of green money.

Not only is the price gap between the highest and lowest currency very large, but it is also skewed. For instance, in early 1979 the MCA percentages operating in the Community were as follows:

Germany	Benelux	Denmark	Ireland	France	Italy	UK
+10.8%	+3.3%	—	−1.4%	−6.5%	−17.7%	−26.2%

This demonstrates that the negative MCAs are much larger than the positive MCAs and this is so despite more numerous adjustments in the green rates of depreciating currencies. The reason for this distortion is the continual upward movement of the AUA, linked as it is to the joint float, which widens the gap between it and the depreciating currencies.

The Commission has tried to get over the problem of the size of the gap by proposing that existing MCAs should be abolished over a period of years and that new MCAs should be of short-term duration. It made proposals along these lines in 1976 [19], 1977 [25] and 1979 [43]. Its 1979 proposals were overtaken by events on the wider monetary front, but it is doubtful if they would have made much progress, as the earlier

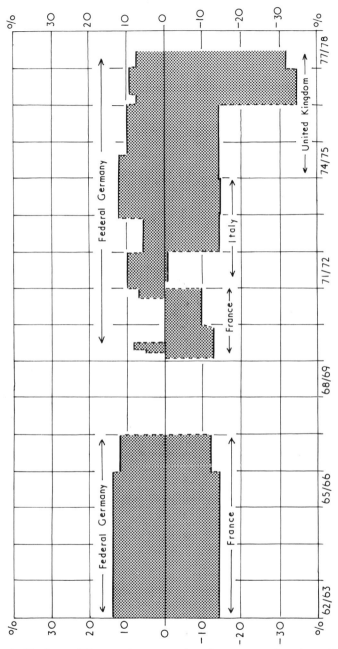

Fig. 4: Maximum differences in target prices for common wheat in national currencies in the Community since the 1962/63 marketing year, taking into consideration monetary fluctuations since 1968.

proposals foundered on the unwillingness of the Council of Ministers to accept the implications which such a return to normality would have on their ability to exert control over farm and food prices.

If the Commission's proposals were accepted, a decision would have to be taken as to the level of common prices to which all Member States would move. Should it be to the existing common level at present applied only in Denmark, or should it be to a level which approximates more closely to the upper limit of the range, so that German farmers do not suffer too drastic a price fall, or should it be to a level more in line with UK prices, so as to lower food prices for the majority of Community consumers? As a House of Lords report puts it [54]: 'Each country would no doubt be content to return to a system of common prices if other members would accept its view of the "correct" price levels on which to harmonise.'

Although the phasing-out of MCAs would have advantages in returning the Community to common pricing, thereby removing the trade distortions which have been created, it would not, of itself, reduce FEOGA expenditure. For instance, a return to common prices based on the present common (or Danish) level would raise the average level of prices in the Community as the devaluing currencies came into line. Their upward movement would outweigh the downward realignment of the strong currencies. Such a price rise could have a dynamic effect on production, leading to greater expenditure on market support. But even without any dynamic effect, the cost of export refunds would rise as the gap between Community and third country prices widened.

Even if this issue of the correct common price level could be resolved, there remains the important political fact that the existence of MCAs has reintroduced an element of national control over price fixing which the Member States are loathe to lose. Any scheme to phase out MCAs would clearly curb the powers of the Member States and remove a bargaining weapon which they have found a very useful addition to their armoury. Their present attitude can be seen clearly in the way in which they use proposed modifications of the MCA levels to further their national interests during the annual farm price-fixing negotiations. This subject is further discussed in chapter 7.

Meanwhile various developments have been taking place on the wider monetary scene which may ultimately have a considerable bearing on the whole question of green money. In chapter 5 we saw how the Community moved from the unit of account based on gold to the EUA based on a basket of currencies for budgetary purposes. In a report issued in 1977 [24], the Commission pointed out the advantages of switching to the use of the EUA in agriculture. When the green rate of exchange is based on the joint float currencies common prices are continually dragged upwards in the wake of the appreciating German mark. If they were linked instead to the EUA, which is based on a basket of all Community currencies, their upward movement would be slowed. But substitution of the EUA for the AUA involves a decision as to the conversion rate and hence on the level of common prices towards which Member States would have to harmonise their national prices as they eliminated existing MCAs. The Commission felt unable to make a formal proposal on this sensitive issue.

At this point events caught up with the Commission's deliberations with the proposal late in 1978 for the creation of a European Monetary System (EMS). The introduction of EMS has the effect of restoring fixed exchange rates between the Member States which join it. This is achieved by the re-introduction of fixed margins of fluctuation around a central rate. The new system is based on the ECU (European Currency Unit) which, initially at least, is of the same value as the EUA used for budgetary and other purposes. In December 1978, eight out of the nine Member States agreed to join the EMS from the beginning of 1979 (the UK being the one exception).

As with the Commission's earlier proposals concerning the use of the EUA in agriculture, the introduction of EMS involved a decision as to whether it should be extended to agriculture and, if so, at what level to fix common prices in terms of the new ECU. At its meeting in December 1978, the European Council agreed [1] that 'the introduction of the EMS should not of itself result in any change in the situation obtaining prior to 1 January 1979 regarding the expression in national currencies of agricultural prices, monetary compensatory amounts and all other amounts fixed for the purposes of the common agricultural policy.' As the market value of the AUA (based on the joint float currencies) is higher than the value of the ECU (based on the basket), common prices expressed in the new currency unit would have to be numerically higher (by about one-fifth) in order to achieve the European Council's aim.

The European Council also made a declaration stressing 'the importance of henceforth avoiding the creation of permanent MCAs and progressively reducing present MCAs in order to re-establish the unity of prices of the common agricultural policy, giving also due consideration to price policy.'

The French held up the introduction of EMS until March 1979 in an effort to get some movement on the MCA front. The steps which were agreed were that in future there would be a 1 per cent franchise on new positive MCAs and that such new MCAs would be phased out over two years providing this did not mean a price fall in the country concerned. The meaning of the 1 per cent franchise is that if the central rate of a revaluing currency moves upward while the green rate remains the same, the resulting increase in MCAs would not fully compensate for the change but rather it would rise by 1 per cent *less* than the extent of the revaluation. The Regulation giving effect to these changes is No. 652/79 *on the impact of the European monetary system on the common agricultural policy* (OJ L84, 4 March 1979).

Notes to Chapter 6

20. *On the value of the unit of account and the exchange rates to be applied for the purposes of the common agricultural policy* (Sp. OJ 1959–1962).

21. *On certain measures of conjunctural policy to be taken in agriculture following the temporary widening of the margins of fluctuation for the currencies of certain Member States* (Sp. OJ 1971(1)).

22. *On the exchange rates to be applied in agriculture for the currencies of the New Member States,* OJ L27, 1 February 1973.

23. *Amending Regulation (EEC) No. 974/71 on certain measures of conjunctural policy to be taken in agriculture* ... OJ L114, 30 April 1973.

24. The French left the joint float in 1974, re-entered it briefly in 1975, but left it again.

CHAPTER 7

The composition of the price and market regimes

The choice of market and price regimes

From earlier chapters we have learned two important facts about the CAP: (a) that the designers of the European Community envisaged a managed market for agriculture rather than the free market being created for other sectors; and (b) that from its inception the Community concentrated most of its efforts in the agricultural sphere on the development of the market and price policies.

There is nothing unique or even unusual about these two facts: while countries differ widely in the level of support which they can afford to give their farmers and while their methods differ, no country operates a completely free market in agricultural products and all countries tend to concentrate a high proportion of their income support measures on the organisation of prices and markets rather than on structural and social measures. It would have been extremely surprising if the new Community had acted contrary to conventional practice. It must also be borne in mind that the designers of the CAP had to reconcile six different support systems and six different levels of support.

The market system which was favoured for the major commodities was not too different from that which was already in operation in a number of Member States. It was more difficult to choose the level of support prices. The existing range in the Member States was wide. Federal Germany and Italy, which were large importers of agricultural products, had high internal support prices, while France and the Netherlands, with large export markets, had much lower levels of internal support.

While the eventual compromise differed from one commodity to another, the overall result was a significant increase in the prices received by large numbers of the Community's farmers. This was particularly so in that the common price levels chosen tended not so much to the mean but rather towards the upper end of the range of the existing price levels in the individual Member States. The reason for this upward bias lay in the ability of the Germans to prevent major price–and therefore income–falls for their farmers. However, in the longer term the major beneficiary was France, where the potential for expansion was greatest.

The upward tendency in prices was accompanied (quite unintentionally) by an era of massive technological innovation in European agriculture which started in the 1950s and gathered momentum during the 1960s. The outcome has been a significant rise in the Community's levels of self-sufficiency as table 8 illustrates.[25]

The Community market and price regimes are based on a two-pronged approach which involves insulating Community farmers from world market influences, to an extent which varies by commodity, through a system of frontier measures and, internally, which provides them with minimum levels of support achieved through the underpinning of prices in various ways. Within this framework prices at all stages of marketing are free to move. The outcome should be an intensification of the comparative advantage of different regions of the Community to produce particular products resulting, over a period of time, in a shift in the geographic location of production.

TABLE 8

Levels of self-sufficiency in some commodities

Product	Degree of self-sufficiency in %	
	Average 1954/55–1958/59	1973/74 or 1974
Total cereals	85	97
Rice	91	109
Potatoes	102	101
Sugar	101	111
Beef and veal	94	96
Pigmeat	102	99(a)
Eggs	91	100
Cheese	100	106
Butter	100	116

(a) = pork

Note: These figures are for a Community comprising the original six Member States only.

Source: [12 & 48]

This system of market management is simple in concept but complicated in practice and it has not operated fully as intended for a number of reasons.

Firstly, the problems which have arisen from the development of structural surpluses have produced a plethora of schemes intended to dispose of the excess supply by raising demand. These schemes have, to some extent, blurred the original framework of the commodity regimes concerned.

Secondly, the high level of self-sufficiency has resulted in weak market prices which in turn has meant that far greater use has been made of intervention buying and storage subsidies to support the market than was originally intended.

Thirdly, while there have been periods of shortage on world markets for certain commodities, the general picture of the 1960s and 1970s has been one of adequate supply and sluggish prices. This has meant that the exportation of Community surplus production has been more difficult and more costly than anticipated.

Fourthly, because the Community was established in an era of fixed exchange rates, common prices were based on such a system. Despite the changes which have been made in the operation of the green money system, nevertheless fundamentally agriculture is still operating on the basis of fixed exchange rates. The reality of the money market is different, and so the CAP has had to cope with MCAs. As described in chapter 6, this situation has greatly distorted the principle of comparative advantage and has resulted in major anomalies of price when expressed in national currencies.

The types of measure used

Various ways can be used to analyse the types of measure in force under the market and price regimes. Two methods are used here. The first is to categorise the main commodities according to the range of price and market measures used. This is done in summary form in table 9. The second, which is an extension of the first, is to group the commodities according to the firmness of internal price support and to the level of protection from third country competition.

Taking the first method of classification, we find in table 9 a list of the

TABLE 9

Commodities according to the main measures applied under the price and market regimes

Product	Target price	Guide price	Norm price	Basic price	Intervention price	Withdrawal price	Minimum price	Production aid	Deficiency payment	Threshold price	Sluice-gate price	Reference price	Variable levy	Supplementary levy	Customs duty	Export refund
Common wheat	x				x					x			x			x
Durum wheat	x				x			x(a)		x			x			x
Barley	x				x					x			x			x
Rye	x				x					x			x			x
Maize	x				x					x			x			x
Rice	x				x					x			x			x
Sugar: white	x				x					x			x			x
beet							x									
Oilseeds: colza	x				x				x							
rape	x				x				x							
sunflower	x				x				x							
soya beans		x							x							
linseed		x							x							
castor		x					x		x							
cotton								x								
Peas & field beans	x(b)						x		x							
Dried fodder								x	x							
Fibre flax & hemp							x									
Milk products:																
butter					x					x		x				x
smp					x					x		x				x
cheese(c)					x					x		x				x
Beef: live		x														
meat					x							x			x	x
Pigmeat				x	x						x			x		x
Eggs											x			x		x
Poultry											x			x		x
Fish		x			x(d)	x						x			x	x
Silkworms							x									
Fresh fruit & veg.				x		x						x			x	x
Live plants															x	
Olive oil	x				x			x	x(e)	x		x			x	x
Wine		x			x(f)							x			x	x
Hops								x							x	
Seeds for sowing								x				x(g)				
Tobacco			x		x			x							x	x

(a) certain regions only; (b) activating price; (c) Italy only; (d) sardines and anchovies only; (e) olive oil consumer subsidy; (f) wine storage contracts and distillation; (g) hybrid maize only.

main commodities to which market regimes apply under the CAP. The table should be read across from left to right: an 'x' in any column indicates that the measure concerned is one which is used in the management of the commodity in question. It might be helpful at this stage to define the terms used in the table as we will meet with them again in the next few chapters.[26]

The terms are grouped into three broad divisions:

(a) those which relate to expected internal market prices;

(b) those which relate to means of internal price support;

(c) those which relate to the treatment of imports and exports.

The first group comprises target, guide, norm and basic prices. It is important to understand that in no way do these prices constitute guaranteed prices. Their significance lies in the fact that frontier protection and internal support measures derive from them. In more detail they can be described as follows.

Target price (prix indicatif): a price which represents for certain commodities the internal wholesale price which, given normal marketing circumstances, should be obtainable. It is set for the main cereals, white sugar, olive oil, certain oilseeds, and liquid milk.

Guide price (prix d'orientation): similar in concept to a target price but used for different commodities–some oilseeds, wine, cattle and fish.

Norm price: represents what is regarded as an adequate return to producers given rational management and the economic viability of the farm. It applies to raw tobacco.

Basic price (prix de base): used in two different ways. In the case of fruit and vegetables it represents the price received in the production areas with the lowest prices. In the case of pigmeat it is similar in concept to the guide price for cattle.

The second group relates to the mechanisms available internally to support prices. There are five such mechanisms and some commodities benefit from more than one type of support.

Intervention price (prix d'intervention): a minimum guaranteed price which is set some percentage points below the relevant target, guide, norm or basic price. Intervention agencies (whose functions were outlined in chapter 4) have a commitment to buy all the home-produced commodities offered to them at the price set, providing the products in question meet the necessary quality and quantity specifications.

Intervention prices are set for the main cereals, white and raw sugar, olive oil, some oilseeds, tobacco, butter, skimmed milk powder, certain cheeses, beef and pigmeat.

Intervention fulfils two separate roles. It is primarily a means of supporting prices (and therefore incomes) but it is also a mechanism for managing the internal market. Despite the widespread publicity given to occasional sales of intervention stocks to third countries at knock-down prices by the Community, in fact a substantial proportion of total stocks is sold back onto the Community market at a later date when prices have firmed up. To aid in this process some intervention prices are stepped throughout the marketing year. However, it should not be thought that intervention purchases and sales are always carried out in the interests of better marketing patterns. Intervention agencies are the buyers of last resort and so their stocks tend to accumulate in an unplanned way as the result of market pressures rather than as the result of a consciously designed policy. In fact the requirement to hold stocks on a regular basis is written into only two commodity regimes: sugar and olive oil.

A more obvious example of market management is to be found in the alternative to intervention buying which is provided for under various commodity regimes. This takes the form of subsidies for private storage. These subsidies are paid to traders as a means of persuading them not to market products at periods of heavy supply. They take somewhat different forms depending on the commodity involved but the intentions are always the same: to even out the pattern of stock release over the marketing year and to prevent heavy supplies from having a detrimental effect on market prices.

Withdrawal price: the price at which producer organisations withdraw certain fish and fruit and vegetables from over-supplied markets.

Minimum price (prix minima): applies under certain regimes when the support is paid to the processor who must undertake to pay the grower no less than the minimum price. It is operative for sugar beet, castor seed, potatoes grown for starch, and peas and field beans.

Production aid: a direct payment made to a producer based on physical quantity produced or area grown. It applies to some durum wheat, olive oil, flax and hemp, dried fodder, cotton seeds, seeds for sowing, silkworms and hops.

Deficiency payment: a payment made to bridge the gap between the target or similar price for certain commodities and the lower market price. It differs from a production aid in that it is not a fixed amount paid on area grown or quantity produced but is based on price differences. It is used for most oilseeds, peas and field beans and dried fodder.

The third group of mechanisms operates at the frontiers of the Community to regulate imports of agricultural commodities from third countries or to subsidise the export of products to other parts of the world. On the import side, there are three types of price and two types of levy, as well as customs duties; while on the export side there are refunds.

Threshold price (prix de seuil): a price set at the Community's frontiers which must be reached by imports. It ensures that the target price cannot be undercut by imports from third countries. It can be thought of as the at-border equivalent of the target price. It applies to cereals, sugar, butter, skimmed milk powder, certain cheeses and olive oil.

Sluice-gate price (prix d'ecluse): a minimum import price based on the level of production costs. It is used for pigmeat, poultry and eggs.

Reference price (prix de référence):[27] a minimum import price based on average prices obtained on representative markets over a period of years. It is used for fish, fruit and vegetables and wine.

Variable levy (prélevement): a charge imposed on imports of commodites from third countries which has the effect of raising their price to the threshold price level. The levy equals the difference between the 'world' price (defined as the lowest representative offer price corrected for Community standard quality) and the relevant threshold price.

Supplementary levy: a charge which can be imposed on imports of products subject to sluice-gate or reference prices in order to bring their offer price up to the minimum import price set by the Community.

Customs duty: a charge which takes the form of a designated percentage of the value of the imported item. Customs duties and import levies combined form the Common Customs Tariff (CCT) which surrounds the Community. Comparatively few of the major agricultural commodities are subject to customs duties because external protection is effected through the levy system. Products which are subject to duty are wine, tobacco, fish, fruit and vegetables, beef and hops.

Export refunds or restitutions: these are subsidies paid on certain agricultural commodities exported from the Community. Usually, though not exclusively, they apply to products which are also subject, on the import side, to levies. As a general rule, the unit rate of export restitution per ton is lower than the equivalent import levy because the Community grants no more than the minimum subsidy necessary to enable its produce to compete on world markets. Thus, whereas we saw above, a variable levy represents the difference between the lowest representative offer price to the Community and the threshold price, an export restitution represents the approximate difference between the average world price and the actual internal Community market price.

If we wish to classify the various price and market mechanisms outlined above in terms of their effectiveness at providing support, we find that on the domestic side the most effective support mechanism is that of intervention buying of surplus produce or, as an alternative, the provision of aids for private storage. The second most effective mechanism is the deficiency payment as this fluctuates in sympathy with trends in market prices and it is sometimes also backed by intervention buying. Minimum prices and production aids have the edge over support through the setting of buying-in prices as these latter are fixed at quite low levels and have to be triggered by the prior collapse of the market.

It should be remembered that not all commodities have internal support mechanisms. For instance, although subject to a market regime, eggs and poultry do not receive internal support. Equally, under many market regimes only the major products receive internal support. This is true of cereals, milk, fruit and vegetables, and fish.

Some commodities, although they come under the CAP and have some form of frontier protection, are not subject to a market regime. These are collectively known as the 'Annex II commodities'. For two of them—sheepmeat and potatoes—market regimes have been proposed but so far not agreed.

On the import side, we find that undoubtedly the most effective protective instrument is the variable levy and the least effective is the customs duty. The ultimate purpose behind all frontier measures is to protect the home market, but the effects of the various measures are different. The variable levy makes it impossible for third country supplies, no matter how competitive (either through lower production costs or through high subsidisation), to enter the Community at below the threshold price. The only chink in the armour lies in the trade agreement which the Community has signed with various third countries which permit levy reduction or total waiver.

In terms of effectiveness as a mechanism for excluding produce, variable levies should be contrasted with minimum import prices (i.e. reference and sluice-gate prices). While the purpose of minimum prices is also to raise the landed price of commodities from third countries, the effect is different. They encourage exporters to raise their offer prices to at least the minimum import price level. This means that the exporting country can keep for itself the extra revenue so generated.

Customs duties are applied to many of the lesser agricultural commodites but, as on the industrial side where they are much more common, Community duties are set at fairly modest levels. In many cases their impact is further limited by the granting of concessionary rates of duties by the Community under trade agreements. Thus their effect is limited to the provision of a certain degree of protection for domestic producers but at a level which leaves Community farmers much more open to world price influences than with the levy system.

Taking into account the twin elements of domestic support and external protection, we find that the most effective regimes are those for cereals, sugar, dairy products, beef and veal, and olive oil. Those with the least support are fruit and vegetables. The remaining commodities can be divided into those for which support is firm–pigmeat, poultry, eggs, wine and tobacco–and those for which support is modest–the lesser arable crops, hops, etc.

Secondary market and price measures

Before going on to discuss the manner in which farm prices are fixed each year, it would as well to round off discussion on market mechanisms by mentioning a number of secondary or subsidiary features of the commodity regimes. These secondary measures can be divided into those which are applied internally and those which are concerned with exports.

Subsidies to manufacturers: as we have seen, for certain commodities there is tight regulation of imports, and Community internal prices are well above those prevailing on world markets. The introduction of such a system of support created problems for those industries which use certain agricultural raw materials. Because of this, provision was made under a number of commodity regimes (for instance, cereals and sugar) to subsidise certain home-produced raw materials used by manufacturers of particular products. The outcome is that, for the industries concerned, the normal effects of the price regimes are partially or fully neutralised and the manufacturers obtain domestically produced raw materials at close to world prices. The Commission would dearly like to see an end to these concessions as they are expensive to operate.

Denaturing premiums: these are subsidies which have the effect of diverting produce from an over-supplied market to some other outlet. They take the form of a subsidy on the price of the surplus commodity which makes it attractive to users who could not otherwise afford it. The product in question is 'denatured' by having dye or some other substance added to it so as to prevent it being sold back onto the over-supplied market. The commodity which most commonly used to be denatured was wheat but this practice was stopped in 1974 and the provision enabling denaturing to take place was removed from the cereals regime when it was revised in 1976. Denaturing is still permitted in limited circumstances under the sugar regime.

Consumer subsidies: originally these subsidies were not a feature of the Community regimes, except insofar as provision was made under the fruit and vegetable regime to give away free to certain social groups surplus produce or, under the milk regime, to subsidise milk and milk products for school children. However, during the 1970s a combination of circumstances has encouraged the Community to introduce consumer subsidies on certain commodities. This development was stimulated by two quite different occurrences.

Firstly, there was the 1972–1974 commodity boom during which certain world prices rose above the Community support levels for prolonged periods. The Community reacted by changing its rules on exports (which will be discussed below) and it also introduced subsidies on some commodities for specific groups of consumers who were regarded as least able to withstand the rise in market prices. Secondly, the Community which has been much exercised by the difficulties of disposing of accumulated surpluses has found that the provision of subsidised products for domestic consumers is a much more popular policy than disposing of them to third countries not normally thought of as needy.

The three secondary measures so far outlined are all concerned in one way or another with stimulating the utilisation on the domestic market of Community products. They are, therefore, in the nature of remedial measures which have to be taken as the result of excess production. The Community has also adopted a number of measures intended to forestall excessive production and to these we now turn.

Production quotas: the Community has consistently resisted the use of internal quantitative controls as a means of reducing domestic production—despite discussion of the issue which arises from time to time. However, as an exception production quotas have always applied in the sugar sector. They are, therefore, something of an anomaly and there is no evidence that they might be extended to other commodities in surplus. Far more attention has been given to the introduction and use of indirect means of cutting production.

The dairy sector has been singled out in particular for a series of measures all aimed at encouraging farmers to cut supplies. There have been schemes to promote a switch to beef production; to withhold milk supplies from creameries and to utilise more milk on the farm as a direct livestock feed; to slaughter dairy cows and not to replace them. One of the most recent measures was the introduction of the 'co-responsibility levy' in 1977. Under this scheme, through a levy on the price of milk delivered to the creamery, farmers are made to pay towards the cost of disposing of surplus dairy products.

External measures

The secondary measures so far outlined are all ones which operate internally. Two measures which operate externally should be mentioned: the first is one which is constantly in use, the second is more in the nature of an insurance policy in the event of difficult market conditions.

Food aid: naturally the Community food aid programme does not involve commercial sales but rather it makes available supplies free of charge to countries which need them. The motives behind food aid are mixed in the Community as they are everywhere else in the world. It has been viewed as a moral commitment and as a convenient means of disposing of unwanted surpluses. However, over a period of time the Community has grown increasingly to accept that its food aid commitment should be a continuing one no matter what the state of its internal supply situation.

Export taxes: paradoxically, although the Community is normally concerned with surpluses and their disposal, it has had to take measures in the past to protect its internal supplies at times of high world prices. This occurred during the commodity boom of 1972–1974, as a result of which some of the market regimes were modified so as to provide a means of inverting the normal institutional arrangements at the frontier when world prices rise above Community support levels.

When this happens the Community's first line of defence against the price rise is to lower or even suspend the operation of the levy system, so that imports can enter freely. But if offer prices rise above the threshold level, the variable levy becomes inoperative and the Community must then concentrate on preventing domestic supplies being exported to third countries where they would benefit from higher prices. In such a situation the Community can impose export taxes equal to the difference between world and internal prices. Of course, this action does not increase total supplies in the Community, it merely prevents them from being depleted by exports. Only in one case (sugar) has the Community gone so far as to subsidise imports, but this proved to be a very expensive operation in terms of budgetary cost.

The annual fixing of support prices

Under normal circumstances common prices are reviewed annually in a composite package. The procedure is for the Commission to submit the price proposals in a series of draft Regulations to the Council of Ministers at the end of the calendar year or shortly afterwards. Agreement is reached on them by the Council in the course of the spring. The new prices then come into operation as each commodity marketing year commences. This means that they apply virtually immediately for, say, the dairy and beef sectors and with a gap of a few months for cereals.

The original intention was slightly different. The price proposals were to be submitted well before the new marketing year so that farmers had time to adjust their investment and production decisions. However, in recent years the Commission has delayed its proposals as long as possible so as to have more up-to-date information available when making them. In many cases this means that farmers have already taken decisions for the next farming year before the proposals are announced or before the Council has agreed the new price levels. Obviously this delays the possible impact of the new prices.

The question arises: on what basis does the Commission make its price proposals? Up to 1972/73 it used what it called 'objective criteria' but what these were was not exactly clear. The Commission then revised its approach and introduced the 'objective method' (described below) as the basis of its calculations, but increasingly this is not the only factor taken into account.

For the first few years after the objective method was introduced it was indeed the only basis of the Commission's proposals. But the Commission regards it now as only one of the factors which need to be taken into account. Other factors which are considered are the general economic situation of the Community, the state of overseas markets, and the internal market situation for the main commodities. However, despite these other factors, the objective method remains of great importance because it provides an indicator of farm income levels.

What then is the objective method? It is a means of determining the end price changes necessary to maintain efficient production. The basic philosophy behind the annual price proposals is that the modern (or efficient) farm should be maintained in that status, and that price changes should be used to achieve this end. The modern farm is defined as one yielding an income comparable to that obtainable in non-agricultural full-time employment in the same region. The Commission is interested to find the level of prices which, allowing for changes in costs and increases in farm productivity, and taking movements of non-farm earnings into account, will allow efficient farms to remain so.

In order to find such a price level, the Commission first examines the cost structure of a sample of 'reference farms' (modern farms) which covers all the main types of farming and regions within the Community. This information is obtained from the Farm Accountancy Data Network. The Commission measures the farm cost changes which have occurred over a three-year reference period and combines these with the movement of non-agricultural earnings to show the rise needed if agricultural incomes on modern farms are to be maintained. From the resulting figures certain deductions are then made. These are: an arbitrary 1.5 per cent per annum to represent the rise in productivity on farms; any increases in prices which have already been awarded; and any changes in support prices due to the movement of green rates of exchange.

In recent years, faced with the continuing problems generated by surplus production, the Commission has put forward increasingly modest price proposals, which explains its introduction of considerations other than the objective method. But as will be remembered from chapter 3, it is the Council of Ministers which takes the final decision as to the level of prices. There has been a regrettable tendency for the Council to use the Commission's figures as no more than a basis for negotiation and to bid up the prices for political and nationalistic reasons.

This tendency has been accentuated by the increasing difficulty which the Council has had in recent years in taking decisions at all. The package method of setting prices has given individual Member States many opportunities to hold up agreement on the whole in order to achieve agreement on some minor matter of particular interest to themselves. Equally it has increased the opportunities for trade-offs between Member States which agree not to object to certain matters in return for support on some project of interest to themselves.

To some extent the Commission is also to blame as it frequently couples proposals on structure with those on prices. Sometimes these are new structural proposals, but on other occasions they are matters which have lain unresolved for months or even years. Sometimes a Member State resurrects an old issue as a bargaining tool. Thus, the level of prices becomes only one element (albeit still the most important) in a package designed to give something to each Minister for Agriculture to bring back home in triumph.

All of this leads to the final price level being higher than the

Commission's proposals. Possibly in the past few years there has been a greater awareness on the part of the Council of the need for caution in the fixing of price levels, but no matter how much prudence is used there still remains one further major outstanding problem—namely, the incidence of MCAs and the effects of green currencies on the actual prices received by farmers.

This can be demonstrated by considering the effect of the adjustments to the green rates which accompanied the price changes for the 1978/79 farm year as illustrated in table 10. The average rise in common prices was just over 2 per cent when expressed in units of account, but the picture was quite different when the impact of green rate changes were added in.

TABLE 10

Make-up of the 1978/79 price changes: common price and green currency rate changes

Member States	Changes in common prices (% in units of account)	Effects of changes in green rates (% in national currency)	Combined effect (% in national currency)
FR Germany	+2.1	− 0.30	+ 1.79
Benelux	+2.1	—	+ 2.10
Denmark	+2.1	+ 5.26	+ 7.47
Ireland	+2.1	+ 6.38	+ 8.61
France	+2.1	+ 7.69	+ 9.95
Italy	+2.1	+12.04	+14.39
UK	+2.1	+ 8.11	+10.38

Source: [51]

The effects are not the same for all countries. For a country with a depreciating currency, devaluation of its agricultural exchange rate has the effect of a support price increase when the common prices are converted into the national currency. Such a country—the UK is a prime example—is very willing to support any Commission efforts to restrain rises in common prices because it is cushioned from the full impact of such restraint by the possibility of green currency devaluation. A country with an appreciating currency faces quite a different situation and one which is inherently much more difficult to resolve. Any realignment of its agricultural exchange rate to bring it closer to the market rate has the effect of lowering support prices when they are converted into its national currency. Consequently, such a country–Federal Germany, for instance–has to depend on the increase in common prices for any rise in the support received by its farmers and it cannot rely on any cushioning through agricultural exchange rate manipulation.

Notes to Chapter 7

25. The Community is often accused of having as one of its aims the raising of self-sufficiency levels. This is not really true. What is much more relevant is that the Community has been far too slow in taking action to head off the development of potential structural surpluses and such action as it has taken has been inadequate.
26. It should not be thought that these are the only terms used in the price and market regimes but they are the most important. Others will be explained where necessary in chapters 8, 9 and 10.
27. This is a particularly confusing term as it is also used on the internal market in a number of different meanings.

CHAPTER 8

Price and market mechanisms for field crops

We come now to the start of a more detailed description of the market and price regimes in operation for the various commodities. Immediately a problem arises as to how the commodities can best be grouped. In chapter 7 they were grouped according to the type of regime but this is not a particularly suitable classification for our present purposes. The grouping chosen raises as many difficulties as it solves and will probably satisfy no one.

This present chapter covers the regimes for cereals, rice, sugar, isoglucose, all oilseeds and other sources of protein feedingstuffs, as well as the proposed potato regime. Chapter 9 covers all the livestock and livestock products, i.e. milk and milk products, beef, pigmeat, poultry and eggs; the proposed sheepmeat regime and—by stretching a point—fish and silkworms. Chapter 10 is devoted to horticultural crops, wine, olive oil, tobacco, hops, seeds for sowing; and the proposed regime on ethyl alcohol.

The reader should be absolutely clear that what follows in this and the next two chapters is an outline of the market and price regimes only. Many details must be left unstated and the regimes are subject from time to time to small amendments which cannot be covered here. What is provided is a full reference to the title and source of each of the basic Regulations and to all the major amendments which have taken place, so that the reader who wishes to pursue the matter further is equipped with some basic tools. It should also not be overlooked that basic Regulations (which are what we will be discussing) are followed by further Council and Commission implementing Regulations setting out detailed administrative procedures. These are not covered here.

The pattern of discussion is the same for all commodities. Each section begins with a list of the important Regulations. For some commodities this means starting with an original Regulation passed in the 1960s under which the Member States transitted to the common regime. In a number of instances the basic Regulation under which the common regime was set up has been superseded by a later one. This is usually because the basic Regulation had been amended so frequently that it had lost much of its clarity. Thus in the interests of intelligibility a new, consolidated Regulation was passed. Sometimes, of course, the basic Regulation has been superseded because it was found to be unsatisfactory in operation. The basic or consolidated Regulation is followed where relevant by a list of important amendments and a statement of the marketing year for the commodity concerned. Having set out the tools we are then ready to tackle the regime itself.

We start with cereals because of the fundamental importance of this regime. Historically it was the first regime and it represents a support model on which many other regimes are founded and on which some are actually dependent.

Cereals

Original Regulation: No. 19 *portant établissement graduel d'une organisation commune des marchés dans le secteur des céréals*, JO 30, 20 avril 1962.
Basic Regulation: No. 120/67/EEC *on the common organisation of the market in cereals*, Sp. OJ 1967.
Consolidated Regulation (EEC) No. 2727/75 *on the common organisation of the market in cereals*, OJ L281, 1 November 1975.
Important amendments: Regs. 1143/76; 1157/77; and 1125/78.[28]
Marketing year: August–July.
The range of products involved is very wide and they are listed in four groups under Art. 1 of Reg. 2727/75 as follows:
   (a) common wheat and meslin, rye, barley, oats, maize (other than hybrid for sowing), buckwheat, millet, canary seed, grain sorghum, and other cereals;
   (b) durum wheat;
   (c) wheat or meslin flour, rye flour, wheat groats and meal (of both common and durum wheat);
   (d) the processed products listed in Annex A of the Regulation.
Despite the length and complexity of this list we can concentrate quite easily on the essentials which are the regimes for the major grains. These in turn can be subdivided for certain purposes into feed grains,

bread wheat, and durum wheat (the type of wheat used in the manufacture of *pasta*). We should also distinguish between the measures taken internally and the measures operating at the Community's frontiers.

Target and intervention prices are set annually for common wheat, durum wheat, barley, maize and rye. The target prices are set at Duisburg (a city in the Ruhr district of Federal Germany), which, as it is situated in a highly industrialised area, represents the point of maximum deficit in the Community. Prices are fixed for a standard quality of each grain. They are based on the relevant intervention price set at Ormes (a city in the Paris Basin, the area of maximum cereals surplus in the Community). The difference between a target and intervention price reflects, firstly, the transport costs between Ormes and Duisburg, and secondly, an element to take account of the difference between the market price and the intervention price to be expected in the Ormes area in a normal year.

The setting of intervention prices has been much simplified in recent years and today there is a single common intervention price for common wheat, barley and maize, and a separate intervention price for rye, which is being brought gradually into line with that of the other feed grains. There is also an intervention price for durum wheat and a reference price[29] for wheat of bread-making quality. This last can best be described as a super intervention price. It is set 13 per cent above the intervention price for common wheat, barley and maize and is intended to reflect the fact that, because wheats of bread-making quality have lower yields than other varieties, the farmer should be compensated for this through a higher floor price in the market. In order to qualify for intervention at the higher reference price, the wheat must pass special tests to determine its suitability for bread-making.

The Community operates two types of intervention. Firstly, there is Intervention A which is the purchase by intervention agencies of all cereals harvested in the Community which are offered to them, providing such offers comply with the rules laid down concerning quality and quantity. Mandatory intervention on bread wheat applies only during the first three months of the marketing year. Secondly, there is Intervention B. This is a form of preventative action whereby an intervention agency can forestall a glut on the market by offering storage contracts to merchants to withhold grain from the over-supplied market. Clearly, this is a much cheaper form of intervention as it involves the cost of storage only and not the total cost of the grain, as the grain remains in the ownership of the merchant. The most usual cereal to benefit from Intervention B is common wheat, although occasionally it is used also for barley.

Two other measures operate internally. Firstly, some durum wheat benefits not only from a target and intervention price but also from a flat rate payment per hectare harvested. This applies in certain regions of Italy, the criterion being that they have below average yields.

Secondly, production refunds are made available for certain raw materials which have increased in price due to the operation of the cereals regime, thus allowing Community starch manufacturers to compete with products made from raw materials from outside the Community, e.g. oil. The refunds are available for maize, common wheat, rice and potatoes used for starch manufacture; and for maize groats and meal used in the brewing industry. The payment of the production refund on potato starch is subject to the requirement that the manufacturer has paid a minimum price for the potatoes. This minimum price varies with the starch content of the potatoes and is related to the price for maize.

We turn now to look at the measures which operate at the frontier. Threshold prices are set not only for the most important grains, for which target and intervention prices are also set, but for lesser grains and processed cereals as well. For the main grains (i.e. common wheat, durum wheat, barley, maize and rye), threshold prices are fixed in such a way that the selling price of the imported grain on the Duisburg market is the same as the target price for home-produced grain. The threshold price is therefore the target price less the sum of the transport costs between Rotterdam and Duisburg, together with the discharge costs and a commercial margin. The costs are based on the cheapest available which is river freight on the Rhine in barges of 1000–1500 tonnes [42].

For the lesser grains (e.g. oats, buckwheat, millet, canary seed and grain sorghum), the threshold prices are set in such a way that they do not undercut the main grains with which they compete. The same principle applies for the main flours and meals, and account is also taken of the need to protect the Community's processing industry.

Levies are charged on all imports of cereals and cereal products for which threshold prices also apply. As we saw in chapter 7, the levy is equal to the threshold price minus the c.i.f. price at Rotterdam, calculated daily on the basis of the lowest representative offer price, corrected for Community standard quality (see fig. 5).

Levies are also charged on the products listed in Annex A of Reg. 2727/75. These levies are made up of two components: one is a variable element based on the levy in the preceding month for the relevant primary cereal, multiplied by a technical co-efficient. The other—which is a fixed element—is intended to protect the Community processing industry. In fact, very little trade takes place in processed cereal products, as practically all imports are of primary grains.

A special derogation from the normal level of levies is made on imports to Italy by sea of barley, oats, maize, grain sorghum and millet. The extent of the levy reduction is fixed annually and is matched by a subsidy on deliveries by sea of the same cereals from other Member States. The basis of this derogation—which is regarded as temporary although it has existed since 1967—has changed over time. It is now said to be a compensation for the higher handling costs at Italian ports.

Levy concessions are also available throughout the Community for imports coming from the ACP states under the Lomé Convention. These states are countries in Africa, the Caribbean and Pacific (hence ACP). The Lomé Convention, signed by the Community, covers trade and aid arrangements between the parties concerned. At the time of writing it was being renegotiated for a further period. The concessions are detailed in Reg. (EEC) No. 706/76,[30] and as far as cereals are concerned relate to reduced levy rates on cereals and processed products originating in ACP states.

On the export side, provision is made for the payment of export refunds on any product listed in Art. 1 of Reg. 2727/75 or on the goods listed in Annex B of the same Regulation. Refunds are based on the difference in the price of the cereal or cereal product on the world market and the price in the Community (see fig. 5). Refunds are the same for the whole Community but can vary according to destination.

Apart from the Community's commercial export sales, it also operates a major food aid programme. Provision is made under Reg.

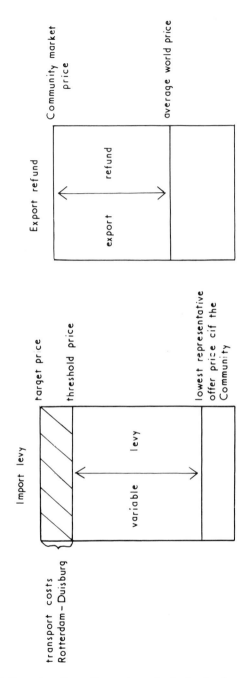

Fig. 5: Operation of import levy and export refund system for cereals.

2727/75 for the purchase of the products coming under Art. 1 for use in this programme. Purchases can be made on the Community market or through the use of cereals held by intervention agencies, or—in exceptional circumstances—by purchases on world markets.

Rice

Original Regulation: No. 16/64/EEC *portant établissement graduel d'une organisation commune du marché du riz*, JO 34, 27 février 1964.
Basic Regulation: No. 359/67/EEC *on the common organisation of the market in rice*, Sp. OJ 1967.
Consolidated Regulation: (EEC) No. 1418/76 *on the common organisation of the market in rice*, OJ L166, 25 May 1976.
Important amendments: Regs. 1158/77; and 1126/78.[31]
Marketing year: September—August.

The only producer of rice in the Community of any size is Italy, (France is a producer on a minor scale) but despite the geographical limitation of production, the rice regime is modelled closely on that of cereals. Under Art. 1.1 of Reg. 1418/76 the regime covers three groups of products:

(a) paddy, husked, semi-milled and wholly milled rice;

(b) broken rice;

(c) rice flour, groats and meal, flaked rice, rice pellets and starch.

The target price is set for husked rice and relates to the Duisburg market. The intervention price is determined for paddy rice (i.e. rice which still retains its husk after threshing) and relates to the Vercelli intervention centre in northern Italy. As the intervention price is set for an earlier stage of processing than the target price, the difference between the two reflects not only price trends at Vercelli and the cost of transport from there to Duisburg, but also an element which represents the milling costs of converting unhusked into husked rice (less the value of by-products).

Both Intervention A and B can take place throughout the year but in fact little use is made of either procedure. In line with the cereals regime, provision is made for a production refund for broken rice used in the manufacture of starch and for brewing beer.

Most activity under the rice regime is concentrated at the frontier. Each year, the Community establishes five threshold prices: for round, husked grain; long, husked grain; round grain wholly milled; long grain wholly milled; and broken rice. The threshold price set at Rotterdam for round, husked rice is in a sense the basic one and is derived from the target price for round-grained husked rice. The other threshold prices (except for broken rice) are derived from the round, husked price, while the broken rice threshold price is related to the threshold price for maize.

Levies are set for paddy, husked, semi-milled, wholly milled and broken rice calculated daily on the difference between the current representative c.i.f. offer price and the relevant threshold price. Levies are also charged on the items listed at (c) above and contain a variable element related to the grain type and a fixed element intended as a protection for the Community processing industry.

Export refunds are available on all the products listed in Art. 1 of Reg. 1418/76 in the state referred to in that Article, and also in the form of the good listed in Annex B of the same Regulation. The arrangements governing the availability of export refunds and rice for the food aid programme are similar to those for cereals.

Sugar

Original Regulation: No. 44/67/EEC *concernant certaines mesures d'organisation commune des marchés dans le secteur du sucre pour la campagne 1967/68*, JO 40, 3 mars 1967.

Basic Regulation: No. 1009/67/EEC *on the common organisation of the market in sugar*, Sp. OJ 1967.

Consolidated Regulation: (EEC) No. 3330/74 *on the common organisation of the market in sugar*, OJ L359, 31 December 1974.

Important amendments: Regs. 1487/76; 1110/77; 705/78; and 1396/78.[32]

Marketing year: July–June.

Although basically modelled on the cereals regime, the sugar regime has a number of special features. Firstly, sugar producers are the only group of farmers in the Community who are subject to production quotas. Secondly, the regime is unusual in that the degree of self-financing of support arrangements is much higher than in other regimes, and thirdly, because of the Community's commitment to import sugar under the Lomé Convention, the regime is subject to outside influences unknown for any other commodity.

Under Art. 1.1. of Reg. 3330/74 the sugar regime covers five groups of products as follows:

(a) beet and cane sugar;

(b) sugar beet and sugar cane;

(c) molasses;

(d) other sugars (excluding lactose and glucose); sugar syrups (excluding lactose and glucose syrups); artificial honey; caramel; flavoured sugars, syrups and molasses (excluding lactose and glucose syrups and excluding fruit juice containing added sugar);

(e) beet-pulp, bagasse and other waste.

A target price is set each year for white sugar in the Community's area of greatest surplus (northern France). An intervention price is set for the same region and provision is made for derived intervention prices which are fixed for the deficit areas of Ireland, Italy and the UK. Derived raw sugar and white sugar prices are also set for the French overseas departments: Réunion, Martinique, Guadeloupe and Guyane (*Départments d'Outre Mer* (DOM)).

Each year the Community sets two minimum prices for sugar beet. One relates to production within the basic quota (the A quota), the other covers production in excess of the basic quota but within the maximum quota (the B quota). The minimum price for A quota beet is related to the intervention price for white sugar but takes into account the sugar yield from beet, the costs of processing (less receipts for molasses), and, where relevant, the cost of delivering the beet to the factory. Sugar manufacturers are required to pay at least this minimum price to the producer (variations up or down based on beet quality being allowed).

The price arrangements in Italy are slightly different: until the 1979/80 marketing year producers are entitled to an extra aid over and above the minimum price. Part of the aid may be retained by the processing industry, and an upper limit is placed on the tonnage on which the aid can be paid. Conditions for the purchase of sugar cane in DOM are governed by agreement between the growers and manufacturers.

Sugar manufacturers pay a levy on each tonne of sugar sold. This levy is intended to finance the reimbursements of the storage costs payable on white and raw sugar and certain syrups. This levy/reimbursement system is operated in the interests of orderly marketing and is intended to achieve the same results as in, for instance, the cereals regime where intervention prices move up in monthly steps throughout the marketing year. If a manufacturer sells early in the marketing year, he is penalised as he will have to pay the levy but will have received little or no reimbursement of the storage costs. If a sugar manufacturer sells into intervention, he pays no levy, so effectively the floor market price is the intervention price plus the levy. Intervention is not resorted to very much as the Community tends to dispose of surplus sugar on world markets with the aid of export restitutions.

Two other internal support measures should be mentioned. Firstly, denaturing premiums are provided for in the basic Regulation but are currently used only on sugar for feeding to bees. Secondly, production refunds are available for sugar used in the manufacture of certain specified products in the chemical industry. These refunds are related to the starch refunds under the cereals regime.

As already mentioned, sugar production is subject to quotas. New arrangements were laid down in Reg. 3330/74 to cover the marketing years 1975/76 to 1979/80 inclusive. Arrangements to be made for subsequent years must be finalised before the start of 1980. Each Member State is allocated a basic quantity of white sugar which it may produce. This is then divided up within each Member State and separate quotas (the A quotas) are allocated to each factory. In turn, each factory allocates to farmers growing contracts which reflect its own quota allocation.

Apart from the A quota, each factory is allocated a B quota, i.e. a quota over and above the basic A quota. B quota sugar is subject to a production levy which may not exceed 30 per cent of the intervention price. This levy is intended to help finance the cost of export restitutions. If, however, a factory produces outside the maximum quota (i.e. A+B quotas), it must export the excess sugar outside the Community within six months of the end of the marketing year and no export refunds are available to assist the sales.

Threshold prices are set each year for white sugar, raw sugar, and molasses. In the case of white sugar, the threshold price must equal the target price plus the storage levy and the transport charges (calculated at a flat rate) between northern France and Palermo (i.e. between the points of maximum surplus and deficit). The raw sugar threshold price is derived from that for white sugar; the molasses threshold price is related to the value ascribed to receipts for molasses used in fixing the minimum price for beet.

Levies on white and raw sugar, and on molasses are based on the difference between the relevant threshold price and the lowest representative world price. The levies charges on items falling under Art. 1.1(b) and (d) listed above are calculated on a combination of sucrose content and the levy on white sugar. The only exception is maple sugar and syrup, for which there is a special limitation on the import charge agreed under the rules of GATT.

Because of the Community's experience in the early 1970s when sugar was extremely scarce, provision is made for a system of minimum stock holding in order to ensure normal supplies. In principle, the minimum stock is equal to 10 per cent of the basic quota, or to 10 per cent of production if this is lower, of each processor of Community sugar and refiner of preferential sugar (i.e. sugar entering the Community under the Lomé Convention). Costs incurred in maintaining this stock are taken into account when fixing the sugar price.

Export refunds are available on all products listed in Art. 1.1(a), (c) and (d) either in the form as described in that Article or in the form of the products listed in Annex 1 of Reg. 3330/74 (as revised by Reg. 705/78). Refunds on most of the sugar exported from the Community in the natural state (i.e. white and raw sugar) are awarded in a weekly competitive tender.

Under Protocol No. 3 attached to the Lomé Convention [64] the Community agreed for an indefinite period to purchase and import from the sugar-producing ACP states a guaranteed quantity of sugar annually at a price withing the range of prices fixed for home-produced sugar. The annual quantity was fixed at 1.2 million tonnes expressed in terms of white sugar (although much of the ACP sugar is actually imported raw for subsequent refining). ACP sugar may be freely sold commercially within the Community at or above the guaranteed price, but if markets are unobtainable, intervention buying is permitted in the same way as for home-produced sugar, although the necessary rules for intervention buying of ACP sugar have not yet been determined by the Council. ACP sugar also participates in the production levy/storage reimbursement scheme, but as this sugar is normally stored for short periods only, the levy charged is lower than that charged on Community produced sugar. Refiners of ACP sugar are required to hold minimum stocks in the normal manner.

The Community has entered into similar but separate agreements on sugar with India, and with the overseas countries and territories (OCT), i.e. dependencies of Member States. Quotas agreed under these arrangements total about 80,000 tonnes.

Isoglucose

Basic Regulation: (EEC) No. 1111/77 laying down certain provisions for isoglucose, OJ L134, 25 May 1977.
Important amendment: Reg. 706/78, OJ L94, 8 April 1978.

Isoglucose is obviously not a field crop but rather a glucose syrup with a high fructose content which is obtained from the processing of starch. It is a direct substitute for liquid sugar produced from beet or cane, hence its inclusion here alongside the sugar regime. The market regime was introduced as a response to the threat posed to the Community's sugar market from the technical developments which had led to the feasibility of isoglucose production. The fear was that its production would expand as fast in the Community as it had already done in the USA.

Not unnaturally, no internal support measures are granted for isoglucose production, but rather its manufacture was made subject to a levy per kilogram of dry matter produced. This was equal to the production levy on sugar. In 1978, the Court of Justice gave a ruling in the Joined Cases 103/77 and 145/77: 1. Royal Scholten-Honig (Holdings) Ltd; 2. Tunnel Refineries Ltd *v* IBAP (OJ C285, 29 November 1978); which stated that while the principle of applying an isoglucose levy was valid, the level at which it was set was not. This meant that the levy was put in abeyance pending a review of the situation by the Commission.

Provision is also made in Reg. 1111/77 for the imposition of an import levy based on the sugar and cereal regimes, but its existence is rather irrelevant. This is because, to date, isoglucose is only available in liquid form and its transport costs are such as to prohibit the development of any significant international trade. Export refunds are also available, but again because of transport costs they are of importance only in the context of processed product exports.

Early in 1979 the Commission put forward a proposal to amend Reg. 1111/77 (OJ C78, 24 March 1979) the effect of which would be to bring the isoglucose regime into line with that for sugar, thereby avoiding the discrimination which gave rise to the actions pursued before the Court of Justice. The most important suggested revision is the allocation to isoglucose manufacturers of basic and maximum production quotas (analagous to the A and B quotas of the sugar regime). Production of B quota isoglucose would be made subject to a production levy equal to the share of the sugar production levy borne by the sugar manufacturers. Production of isoglucose which exceeded a manufacturer's maximum quota (i.e. the sum of the A and B quotas) or which was produced by a manufacturer to whom a basic quota had not been allocated would have to be disposed of in its natural state outside the Community without the benefit of an export restitution.

Oilseeds

Basic Regulation: No. 136/66/EEC *on the establishment of a common organisation of the market in oils and fats.* Sp. OJ 1965–1966.
Marketing years: colza and rape seed: July–June
                      sunflower seed: September—August

Reg. 135/66 covers colza, rape and sunflower seed, and olive oil. This last is a very different crop and has a completely separate regime and is outlined in chapter 10 along with the other permanent crops. The oilseed group has been added to down the years and the additional crops are outlined below. Art. 1.2 of Reg. 136/66 covers five groups of products, of which three relate to olives and olive oil, the remainder are as follows:

  (a) oil seeds and oleaginous fruit other than for sowing;
  (b) flours and meals of oil seeds and oleaginous fruit, fats and oils of fish and marine mammals, fixed vegetable oils (excluding olive oil), animal or vegetable oils and fats, margarine, imitation lard and other prepared edible fats, residues resulting from the

treatment of fatty substances or animal or vegetable waxes (excluding those containing oil having the characteristic of olive oil).

Despite the extensiveness of this list, our discussion can be reduced quite simply to colza, rape and sunflower. The regimes covering them and the remaining oilseeds outlined below are very light in terms of levels of protection in keeping with the Community's deficit status.

Colza is a plant similar to rape and the two can be considered as one. Target, basic and derived intervention prices are set each year. Owing to health fears concerning erucic acid, the Community discourages the production of rape seed with a high erucic content by limiting intervention to those seed varieties with a low acid content.

A production subsidy—or deficiency payment—payable to the crusher is available for rape and sunflower seeds. This subsidy represents the difference between the target price and the world market price. In 1979 the rules are being changed so that aid in future will be available only on low erucic varieties and on other varieties, providing the oil extracted from them is contracted to the chemical industry. All oilseeds and oil meals used in animal feed are zero-rated under the CCT. Customs duties are payable on oil flours.

Cotton seeds: Regulation (EEC) No. 1516/71 *introducing a system of subsidies for cotton seeds* (Sp. OJ 1971(11)) was designed to assist growers in southern Italy and Sicily. The marketing year is August–July. The only form of aid available is a flat rate area payment per hectare of land sown and harvested. The payment is made direct to the grower.

Soya beans: under Regulation (EEC) No. 1900/74 *laying down special measures for soya beans* (OJ L201, 23 July 1974) the Community introduced a guide price for soya beans. The marketing year is November–October. A subsidy is paid to producers, which equals the difference between the guide price and the world price. The subsidy is based not on actual production but on an imputed production. Each year an indicative yield (i.e. a sort of standardised yield) is set and the subsidy is paid on the number of hectares sown and harvested multiplied by the indicative yield. There is a possibility that this regime may be changed as the French (the main producers) believe it to be unsatisfactory as it tends to penalise the efficient grower, and in this regard a proposal to change the regime has been included in the 1979/80 price proposals [42]. If this were adopted the soya regime would be similar to that for castor seed (see below).

Linseed: a regime very similar to that for soya beans was established for linseed under Regulation (EEC) No. 569/76 *laying down special measures for linseed* (OJ L67, 15 March 1976). The marketing year is August–July. The subsidy applies not only to seed grown for oil, but also to the seed which is a by-product of fibre flax production. The indicative yield on which the subsidy payment is based varies according to different zones in the Community. This variation is intended to reflect the difference in natural ability to grow flax for linseed. The French have the same objections to the linseed regime as they have to the soya bean regime and it may be changed as a result of proposals in the 1979/80 price proposals [42]. It, too, would become similar to the castor seed regime.

Castor seed: the regime set up under Regulation (EEC) No. 2874/77 *laying down special measures in respect of castor seed* (OJ L332, 24 December 1977) differs somewhat from those for soya beans and linseed. The marketing year is October–September. The production aid is paid to the crusher rather than to the farmer and is based on the difference between the guide price and the world market price in the months in which castor seed is sold. The aid is subject to the payment by the crusher of a contract price to the producer which is at least equivalent to the minimum price required under the Regulation. This minimum price is set a little below the guide price.

Peas and field beans

Basic Regulation : (EEC) No. 1119/78 *laying down special measures for peas and field beans used in the feeding of animals*, OJ L142, 30 May 1978.

Marketing year: July–June.

The regime covers peas (excluding chick peas) and field beans and it was instituted to help increase the Community's supplies of proteins and also to assist farmers in Mediterranean regions. The aid provided under the regime is paid to the manufacturer of animal feedingstuffs but, in order to qualify, he must purchase peas and field beans from growers under contract and pay them at least the stipulated minimum price.

Each year the Community sets an activating price (i.e. a target price) for peas and field beans. The aid–which is in the form of a deficiency payment–is calculated on the basis of the difference between the world price of soya meal and the activating price. The subsidy is equal to 45 per cent of the difference between these two prices. The reason why it is 45 per cent rather than 100 per cent is to take account of the difference in protein content of soya meal and peas and field beans.

Dried fodder

Original Regulation: (EEC) No. 1067/74 *on the common organisation of the market in dehydrated fodder,* OJ L120, 1 May 1974.
Basic Regulation: (EEC) No. 1117/78 *on the common organisation of the market in dried fodder,* OJ L142, 30 May 1978.
Marketing year: July–June for potatoes
                        April–March for remaining fodder crops.

The original regime, which was set up in 1974, proved unsatisfactory in operation and so a new regime was introduced in 1978. It covers the following crops:

(a) potatoes, artificially dehydrated, unfit for human consumption potato flour, meal and flakes, unfit for human consumption;

(b) lucerne, sainfoin, clover, lupines, vetches and similar fodder products artificially dried, except hay and fodder kale and products containing hay, lucerne, sainfoin, clover, lupines and vetches otherwise dried and ground;

(c) protein concentrates obtained from lucerne juice and from grass juice.

There are two types of aid under this regime. The first is a production aid paid on a flat rate basis per kilo. The second is a deficiency payment or variable aid which is based on the relationship between the guide price (which is fixed annually) and the world price. The actual level of payment is 70 per cent of the difference between the two prices in the case of artificially dried products and 40 per cent in the case of sun-dried products.

The aid is paid to processors who must produce dried fodder of a minimum quality and satisfy all the requirements of entitlement to aid, in particular that they have concluded contracts with growers, or that they are processing their own crops or, in the case of a group or co-operative, the crops of their members.

Fibre flax and hemp

Basic Regulation: (EEC) No. 1308/70 *on the common organisation of the market in flax and hemp*, Sp. OJ 1970 (11)
Important amendment: Regulation (EEC) No. 814/76, OJ L94, 9 April 1976.
Marketing year: August–July.

The commodities covered under Art. 1.1 of Reg. 1308/70 are:

(a) flax, raw or processed but not spun; flax tow and waste;

(b) true hemp, raw or processed but not spun; tow and waste.

The aid available is in the form of a fixed payment per hectare of flax, grown mainly for fibre, and of hemp sown and harvested. If the market for flax or hemp fibre is temporarily imbalanced, provision is made for the concluding of private storage contracts. While not normally needed, this provision has been availed of in the past.

Proposed regime for potatoes

The Commission originally proposed the introduction of a potato regime in 1975. Its proposals have been revised a number of times since then and the draft outlined here is the latest which was to hand at the time of writing [41].

The proposed regime, which bears a strong resemblance to those already in force for fish and fruit and vegetables, would cover seed potatoes, new potatoes, those grown for starch manufacture, and other potatoes including those processed and preserved. The regime would lay down quality standards and would provide for the establishment of producer groups (see chapter 12 for a discussion of these in other sectors). These would be intended to improve the marketing of their members' crop and to assist in improving the cultivation and harvesting of the crop. Aid would be made available to help launch these groups.

Each year the Commission would make an estimate of the Community requirements of main-crop potatoes. If production looked as though it were going to exceed requirements, an aid might be granted, either to remove the potatoes from the market by denaturing or to remove them by providing funds for their dehydration.

The proposal also envisages aid for new potatoes harvested in the April–July period. A producer target price would be set each month. If the average prices recorded on representative producer markets fell on three consecutive days of the same month to less than 10 per cent of the producer target price, a standard aid would be granted to recognised producer groups. The aid would equal the difference between the average market price on the three days referred to above and the producer target price. An upper limit on the amount of aid would be fixed annually by the Council.

On the import side reference prices for new potatoes would be fixed each year. These prices would correspond to the average prices on representative markets in the production areas with the lowest prices during the three previous years, plus a fixed amount to cover transport costs between the production areas and representative consumption centres in the Community. If the entry price of third country potatoes were to fall to at least 0.5 UA below the reference price for two consecutive market days, the Community would impose a countervailing charge. This would be levied in addition to the normal customs duties in force. Export refunds would be available.

Notes to Chapter 8

28. OJ L130, 17 May 1976; OJ L136, 17 May 1977; and OJ L142, 22 May 1978.
29. This reference price should not be confused with the reference price which operates at the frontier in the fish and fruit and vegetables sectors. They serve quite different purposes.
30. *On the arrangements applicable to agricultural products and certain goods resulting from the processing of agricultural products originating in the African, Caribbean and Pacific States or in the overseas countries and territories*, OJ L85, 31 March 1976.
31. OJ L136, 2 June 1977; and OJ L142, 30 May 1978.
32. OJ L167, 26 June 1976; OJ L134, 28 May 1977; OJ L94, 8 April 1978, and OJ L170, 27 June 1978.

CHAPTER 9

Price and market mechanisms for livestock and livestock products

This chapter is concerned with livestock and livestock products, as well as with fisheries and silkworms. As with field crops, the reader will find the regimes described here differ considerably one from another. For instance, both the dairy and beef regimes have high levels of protection at the frontier and considerable internal support measures as well. In contrast, poultry and eggs have no internal support and the measures which are available for pigmeat are infrequently used. The fisheries regime is the first of two (fresh fruit and vegetables being the other) in which intervention on the domestic market is carried out, not by the intervention agencies, but by producer groups for the benefit of their members. The difficulties which the Community faces in the milk sector are reflected not so much in a complicated regime as in the numerous schemes which have been devised to increase milk and milk product utilisation. The beef regime has undergone some major amendments in recent years, reflecting disatisfaction with its performance in the difficult marketing circumstances of the 1970s.

Milk and milk products

Original Regulation: No. 13/64/EEC *portant établissement graduel d'une organisation commune des marchés dans le secteur du lait et des produits laitiers*, OJ 34, 27 février 1964.
Basic Regulation: (EEC) No. 804/68 *on the common organisation of the market in milk and milk products*, Sp. OJ 1968 (1).
Important amendments: Regs. 465/75, 740/75, 559/76, 2560/77, 1037/78, 1038/78, 1421/78 and 1761/78.[33]
Marketing year: April–March.

Under Art. 1 of Reg. 804/68 the following broad groups of products are included:

(a) fresh milk and cream, not concentrated or sweetened;

(b) milk and cream preserved, concentrated or sweetened;

(c) butter;

(d) cheese and curd;

(e) lactose and lactose syrup;

(f) sweetened forage.

Each year a target price is set for milk of 3.7 per cent fat content, delivered to dairy. Five intervention prices are fixed: one for butter, one for skimmed milk powder (smp), two for the Grana Padano variety of cheese (the price depending on the age of the cheese), and one for Parmigiano Reggiano cheese. The cheese intervention price applies only in Italy and replaces butter and smp arrangements which are more suited to the pattern of milk utilisation in Northern Europe.

Intervention measures for all three groups of products take the form either of buying-in or of aids to private storage. Cream also benefits from private storage aids, as does the Provolone, Emmental and Gruyère varieties of cheese.[34]

In order that milk products are able to compete with vegetable proteins in the composition of animal feed, disposal subsidies are available for skimmed milk (including butter milk) and smp (including buttermilk powder) used as a feed either directly in the case of the fresh product or in processed form. Aids are also available for skimmed milk used in the production of casein. Other measures are in force which are intended to increase consumption of milk products and these are outlined below.

Each year the Community fixes threshold prices for what are termed 'pilot products'. These represent the main types of milk product and there are twelve altogether. To these are related a whole series of 'assimilated products'. The threshold prices of the pilot products are set in order that the import levies can be fixed so that the price of imported processed products does not undercut the target price for liquid milk. This is done through the application of a series of coefficients. The levy for an assimilated product is usually the same as the levy on the relevant pilot product. The world price on which the levy is based is the lowest representative offer price to the Community.

Export refunds are available on all products listed in Article 1 of Reg. 804/68 in the form in which they appear there or in the form of the goods listed in the Annex to the Regulation. Although food aid is not specifically referred to under Reg. 804/68, nevertheless such aid in the form of butter oil and smp is made available on a regular basis.

One of the problems which arose when the UK joined the European Community was the anomalous position of the Milk Marketing Boards (MMBs) operating in that country, some of whose activities were thought likely to be contrary to the Rome Treaty. Because the Community believed that the MMBs perform a useful function in relation to maintaining the consumption of milk in the UK, Reg. 804/68 was amended under Reg. 1421/78 to allow for the existence anywhere in the Community of marketing organisations of a particular kind under rules set out in Art. 25. The actual conditions under which the MMBs are permitted to operate are spelled out more fully in Regulation (EEC) No. 1422/78 *concerning the granting of certain special rights to milk producer organisations in the United Kingdom* (OJ L171, 28 June 1978).

The milk market has suffered from chronic over-supply for many years and the Community has taken various steps from time to time to try to increase consumption and reduce supplies. On the consumption side, apart from the measures referred to above concerning skimmed milk used in animal feed and in casein production, there have been a number of schemes to subsidise milk and milk products going into final consumption. At the time of writing the following schemes listed in order of their introduction, which is not necessarily the order of their importance, were in operation:

1. Regulation (EEC) No. 1281/72 *on the sale of butter at a reduced price to the army and similar forces*, Sp. OJ 1972 (II).
2. Regulation (EEC) No. 1717/72 *on the sale of butter at a reduced price to non-profit-making institutions and organisations*, Sp. OJ 1972 (III).
3. Regulation (EEC) No. 349/73 *on the sale at reduced prices of intervention butter for direct consumption as concentrated butter*, OJ L40, 13 February 1973.
4. Regulation (EEC) No. 471/75 *on the sale of butter at reduced prices to persons receiving social assistance*, OJ L52, 28 February 1975.
5. Regulation (EEC) No. 880/77 *on the granting of a consumer subsidy for butter*, OJ L106, 29 April 1977.[35]

6. Regulation (EEC) No. 1080/77 *on the supply of milk and certain milk products at reduced prices to school children*, OJ L131, 26 May 1977.[36]

The titles of these Regulations speak for themselves. Not all Member States operate all of the available schemes nor are they all operative the whole time. Other schemes have come and gone over the years but the intractable problem of surplus dairy products goes on.

On the supply side, two measures are currently in operation. The first of these is a structural measure and is outlined in chapter 11. The second is the co-responsibility levy introduced in 1977 under Regulation (EEC) No. 1079/77.[37] Initially this scheme is to run until the end of the 1979/80 milk year. Under it a levy payable by milk producers on milk sold for any kind of processing was introduced. The levy is not payable in mountain and hill areas falling under the disadvantage areas Directive (see chapter 11). The actual level of the levy is fixed annually by the Council but it must not exceed 4 per cent of the target price. The buyer of the milk is responsible for its deduction from the payments made to producers. The levy is also payable on milk products made on the farm. Proceeds from the co-responsibility levy are used for the expansion of markets, both inside and outside the Community, and to assist in the search for new outlets and improved products.

Under the price proposals for 1979/80 [42] the Commission put forward suggestions for considerable amendments to the operation of the co-responsibility levy. Firstly, it should be made permanent. Secondly, the rate of the levy should vary with the extent of surplus production. Thirdly, the range of producers exempt from payment, which is currently confined to those in disadvantaged areas, should be extended to include certain low-income farmers, those with small-scale enterprises and on grounds of age.

While the Community makes these various efforts to increase consumption of its own butter and to reduce its total supplies of milk, it is ironic that it also operates special import arrangements for butter from New Zealand. Among the matters which had to be resolved during the negotiations for UK membership of the Community was the position of New Zealand as a major supplier of butter and cheese to the UK market. As the Community was in surplus, it did not welcome supplies of these products on its internal markets but it recognised that because the quantities were large New Zealand would have considerable difficulty in finding alternative markets in other parts of the world. Provision was made, therefore, in the Treaty of Accession [52] for the UK to continue to import New Zealand butter and cheese on a decreasing basis over the transition period ending in 1977. These imports came in at a reduced levy rate. In 1976 the arrangements for New Zealand butter were extended to the end of 1980 again on a reduced levy basis under Regulation (EEC) No. 1655/76 *extending the transitional arrangements for the import of New Zealand butter into the United Kingdom* (OJ L185, 9 July 1976).

Beef and veal

Original Regulation: No. 14/64/EEC *portant établissement graduel d'une organisation commune des marchés dans le secteur de la viande bovine,* JO 34, 27 février 1964.
Basic Regulation: (EEC) No. 805/68 *on the common organisation of the market in beef and veal,* Sp. OJ 1968 (1).
Important amendments: Regs. 2822/72, 425/77 and 995/78.[38]
Marketing year: first Monday in April to the preceding Sunday in the following year.

The products covered by the beef and veal regime are set out in Art. 1.1 of Reg. 805/68 as amended by Reg. 425/77. They include:

- (a) live cattle other than pure-bred breeding animals; beef and veal fresh, chilled, salted, in brine, dried or smoked; other prepared or preserved meat or meat offal containing bovine meat or offal, uncooked;
- (b) live cattle, pure-bred breeding animals; edible offals fresh, chilled, frozen, salted, in brine, dried or smoked; unrendered and rendered fat; other prepared or preserved meat or meat offal, containing bovine meat or offal, other than uncooked.

Each year the Community sets a guide price for adult cattle. This price is fixed in the light of past experience, the future trends in the beef market and the situation on the milk market. Intervention arrangements, which consist of aids for private storage and buying-in of surplus beef, differ quite considerably from the type already described for other products. Intervention measures can in theory be taken on live cattle as well as on primal cuts but in practice the former never occurs. The intervention price is set at 90 per cent of the guide price, but this is not the price paid to the producer, rather he receives the buying-in price. This latter price operates for different qualities of animals; each quality has a band composed of upper and lower buying-in prices which are linked to the intervention price by coefficients and the killing-out percentage.

Intervention can take place in two quite separate sets of circumstances. Firstly, it must take place over the whole Community when the price of adult cattle on representative markets falls below 93 per cent of the guide price. Secondly, regional intervention may take place when it is triggered by the occurrence of two events simultaneously. These are: that the price of adult cattle recorded on representative markets is below 98 per cent of the guide price and that the price of certain products on the representative market(s) of a Member State are below the intervention level.

If a Member State's reference price (i.e. the price of adult cattle on the representative markets) for any particular category of intervention beef rises above 100 per cent of the upper buying-in price for that category for a period of three consecutive weeks, then the Commission may suspend the buying-in operations for that category in the country concerned. Once the suspension has been imposed, if the price then falls to 100 per cent or less of the upper buying-in price for a period of two weeks, the Commission must reintroduce buying-in operations.

Community frontier arrangements on imports normally involve either a customs duty or a levy, but beef is unusual in that imports are subject not only to customs duties, but also to levies. (Levies, however, do not apply to pure-bred breeding animals, edible offals and fats.) Basic levies are worked out monthly for live animals and, through a series of coefficients, for the types of meat listed in the Annex sections (a), (c) and (d) of Reg. 805/68 as amended by Reg. 425/77. The basis of this levy is the difference between the guide price and the most representative offer price plus the amount of customs duty. The levy for frozen meat, referred to in the Annex section (b) of the Regulation, is based on three components: firstly, the fresh meat guide price adjusted to take account of the price relationship in the Community between fresh and frozen meat; secondly, the free-at-frontier price of frozen meat duty paid; and thirdly, a fixed sum to represent import handling charges.

The whole of the basic levy is not always applied. The percentage which is applied is determined by the relationship between the reference price and the guide price. For instance, if the reference price is less than or equal to 102 per cent of the guide price, then 75 per cent of the basic levy is applied. This percentage falls in steps as the reference price rises, so that when the reference price is more than 106 per cent of the guide price, no levy is charged. Analogous arrangements are enforced when the reference price is at or below 100 per cent of the guide price. In these circumstances the proportion of the basic levy charged rises in steps as the reference price falls, until 114 per cent of the basic levy is charged when the reference price falls to below 90 per cent of the guide price.

Fig. 6 illustrates the relationship of the guide price for cattle to the basic levy and the relationship of the reference price to the actual levy charged. While the mechanisms are the same, the relative sizes of the levy and offer price would be quite different for beef carcases or primal cuts.

Various concessionary arrangements are made on imports. The first relates to an undertaking in GATT to import levy-free a fixed quantity of frozen beef annually. The second is concerned with imports of manufacturing beef. Each year the Community draws up a balance sheet indicating requirements and availability of this quality of beef. The deficit on availability can then be imported either by paying no levy or by paying a reduced levy.

Young male cattle for fattening are imported at nil or reduced levy rates in order to make up the Community's deficit in these livestock. Under the Lomé Convention an annual quota of beef from Botswana, Kenya, Madagascar and Swaziland is admitted duty free, and part of the quota is also admitted under reduced levy arrangements. Baby beef is imported from Yugoslavia at reduced rates of levy. Besides these arrangements there are also minor concessions under agreements with Malta, Latin America, EFTA and so forth.

A number of internal schemes other than the basic regime outlined above also exist in the Community. One, on the conversion of dairy herds into beef is part of the non-marketing of milk scheme and is

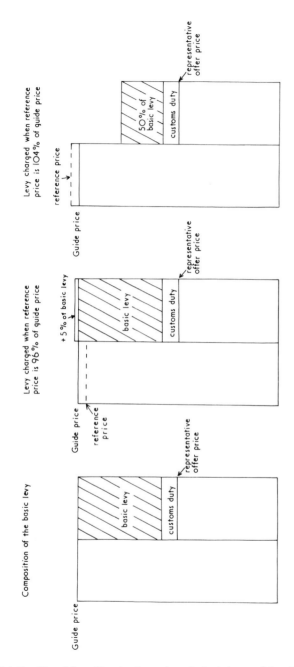

Fig. 6: Relationships of the guide price for cattle to the basic levy, and the relationship of the reference price to the actual levy charged.

described in chapter 11. Besides this there is a calf retention scheme, introduced in 1975 under Regulation (EEC) No. 464/75 *establishing systems of premiums for producers of bovine animals*, OJ L52, 28 February, 1975. It applies in Italy only. The other schemes set up under the same Regulation have since expired or been superseded. One of these was the slaughter premium scheme for adult cattle other than cows (sometimes called the variable premium scheme). Originally this was a nationally financed scheme but in 1976 it became a Community scheme by virtue of its inclusion under Regulation (EEC) No. 797/76 (*Authorising Member States to grant a premium on the slaughter of certain adult bovine animals intended for slaughter during the 1976/77 marketing year*, OJ L93, 8 April 1976.). This scheme is renewed annually and to date has been applied only in the UK. The slaughter premium varies with the market price and also seasonally. Within certain limits, it represents the difference between the market price and a target price but it must not exceed a given amount per head nor must it exceed, over the year as a whole, 85 per cent of the guide price. Any premium paid is deducted from the intervention buying-in price.

Proposed sheepmeat regime

Sheepmeat is one of the few commodities of any significance for which there is no price and market regime. For some years past the Commission has wished to see the introduction of such a regime and its desire was strengthened as a result of ruling in the Court of Justice in the Charmasson case (OJ C75, 5 April 1975).[39] The Court declared that the maintenance of quota arrangements for a commodity subject to a national regime was illegal once the transition period was ended.

The Commission's first proposals on sheepmeat were rejected by the Council and they were withdrawn by the Commission. In 1978 it made fresh proposals for a sheepmeat regime [34] but discussions on them have, to some extent, been overtaken by events. The Commission has taken France to the Court of Justice on the grounds that its national sheepmeat regime discriminates against imports from the UK. The outcome of this case could have important implications for the sheepmeat proposals and could prompt the Council to take action more quickly on the introduction of this regime.

As they stand, the proposals envisage the establishment of a basic price each year for fresh and chilled sheep carcases. Intervention in the form of buying-in would not be available, but aids for private storage would be available when prices on representative Community markets fell to less than 90 per cent of the basic price. Provision would be made for the granting of a production premium to sheep producers which could vary regionally. The intention would be to compensate producers for any fall in their incomes caused by the introduction of the common regime.

At the moment, protection at the Community's frontiers is achieved by the imposition of customs duties which are bound in GATT (i.e. they cannot be raised). The Commission is proposing their replacement by levies of similar effect. Export refunds would not be available.

Pigmeat

Original Regulation: No. 121/67/EEC *on the common organisation of the market in pigmeat*, Sp. OJ 1967.

Consolidated Regulation: (EEC) No. 2759/75 *on the common organisation of the market in pigmeat*, OJ L282, 1 November 1975.

Important amendment: Regulation (EEC) No. 1423/78 (OJ L171, 28 June 1978).

Marketing year: November–October.

As with the regimes for poultry and eggs outlined below, the regime for pigmeat is based on the premise that the products covered are in the nature of processed cereals and so the provisions made for pigmeat reflect very clearly this dependence on cereals.

Art. 1.1 of Reg. 2759/75 lists the products covered by the pigmeat regime and, in outline, these are:

(a) live pigs other than pure-bred breeding stock;

(b) pigmeat fresh, chilled or frozen;

(c) offals fresh, chilled or frozen;

(d) pig fat, fresh, chilled, frozen, salted, in brine, dried or smoked;

(e) pigmeat and edible offal, salted, in brine, dried or smoked;

(f) lard and other pig fat;

(g) sausages and other preserved meat or meat offal.

Each year a basic price is set for carcases or half carcases of a standard quality. When fixing this price the Community must have regard to the costs of pigmeat production and must avoid setting the price at a level which would lead to the creation of structural surpluses of pigmeat. However, these considerations are in the nature of factors to be borne in mind and are not based on any strict formula which must be followed.

Intervention can take the form of buying-in or aids for private storage. Buying-in, which covers a small range of products, is much less frequently used than aids for private storage. Intervention is not automatic and has to be triggered by the fall in the reference price (i.e. the weighted market price) to below 103 per cent of the basic price. When this occurs, the Commission may introduce intervention measures but it is not obliged to do so and there have been long periods of time during which prices were below the trigger level but no market support was provided.

The intervention price (or as it is called in the pigmeat regime, the buying-in price) is set at the range of 78 to 92 per cent of the basic price. Because of the infrequency of buying-in operations, this price is of importance only in relation to the calculation of MCAs which are based on intervention price levels.

The main and continuous support for the Community pigmeat sector comes in the arrangements at the frontier. Each quarter (starting on the first day of February, May, August and November) a sluice-gate price for carcases is set which acts as a minimum import price. It is composed of three elements: a variable amount to represent the world market value of the quantity of cereals required to produce one kilogram of pigmeat abroad; a fixed element to represent the cost of other protein feed used in producing the same kilogram; and a further fixed element to represent overhead, production and marketing costs. To this sluice-gate price is added a levy which represents the difference in cost between producing one kilogram of pigmeat in the Community and in third countries. The levy contains two components: one element represents the difference in price inside and outside the Community of the cereals used to produce one kilogram of pigmeat; the other element, which is equal to 7 per cent of the average sluice-gate price over the preceding twelve months, is intended to protect the domestic processing industry.

If the free-at-frontier price falls below the sluice-gate price, a supplementary levy may be charged on the imports equal to the difference between the offer price and the sluice-gate price. Fig. 7 illustrates the composition of the sluice-gate price and the operation of the basic and supplementary levies. Sluice-gate prices and levies for commodities other than carcases are derived from those for carcases by the application of coefficients, which are intended to reflect the price relationships within the Community of the products concerned to that of the basic product which is the pig carcase.

Eggs

Basic Regulation: No. 122/67/EEC *on the common organisation of the market in eggs*, Sp. OJ 1967.

The products covered by the regime are set out in Art. 1.1 of Reg. 122/67 as follows:

(a) poultry eggs in shell, fresh or preserved;

(b) poultry eggs not in shell and egg yolks, suitable for human consumption, fresh, preserved, dried or sweetened.

There are no internal support measures. Each quarter starting on the first day of February, May, August and November, sluice-gate prices are set for eggs in shell and they are determined in the same way as are the sluice-gate prices for pigmeat. Sluice-gate prices for hatching eggs are calculated in similar fashion and derived sluice-gate prices are calculated for the products in Art. 1.1 (b).

A levy is charged on imports and is determined in a manner similar to that for pigmeat, i.e. it represents the difference in cost between producing one kilogram of eggs in shell in the Community and in third countries, together with a fixed amount to cover other feed costs and overheads. Levies are also imposed on hatching eggs and derived levies are imposed on the products under Art. 1.1 (b). If the offer price falls below the sluice-gate price, a supplementary levy is imposed equal to the difference between the two. Export restitutions are available for the products listed in Art. 1.1 and for the group of products listed in the Annex to Reg. 122/67.

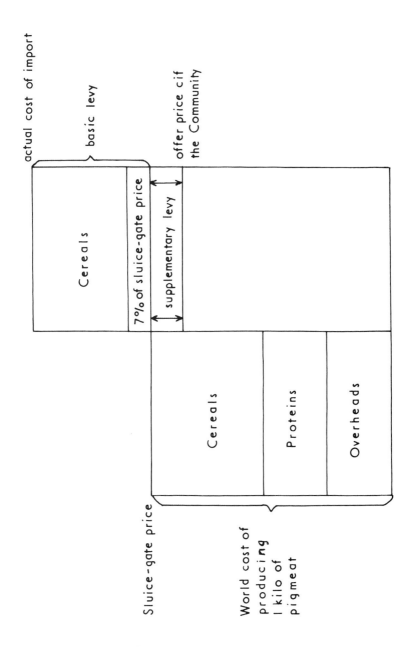

Fig. 7: Operation of import mechanism for pigmeat.

Poultry

Basic Regulation: No. 123/67/EEC *on the common organisation of the market in poultry meat*, Sp. OJ 1967.

The products covered by the regime are listed in Art. 1.1 as follows:
(a) live poultry;
(b) dead poultry and edible offal except liver, fresh, chilled or frozen;
(c) poultry liver, fresh, chilled, frozen, salted or in brine;
(d) unrendered poultry fat, fresh, chilled, frozen, salted, in brine, dried or smoked;
(e) rendered poultry fat;
(f) other prepared or preserved poultry meat or poultry offal.

There are no internal support arrangements. Sluice-gate prices are calculated in the same manner and for the same periods as those for pigmeat and eggs. Supplementary levies are payable on imports not observing the sluice-gate price as a minimum entry price. Levies on slaughtered poultry and live chicks are calculated as under the pigmeat and eggs regimes, and derived levies are based on the slaughtered poultry levy adjusted by coefficients. Export refunds are available on the products listed in Art. 1.1.

Silkworms

Basic Regulation: (EEC) No. 845/72 *laying down special measures to encourage silkworm rearing*, Sp. OJ 1972 (II).
Marketing year: April–March.

This regime is of direct interest only to Italy. It consists of an annual production aid paid to growers per box of silkworm eggs. The aid is paid on condition that the boxes contain a minimum quantity of eggs and that the worms have been successfully reared.

Fishery products

Original Regulation: (EEC) No. 2142/70 *on the common organisation of the market in fishery products*, Sp. OJ 1970.
Consolidated Regulation: (EEC) No. 100/76 *on the common organisation of the market in fishery products*, OJ L20, 28 January 1976.

The regime covers seven broad groups of products under Art. 1.2 as follows:

(a) fish, fresh (alive or dead), chilled or frozen;

(b) fish, dried, salted in brine, or smoked;

(c) crustaceans and molluscs;

(d) fish, crustaceans and molluscs unfit for human consumption;

(e) prepared or preserved fish;

(f) crustaceans and molluscs, preserved or prepared;

(g) flours and meals of fish, crustaceans or molluscs.

As with fresh fruit and vegetables outlined in chapter 10, the fishery regime is unusual in two ways: firstly, it includes rules on marketing standards, and secondly, it uses the device of producers' organisations to carry out certain market management functions. The common marketing standards are intended to keep products of unsatisfactory quality off the market and to improve profitability. Producers' organisations have a dual function: they help to improve marketing and processing by carrying out these activities on behalf of their members (see chapter 12) and they act as the equivalent of intervention agencies in withdrawing surplus products from over-supplied markets.

Each year guide prices are set for the species of fish listed in Annex 1 (A) and (C) of Reg. 100/76 (these are herring, sardines, redfish, cod, coalfish, haddock, whiting, mackerel, anchovies, plaice, hake and shrimps). The guide prices are based on the average of prices recorded on representative wholesale markets or at representative ports in the three fishing years immediately preceding the year in question. Withdrawal prices are set for the same species of fish within a band of between 60 and 90 per cent of the guide price. If first-hand market prices for fish for human consumption fall to below the level of the withdrawal price, the fish may be withdrawn from the market by producers' organisations. The withdrawal price is not quite the same as an intervention price, as producers do not receive the withdrawal price but rather, when prices fall to that level, they receive compensation payments through their organisation which are related to the non-human consumption market outlet which they actually do find for the fish. Special withdrawal prices are fixed for remote areas distant from main centres of consumption, analogous to derived intervention measures under some of the other commodity regimes.

Guide prices are also fixed for the products set out in Annex II of Reg. 100/76 (these are frozen sardines, seabream, squid, cuttle fish and octopus). As with the guide prices referred to above, this group is fixed on the basis of prices over the three preceding years. When market prices for this group fall below 85 per cent of the guide price, private storage aids may be granted to cushion producers during the poor market conditions.

A producer price for tunny intended for canning is set every year, again based on average prices over a three-year period. If prices fall below this level, a compensatory payment may be made if it is thought necessary but in fact little use is made of this provision.

Intervention prices are set only for fresh or chilled sardines and anchovies. They are set at the very low level of between 35 and 45 per cent of the guide price. Intervention arrangements are not automatic as they are under many other regimes but have to be triggered by the collapse of the market price on representative markets to below the intervention level for three consecutive market days. When this happens, the Commission must declare the market to be in a state of serious crisis, and at that stage the intervention agencies must buy in fish offered to them providing it is of the required standard and has not been withdrawn from the market already under the withdrawal arrangements referred to above. Except in special circumstances, products bought in must be disposed of for purposes other than human consumption. Buying-in operations are suspended as soon as prices remain at or above the intervention level for three successive market days.

Most fish imports are subject to customs duties but a few are zero-rated, either seasonally or on a permanent basis. In addition, some duties may be temporarily reduced if the supply situation in the Community warrants it. Imports from third countries are governed by a series of reference prices for the species of fish coming under Annexes I, II, III(A) and IV(B) of Reg. 100/76. These prices are intended to protect the Community markets from de-stabilising influences and act as a kind of minimum import price. For products for which a withdrawal price is also fixed, the reference price equals the withdrawal price. For sardines and anchovies the reference price also equals the withdrawal price, and for tunny the reference price is based on representative c.i.f. import prices over a three-year period. A separate reference price for carp may be fixed each year but it is not mandatory. If the entry price of imports lies below the relevant reference price, the Community may either ban imports of the particular species or it may apply countervailing duties. Export restitutions can be made available for all the products listed in Art. 1.2.

Notes to Chapter 9

33. OJ L52, 28 February 1975; L74, 22 March 1975; L67, 15 March 1976; L303, 28 November 1977; L134, 22 May 1978; L134, 22 May 1978; L171, 28 June 1978; L204, 28 July 1978.
34. Emmental and Gruyère benefit under Regulation (EEC) No. 508/71 *laying down general rules on private storage aid for long-keeping cheeses* (Sp. OJ 1971 (1)). This Regulation also extends private storage aids to long-keeping sheep's cheese.
35. Amended under Reg. 1040/78 (OJ L134, 22 May 1978).
36. Amended under Reg. 1039/78 (OJ L134, 22 May 1978).
37. *On a co-responsibility levy and on measures for expanding the markets in milk and milk products*, OJ L131, 26 May 1977.
38. Sp. OJ 1972 (III); OJ L61/1, 5 March 1977; and OJ L130, 18 May 1978.
39. The *Official Journal* contains the judgement only. The details of the case are to be found in *Reports of Cases before the Court*, Part 8, 1383–1404.

CHAPTER 10

Price and market mechanisms for horticultural and perennial crops

We come now to the last of the three chapters devoted to outlines of the commodity regimes. The arrangements for fruit and vegetables are highly reminiscent of the fisheries regime already outlined. Quality standards for many products are laid down, and producer groups play an important part in managing the market. The regime for live plants is minimal. The internal support arrangements for processed fruit and vegetables have one feature in common with the tobacco regime, namely, that processors are compensated for higher Community prices for their raw materials through a production aid. Tobacco is included in this chapter rather than with the field crops in chapter 8 because, in certain respects, its production pattern is quite different from that of other annual arable crops. Similarly, seeds for sowing differ from other field crops in terms of their production pattern, a factor which is reflected in the type of regime devised for them. Hops have a light regime based on a direct payment to the grower.

One of the more important regimes described in this chapter is that for table wine–a commodity which, like milk, suffers from structural surpluses. Its difficulties are reflected in the various schemes which have been put forward to restructure this sector. These are discussed in chapter 11. The extensive provision made for the distillation of surplus table wine has implications for the proposed alcohol regime outlined here. The chapter ends with a description of the regime for olive oil, another commodity which has caused concern in recent years.

Fresh fruit and vegetables

Original Regulation: No. 23 *on the progressive establishment of a common organisation of the market in fruit and vegetables*, Sp. OJ 1959–1962.

Basic Regulation: (EEC) No. 1035/72 *on the common organisation of the market in fruit and vegetables*, Sp. OJ 1972 (II).
Important amendments: Regs. 2454/72; 1154/78 and 325/79.[40]
Marketing year: varies by commodity.

Reg. 1035/72 covers a wide range of activities of which the price and market regime is but one part. It includes the establishment of common quality standards for a range of fruits and vegetables listed in Annex 1 of the Regulation. It also covers the provision of launching aids granted to producer groups, which is outlined in chapter 12.

Our concern here, however, is firstly, with the price and market system established to cover the products listed in Annex II of the Regulation[41] for which basic and buying-in prices are fixed each year and on which withdrawal takes place, and secondly, the products for which reference prices are fixed.[42]

Each year the Community sets basic prices for the main fruits and vegetables, taking into account the development of average prices over the preceding three years on the most representative Community production markets. The buying-in prices are the ones at which, in a state of serious crisis, the intervention agency in a Member State accepts produce from the over-supplied market. The buying-in prices are set at:

40 and 45 per cent of the basic price for cauliflowers and tomatoes;

50 and 55 per cent in the case of apples and pears;

60 and 70 per cent in the case of the remaining Annex II products.

However, this form of intervention buying is rarely if ever used and the market is supported, as in the fisheries sector, by the withdrawal of produce from over-supplied markets by producer groups. These groups are free to operate their own voluntary withdrawal schemes before the market price falls to the official Community withdrawal price level, but in practice most do not. The Community withdrawal price is equal to the buying-in price plus 10 per cent of the basic price. For only two commodities–lemons and cauliflowers–is the withdrawal price operative throughout the year. For the remaining commodities it varies from as little as three months in the case of table grapes to ten months for apples and pears.

Early in 1979 the Community introduced (under Reg. 325/79) an extra supportive measure for apples and pears which can best be described as preventative withdrawal subject to certain conditions. During the early months of the marketing year Member States may authorise producer groups to withdraw a proportion of these fruits coming onto the market. Such withdrawal may be authorised when, over a period, the market price lies somewhere between the buying-in price and 80 per cent of the basic price, and when due to the size of the crop there is the danger of a market collapse and subsequent heavy withdrawals. This measure is to apply, initially at least, until mid-1982.

The Community has considerable difficulties in disposing of withdrawn produce. By the time the withdrawal price becomes operative the market is well and truly weakened and many of the products concerned are highly perishable. Attempts are made to dispose of surpluses for human consumption or as animal feed or to the processing sector but the task is not easy.

Imports from third countries are subject to customs duties, except where these are waived or lowered under trade agreements such as the Lomé Convention or under the agreements with various Mediterranean countries. Imports of certain products are also subject to reference prices. As with withdrawal prices they usually operate for part of the year only, representing the months during which imports from third countries are in greatest competition with Community production.

The reference prices are calculated by taking the arithmetic mean of producer prices in the Community over the immediately preceding three years, corrected by the trend in production costs over the most recent year. If, for two consecutive market days, the actual entry price is at least 0.5 UA below the reference price, then a countervailing charge is imposed, equal to the difference between the two. The charge is withdrawn when the entry price is at least equal to the reference price for two consecutive market days.

Processed fruit and vegetables

Basic Regulation: (EEC) No. 865/68 *on the common organisation of the market in products processed from fruit and vegetables*, Sp. OJ 1968 (1).

Consolidated Regulation: (EEC) No. 516/77 *on the common organisation of the market in products processed from fruit and vegetables*, OJ L73, 21 March 1977.
Important amendment: Reg. 1152/78.[43]

The processed fruit and vegetables regime covers virtually all fruits and vegetables processed or preserved in any way, as well as such items as jams, jellies, marmalades, purée and juices (see Art. 1 of Reg. 516/77 for the detailed list). Starting in 1978/79 the Community introduced a system of production aids for the products listed in Annex Ia to Reg. 516/77 (as amended). These are prunes, tomato concentrates, peeled tomatoes, peaches in syrup, and tomato juice. The purpose of the aid is to compensate processors for having to pay higher prices to producers in the Community than they have to pay for the same raw materials imported from third countries. The amount of the aid is intended to represent the difference between the price of Community products and those from abroad.

In order to qualify for aid, processors must conclude contracts with suppliers and must pay them not less than the stipulated minimum prices. In the event of the Community running into surplus difficulties with the products listed in Annex Ia, provision is made for the Council to decide to limit the production aid to a specified quantity, taking into account the average level of production in the three immediately preceding years.

On the import side, the Regulation stipulates that, besides customs duties, levies must be charged on the added sugar content of the products listed in Annex I of the Regulation. Export refunds are granted in two ways: firstly, on the added sugar content of the products listed in Annex II of the Regulation and secondly, on those products listed in Annex I which do not contain added sugar.

Live plants

Basic Regulation: (EEC) No. 234/68 *on the establishment of a common organisation of the market in live trees and other plants, bulbs, roots and the like, cut flowers and ornamental foliage*, Sp. OJ 1968 (I).
Important additional Regulations: Regs. 3279/75 and 3353/75.[44]

All products coming within chapter 6 of the CCT are covered by the live plant regime. It is an extremely light regime, there being no internal support measures. Imports are subject to customs duties. When the regime came into operation certain quantitative import restrictions were being used by various Member States. These were temporarily retained but were removed in 1975 except in the case of roses and carnations, and unrooted cuttings and slips of vines and grafted or rooted vine plants. Treatment of these items by Member States was standardised at their existing level under Reg. 3279/75 and deadlines were imposed on their final removal which was completed by the end of 1977.

Under Reg. 3353/75 imports of certain products from named countries were made subject to Community surveillance procedures. Such imports must be accompanied by a special import document, the purpose of which is to make easier the monitoring of the volume of imports. The products concerned are rose bushes from Hungary; roses from Israel and South Africa; carnations from Spain, Israel, Kenya, Colombia and Romania; and foliage of asparagus plumosus from Kenya.

Tobacco

Basic Regulation: (EEC) No. 727/70 *on the common organisation of the market in raw tobacco*, Sp. OJ 1970 (1). (The Regulation number is incorrectly stated in the *Official Journal*, Special Edition as 272/70.)
Marketing year: January–December.

The main producers of tobacco in the Community are Italy, France, Federal Germany and Belgium. Under Art. 1 of Reg. 727/70 the regime covers unmanufactured tobacco and tobacco refuse. Each year the Community sets a norm price for leaf tobacco. This is a target price and in setting it account is taken of the previous year's norm price and of the need to promote specialisation in production.

The Community also fixes an intervention price, usually at 90 per cent of the norm price, although it has been lower for particular varieties, the aim being to discourage their production. Intervention is not an open-ended commitment and the intervention agencies may limit the amount of tobacco they take from any one producer. Normally, intervention is concerned with leaf tobacco, but the Regulation makes provision for the setting of derived intervention prices for baled tobacco and use is made of this form of intervention in Italy.

While intervention has been used more since 1976 than formerly, the main source of internal aid is still to be found in the premium paid to the first-hand buyer of leaf tobacco. This premium is intended to compensate the processor for having to pay a price to the Community grower which is well above the world price level. The premium, which is a flat-rate payment per kilogram of leaf tobacco, represents the difference between the world price for the particular variety and the Community production costs.

Customs duties are charged on imports but the levels of the tariffs are bound in GATT. Export restitutions are available.

The arrangements made under Reg. 727/70 for dealing with a situation in which markets are disrupted have proved unsatisfactry in that they are ambiguous and the time scale for action is unrealistic. As part of the price proposals for 1979/80 [42] the Commission put forward a suggested amendment to Art. 13 which it was hoped would clarify procedures and make easier the taking of effective action.

During the early 1970s the intervention agencies bought in a considerable quantity of the Beneventano variety of tobacco and, in order to discourage its continued cultivation, the Council adopted Regulation (EEC) No. 339/77 *laying down special measures in the tobacco sector in respect of the Beneventano variety of tobacco* (OJ L48, 19 February 1977). This programme of measures was scheduled to last for the three harvests 1977–1979.

Under Reg. 339/77 restrictions are placed on intervention buying, limiting purchases to 75, 60 and 35 per cent respectively in the three years concerned of the quantity bought in from the 1975 harvest. At the same time the intervention price for Beneventano was lowered from 90 to 80 per cent of the norm price. Because these changes in the intervention arrangements adversely affected growers' incomes, a special aid per hectare was made available to growers who plant with other varieties the area previously devoted to Beneventano. Growers receiving the aid must undertake not to replant with Beneventano for five years.

Seeds for sowing

Basic Regulation: (EEC) No. 2358/71 *on the common organisation of the market in seeds*, Sp. OJ 1971 (III).
Important amendments: Regs. 597/73; 671/75; 1167/77 and 1346/78.[45]
Marketing year: July–June.

The products covered by the regime are listed in Art. 1 as follows:

(a) dried leguminous vegetables for sowing;

(b) hybrid maize for sowing;

(c) oil seeds and oleaginous fruit for sowing;

(d) seeds, fruit and spores, of a kind used for sowing.

Production aids are available for basic and certified seeds of the varieties listed in the Annex to Reg. 2358/71 (as amended). Currently these include flax, hemp, grasses and legumes. The aid, which is fixed every two years, is on the basis of a flat-rate payment per 100 kilograms of seed produced. If during the two-year period the market becomes disrupted, provision is made for the aid fixed for the second year to be altered.

While no internal support is given to the production of hybrid maize seed, protection at the frontier is afforded to this one type of seed through the use of a reference price system. A reference price for each type of hybrid maize seed for sowing is set each year, based on the free-at-frontier offer prices recorded during the three preceding marketing years. When an offer price (including customs duties, if any) is below the relevant reference price, a countervailing charge is imposed. This charge is limited due to the existence of a GATT binding which prevents the Community from raising its customs duty to over 4 per cent.

Hops

Basic Regulation: (EEC) No. 1696/71 *on the common organisation of the market in hops*, Sp. OJ 1971 (II).

Under Art. 1.1 the regime covers hop cones and lupulin; in addition under Art. 1.2, in so far as trade with third countries is concerned, vegetable saps and extracts of hops are included under the regime.

As with fish and fruit and vegetables, the hops Regulation provides for the setting-up and recognition of producer groups and makes arrangements for granting them launching aids (outlined in chapter 12). Contracts between a producer (or association of producers) and a buyer to supply hops must be registered in the Member State concerned. Aid to hop growers takes the form of a fixed amount per hectare of registered area, the actual level of the aid differing according to the variety. The Commission must make a report on the industry each year and if it appears from this report that there is the risk of a structural surplus, or a disturbance in the supply structure of the market, the aid may be limited to an amount corresponding to the average area cultivated during the three years preceding that under review.

Table wine

Original Regulation: No. 24 *on the progressive establishment of a common organisation of the market in wine*, Sp. OJ 1959–1962.

Basic Regulation: (EEC) No. 816/70 *laying down additional provisions for the common organisation of the market in wine*, Sp. OJ 1970 (I).

Consolidated Regulation: (EEC) No. 337/79 *on the common organisation of the market in wine*, OJ L54, 5 March 1979.

Marketing year: 16 December–15 December.

It is important to realise at the outset that the wine regime does not cover quality wines produced and sold as such. Such wines are expected to fend for themselves. This regime is limited to what is called table wine or *vin ordinaire*.

Art. 1.2 of Reg. 337/79 covers four groups of products as follows:

(a) grape juice (including grape must), unfermented and not containing spirit;

(b) grape must, in fermentation or with fermentation arrested; wine of fresh grapes;

(c) fresh grapes other than table grapes; wine vinegar;

(d) piquette; wine lees; grape marc.

Each year the Community sets a guide price for each type of table wine representative of Community production. In fixing this price the Community takes into account the average prices for the relevant wines in the two preceding years and the price trends during the year in question. The Community also sets an activating (or intervention) price for each type of wine for which there is a guide price. This may not exceed 95 per cent of the corresponding guide price. The purpose of the activating price is to trigger off the possibility of market support through the use of storage contracts. Intervention in the sense of a permanent right to sell surplus produce at the activating price is not available under the wine regime.

There are two types of storage contract. A short-term contract (i.e. for three months) may be entered into between the intervention agency and a producer if the representative price (i.e. the weighted average of producer prices) for a particular type of table wine remains below the activating price for two consecutive weeks. Once the representative price rises above the activating price for two consecutive weeks, no more contracts are entered into. Short-term contracts may also be entered into in a wine-growing zone or part of one if, because of a very heavy harvest, there appears to be an imbalance in supply and demand at the beginning of the wine year.

Long-term contracts may be entered into if estimates at the beginning of the wine year show that supplies (i.e. estimated production plus stocks) exceed foreseeable demand for the year by more than four months' consumption (i.e. that there is the equivalent of a total of sixteen months' consumption available). During the period when long-term contracts may be entered into for a particular wine, the provisions for short-term contracts for the same or closely related wines are suspended.

Short- and long-term private storage contracts are also possible for grape must. In the light of stocks held at the end of the marketing year and the prospects for the new harvest, it may be decided to grant aids for the re-storage of table wines which are the subject of short- or long-term storage contracts. The intention behind this measure is to free the producers' storage capacity for the new harvest.

The other form of internal aid available under the wine regime is aid for distillation. In normal circumstances, two types of distillation aid are available. The first applies only during the period 15 September–15 December. If the total quantity of table wines of all types subject to storage contracts is equal to or in excess of seven million hectolitres, preventive distillation may be introduced. This does not apply to wines produced from table grapes or from certain direct producer hybrids or to wines suitable for making certain potable spirits. The distiller must pay at least the buying-in price which is fixed at 53 per cent of the guide price for wines classified Type A1.

The second possibility for distillation relates to circumstances when the representative price of a type of table wine remains below the activating price for three consecutive weeks at the end of the nine month storage period. In this event the wine leaving store may be re-stored for a further four months and/or producers may be guaranteed the activating price for wine they sell for distillation. A rather special distillation aid may be made available for wines which are normally used for the production of certain potable spirits (cognac) if the volume of such wine exceeds the volume used for cognac production in the previous year by 1 million hectolitres.

If, having exhausted all the possibilities for short-term and long-term storage, and for normal distillation, the market prices are still weak additional distillation provisions must be adopted. In such an event, the conditions under which the distillation may be carried out and the price to be paid for the wine concerned will be laid down. Finally, the Council has recently agreed in principle that if the representative price falls below 85 per cent of the guide price for three consecutive weeks, the sale of table wine at below a minimum price may be banned, in which case distillation would be made available at that minimum price level.

Imports of wine are subject to customs duties unless exempted under preferential agreements. Reference prices (i.e. minimum import prices) are fixed each year for red and white wine. They are based on the guide prices of the most representative types of wines in the Community, plus the costs incurred in bringing the Community wines to the same marketing stage as the imported wines; this is necessary as the guide price is a producer price. Reference prices are also fixed for grape juice (including must), concentrated grape juice (including must), grape must with fermentation arrested by the addition of alcohol, wine fortified for distillation and liqueur (fortified) wine.

If the free-at-frontier price of imports plus the appropriate customs duty is lower than the reference price, then imports of that product may be subject to a countervailing charge equal to the difference between the two. Countervailing duties are not applied, however, to shipments from countries which have given an undertaking to the Community that their exports will meet the reference price (in practice the great majority of suppliers). Any shipments from these countries which nevertheless do fall short of the reference price are not eligible for preferential custom duty rates.

Besides laying down the price and market regime, Reg. 337/79 also contains rules about the control of planting and the various oecological practices allowable. With regard to planting, at the moment in general aids for new planting are prohibited. So, too, are aids for replanting which has the effect of increasing production unaccompanied by improvement in quality. National aids may be allowed on a case-by-case basis in wine-growing regions where wine provides a major element in agricultural income and the granting of the aid is likely to improve that income. As to the processes permitted in the making of wine, the Regulation lays down very detailed rules on such things as raising the natural alcoholic strength of the wine, acidification and deacidification, the sweetening of wine, permitted additives and so forth. Rules are also laid down on the compulsory distillation of marc and lees, and of wine made from table grapes.

Proposed regime for ethyl alcohol

The original proposal for a regime for ethyl alcohol dates from 1972. This was extensively revised in 1976 [18] when the Commission took on board the criticisms of its original proposals and the effects which Enlargement of the Community had had on the ethyl alcohol market. At the time of writing yet another revision was being awaited.

As it stands, the proposed regime is concerned only with (a) ethyl alcohol produced from agricultural raw materials (i.e. synthetic ethyl alcohol is excluded); (b) fruit containing added spirit, and fortified wine; (c) compound alcoholic preparations; and (d) spirituous beverages, vermouths and similar drinks.

The main method of support would be found through reserving the market for certain products of agricultural alcohol. These reserved sectors would be oral consumption (i.e. alcoholic drinks), vinegar and pharmaceuticals. A target price would be set each year for ethyl alcohol of agricultural origin. Throughout the marketing year the intervention agencies could be obliged to buy-in at the target price ethyl alcohol of agricultural origin other than molasses.

The activities of the intervention agencies would not be open-ended; rather there would be a target quantity of agricultural alcohol which would be given a guaranteed market. This target quantity would be allocated to distillers as guaranteed quotas when not sold in the reserved sectors. Production over and above that required for the reserved sectors would have to be sold on the unreserved market with no price support. Import levies and export restitutions would apply to trade in agricultural alcohol and spiritous drinks. Provision would also be made for the imposition of a flat rate levy on the alcohol content of all neutral agricultural spirit and of all spirituous drinks used in the Community (both imported and domestically produced).

Olive oil

Basic Regulation: No. 136/66/EEC *on the establishment of a common organisation of the market in oils and fats,* Sp. OJ 1965–1966.
Important amendment: Reg. 1562/78, OJ L185, 7 July 1978.
Marketing year: November–October.

The olive oil regime is the other half of the regime on colza, rape and sunflower which was outlined in chapter 8. Under Art. 1.2 of Reg. 136/66 it covers:

(a) olive oil;

(b) olives;

(c) residues containing oil having the characteristics of olive oil, oil cake and other residues resulting from the extraction of olive oil.

The internal support system is based on five elements and the way in which support is organised is determined by the fact that olive oil must compete with much cheaper oils. The five elements are: a production target price (PTP), a production aid; an intervention price, a consumer subsidy, and a representative market price (RMP).

Each year an RMP is set at a level which permits olive oil to compete with substitute oils. Above this is the intervention price which is derived from the PTP minus the production aid, making allowance for market

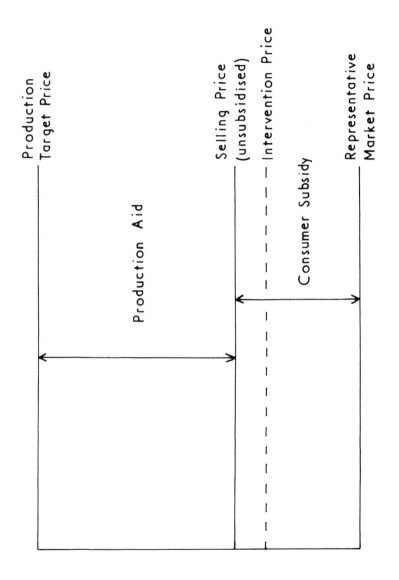

Fig. 8 : Internal support regime for olive oil.

fluctuations and the cost of transporting the oil from the production areas to the consumption areas. If left to its own devices, the normal selling price of olive oil (as with any other commodity) could be expected to lie somewhere between the PTP and the intervention price. But in order to compete with other oils, olive oil must sell at the lower RMP. So that this can happen, a consumer subsidy is applied, which bridges the gap between the PTP minus the production aid, and the RMP. Fig. 8 illustrates the relationship of the various elements of the internal support arrangements

If the producer is a member of a producer group under Regulation (EEC) No. 1360/78, (see chapter 12 for further discussion of this Regulation) the production aid is paid on the actual quantity of oil produced. For other growers, the aid is based on standard rates of yield. No aid is paid on olive groves planted since 31 October 1978.

Intervention agencies will only buy in olive oil offered to them in bulk by producers or producer groups. Both buying-in and storage contracts are available, but the latter are only available to producer groups. Very big stocks are currently held in intervention and, given this, it is perhaps surprising that provision is made for intervention agencies to carry buffer stocks.

A threshold price is set every year in such a way that imports sell in the Community at the same level as the RMP. In the past it proved very difficult to find a representative world price on which to base the levy for untreated oil and, as a result, a new concept was introduced to the CAP, namely, the levy tender. An importer wishing to import olive oil submits a tender to the local intervention agency stating the quantity to be imported and the levy he is prepared to pay. On the basis of all the tenders submitted and taking into account Community requirements, the Commission fixes a minimum levy. If the levy offered in a tender is equal to or greater than the minimum levy set, then the importer's tender is deemed successful and he must import the quantity stated at the level of the levy offered. Levies are also charged on olives and the various olive oil residues. These are derived from the levy on olive oil.

Olive oil used in the manufacture of preserved fish and vegetables benefits either from a production refund or from full or partial suspension of the import levy. Export restitutions are available.

Notes to Chapter 10

40. Sp. OJ 1972 (November); OJ L144, 31 May 1978; and OJ L45, 22 February 1979.
41. Cauliflowers, tomatoes, sweet oranges, mandarins, lemons, table grapes, apples (other than cider), pears (other than perry) and peaches (excluding nectarines).
42. Tomatoes, sweet oranges, mandarins, lemons, table grapes, apples, pears, plums, cherries and cucumbers.
43. OJ L144, 31 May 1978.
44. OJ L326, 18 December 1975 and OJ L330, 24 December 1975.
45. OJ L57, 2 March 1973; OJ L72, 20 March 1975; OJ L137/1, 3 June 1977; OJ L165, 22 June 1978.

CHAPTER 11

On-farm structural and social policy measures

The point was made in chapter 1 that in the proposals on the setting up of the CAP [12] the details of the market and price regimes were more fully worked out than were the measures of a structural and social nature. That serious social and structural problems existed was well known at the time, and the delegates to the Conferences at Stresa [44] and Rome [8] as well as the Commission devoted much thought and many words to these latter aspects of the embryonic policy, but their efforts were not matched by similarly intensive action in the legislative field. Indeed, it would not be unfair to state that much of the subsequent history of the CAP has been concerned with attempts—mostly unsuccessful—to shift the balance of the policy towards measures falling under the Guidance Section of FEOGA and away from the market and price supports under the Guarantee Section. Certainly this is true of the 1967 Community Programmes [9], the 1968 *Mansholt Plan* [10]; the *Improvement* of 1973 [13]; the 1975 *Stocktaking* [16]; and the review of *Mediterranean Agricultural Problems* of 1977 [23].

In the light of the subsequent history of the Guidance Section it is of interest to draw attention to the subordinate role envisaged for it very early on. Under Reg. 25 not only was a ceiling imposed on the annual expenditure from the Guidance Section (albeit a generous ceiling) but also what is more significant it was given a role which was subordinate to that of the EIB and the European Social Fund. Article 2.2 (c) states that FEOGA shall finance 'common measures adopted in order to attain the objectives set out in Art. 39(1)(a) of the Treaty, including the structural modifications required for the proper working of the common market, *provided that those measures do not encroach upon the work of the European Investment Bank and the European Social Fund*' (italics added). As to the ceiling: we have already learned that in 1966 it was made more restrictive by being limited to a fixed sum each year, and today this stands at 325 million EUA with a new ceiling of 720 million EUA from 1980–84. The net result of these restrictions is that there are a great many structural schemes each of which receives comparatively small sums of money from Community sources.

Indeed, so many schemes are involved that it is necessary to devise some system of classification, otherwise the picture is impossibly confused. The Commission distinguishes between 'common measures' and 'special measures'. This is unhelpful and could be misleading: for instance, 'common' in this context does not mean 'universal' as one might expect. The Commission classification is based on a technical, legal point arising out of Reg. 729/70 and does not relate to the purpose of the measures nor to any meaningful generic qualities of the various schemes. For present purposes the schemes have been divided into 'on-farm' discussed in this chapter and 'off-farm' discussed in chapter 12. Needless to remark, the division is somewhat arbitrary here and there.

Before discussing the schemes, attention should be drawn to an important difference between action under the Guarantee Section and under the Guidance Section. For those commodities for which price and market regimes operate, the payments made from the Guarantee Section represent total expenditure on the particular commodities.[46] In other words, Community expenditure has fully replaced the market and price support previously given by the individual Member States. This is not the case with Guidance aids. For these, as will become clear, the Community never pays more than a part of eligible expenditure, the Member States and the individual beneficiary having to pay the remainder.

There is a second point about Guidance Section funding which may not be well understood. The reader will find that for a number of schemes the rate of FEOGA reimbursement to a particular Member State or in a particular region is higher than elsewhere. This special treatment—which seems to be an increasingly frequent aspect of Guidance assistance—is of indirect benefit to the recipient only. The principal beneficiaries are the state treasuries concerned. The effect of a higher percentage reimbursement by FEOGA is to make the operation of the particular schemes involved less costly. It does not mean that the recipients of aid receive additional funds. However, it may mean that the governments concerned—and they are always the poorest ones— can afford to help a greater number of individuals or organisations, as the cost to the exchequer of each separate grant is lower.

Finally, it will be noticed in reading this and the next chapter that, unlike the commodity regimes, many Guidance measures are based on Directives rather than Regulations. It will be recalled from chapter 3 that a Directive is a much more flexible legislative instrument than a Regulation in that it only establishes a framework within which the Member States must formulate their own national legislation. Thus particular aspects of the schemes drawn up in accordance with a Directive vary from one country to another giving a certain flexibility to meet local needs. Indeed, the Commission provides examples of such variations in a report published in 1976 on the application of the three structural Directives of 1972 [17]. The existence of national differences should be borne in mind, as what follows is an outline of the more important features of the Directives and not an account of the specific schemes as applied in the various Member States.

General measures

MODERNISATION OF FARMS

Directive 72/159/EEC *on the modernisation of farms* (Sp. OJ 1972(II)) is intended to help combat two features of Community agriculture: the large number of farms which provide neither a fair income nor living conditions comparable with those of other occupations; and the constantly widening gap between such farms and those that are structurally sound.

In order to be considered as suitable for possible assistance under this Directive a farmer must practise agriculture as his main occupation, have adequate occupational skills, keep farm accounts of a specified kind, and draw up and have approved a farm development plan.

The farm plan—which is the key to the whole scheme—must demonstrate that on its completion the farm will be able to attain, in principle for either a one man or a two man-work unit, a level of earned income at least comparable to that received from non-agricultural work in the same region.

The concept of 'comparable earned income' is defined in Art. 4 as meaning the average gross wage paid to a non-agricultural worker (adjusted if necessary to take account of differences in the social security arrangements as between farmers and those in non-agricultural employment). The earned income to be attained on the farm at the completion of the development plan may include an element derived from non-agricultural activities, providing such an element does not exceed 20 per cent of total income, and providing that the income from the farm business is equal to the comparable earned income for one man-work unit.

Normally, the farm development plan can be spread over a maximum of six years but Member States are free to authorise a longer period in certain regions. Plans may be submitted either by an individual farmer or by a group of farmers in association and Member States are not permitted to discriminate between the two.

Various types of aid are available to farmers whose development plans have been accepted. Three aids are available under Art. 8: the allocation as a matter of priority of land released under the retirement Directive (see below); the provision of interest rate subsidies (or capital grants of equivalent effect) to help finance the investments necessary for carrying out the development plan, and the provision of guarantees for loans where the security provided by the farmer is insufficient. FEOGA reimburses 25 per cent of the eligible expenditure incurred by the Member States in providing these aids.

The interest rate subsidy applies to the whole loan up to a ceiling which is revised from time to time. Aids for investment over this limit are prohibited except when they are intended (a) for the construction of farm buildings; (b) for the transfer of farm buildings to new sites where this is done in the public interest; and (c) for land-improvement works.

For those farmers who intend to concentrate on the production of beef, veal, mutton or lamb, the incentives provided under Art. 8 are supplemented under Art. 10 by the provision of a guidance premium. This takes the form of a degressive hectarage payment within an upper limit per farm per year.[47] FEOGA reimbursement equals 25 per cent of eligible expenditure by Member States. By way of contrast to the favourable treatment of cattle and sheep production, incentives for the production of pigs are severely restricted and no incentives are available in respect of poultry and eggs.

The keeping of accounts of a specified kind is a compulsory feature of an acceptable development plan. In order to help farmers for whom account keeping is a new activity, an aid is provided under Art. 11. The grant is available for at least the first four years during which farm accounts are kept. Once again FEOGA reimburses 25 per cent of Member States' eligible expenditure.

One of the sections of chapter 12 is concerned with the establishment of producer groups intended to improve standards of marketing. Under Directive 72/159 assistance is provided which is intended to encourage the establishment of producer groups at the farm production level rather than at the marketing stage. A launching aid is available under Art. 12 to help defray the management costs of recognised groups. Member States are entitled to a FEOGA refund of 25 per cent of eligible expenditure under this Article.

According to Art. 13 Member States are empowered to introduce special incentives to promote modernisation through schemes to re-parcel land or to provide irrigation. In certain circumstances the Community will reimburse part of the costs of such schemes but subject to an upper limit per hectare.

The basic purpose of Directive 72/159 is to assist farms which could be made viable to achieve that status through the implementation of a development plan. It is not surprising, therefore, that as a general rule under Art. 14.2 Member States are prohibited from granting aids of equal value to other categories of farmers. This means that, for instance, already viable farms, while not excluded completely from investment aids, may not receive as generous an aid as that available to farms on which a development plan is in operation. No FEOGA reim-bursement of expenditure is involved in aiding already viable farms.

While the clear intention is for Member States to concentrate their efforts on helping development farmers, the needs of two other groups are, however, recognised.

Firstly, there are the farmers who are not capable of attaining the level of comparable earned income and who are not yet eligible for a retirement annuity; during the first five years of the operation of the Directive Member States were empowered to grant them temporary aids on the understanding that these could not be more favourable than those available to development farmers under Art. 8. In 1977 the time period was temporarily extended and extended again in 1978; it now runs until the end of 1979. In its proposals to amend the structural Directives issued in November 1977 [28], as amended in 1979 [43a], the Commission suggested that Member States be allowed to continue this aid without any reference to a new time period, but that an upper limit should be placed on the amount of investment for which assistance could be given.

Secondly, there are those farmers who are living 'in certain regions where the maintenance of a minimum level of population is not assured and where a minimum amount of farming is essential in view of the need to conserve the countryside.' It was left to a later decision of the Council to define in detail the permissible regions and systems of aid. In the event, this provision has been overtaken by the introduction of Community aids in disadvantaged areas, discussed below.

Directive 72/159 has been amended on a number of occasions, the most important being the introduction of additional measures in disadvantaged areas (discussed separately below). Other amendments have been necessary in order that the assistance provided should keep pace with inflation: for instance, Decision 76/402/EEC *on the level of the interest rate subsidy . . . to be applied in Italy*, itself subsequently amended by Decision 78/69/EEC (OJ L23, 28 January 1978); and Directive 76/837/EEC (OJ L302, 4 November 1976), which increased the amounts of aid available under Arts. 9 and 11. In 1977 an amendment was made to prohibit the use of the aids provided under Arts. 8 and 14 for the purchase of dairy cows and heifers intended for milk production. (Regulation (EEC) No 1081/77 *on the temporary suspension of aids for the purchase of dairy cows and of heifers intended for milk production* (OJ L131, 26 May 1977). This applies until the end of 1979.)

The modernisation Directive was to run for ten years, with a review of its progress after five years. This review took place in 1977 along with a review of the next two Directives discussed in this chapter. As a result of this review the Commission made certain proposals in 1977 [28] which were superseded by new proposals put forward early in 1979 in COM (79) 122 [43a].

Reference has already been made above to the proposed amendment to Art. 14 of Directive 72/159. In COM (79) 122 the Commission made some further suggestions concerning this Directive. Among these were a proposal to provide Community assistance to farms which would be able to reach no more than 90 per cent of the comparable income level on completion of the development plan. The Commission also proposed the exclusion from Community aid under the Directive of those farms for which the target income at the end of the period of the plan is more than 20 per cent above the comparable income level. The reasoning behind such a restriction is that farms able to achieve such a high level of income could probably finance the necessary expansion out of their own resources without assistance from Community funds. The Commission also suggested that in view of the market situation for certain commodities, investment aid for the construction of glasshouses should be suspended from the beginning of 1980 and that, except in certain limited circumstances, investment aid for pig farming and dairying should also be suspended from the same date.

RETIREMENT AND REALLOCATION OF LAND

Directive 72/160/EEC *concerning measures to encourage the cessation of farming and the reallocation of utilised agricultural area for the purposes of structural improvement* (Sp. OJ 1972 (II)) should be seen as a measure complementary to the modernisation Directive. It must be acknowledged that not all farms can be made viable and not all farmers are in a position to change their occupation. One group with particular job-mobility problems is composed of farmers aged 55–65 years and it is with them that Directive 72/160 is particularly concerned by offering assistance for early retirement. This aid is a means to an important end because through it under-utilised land is released which then becomes available for the purpose of structural improvement on other farms and, in particular, development farms under Directive 72/159.

The aid available under the retirement Directive is an annuity or an equivalent lump sum payable to eligible farmers who apply for it, who are aged between 55 and 65 years, and for whom farming is their main occupation. Member States are free, if they so wish, to grant a premium to retiring farmers as an added incentive. The premium must be calculated in relation to the area of utilised agricultural land released by the retiring farmer and expenditure on it is not eligible for FEOGA reimbursement.

As to the land released by retiring farmers, Art. 5 stipulates that at least 85 per cent of it must (a) be leased or sold to a farmer benefiting under Directive 72/159; (b) failing that, be allocated to other farmers, or (c) be withdrawn permanently from agricultural use. Provision is also made under this Article for the lease or sale of the available land to official agencies which will then carry out the functions referred to at (a), (b) or (c).

Besides the provision of pensions to farmers, the Directive lays down conditions under which an annuity or equivalent lump sum can be paid to a hired or family worker. Such workers must apply for the aid, be aged 55–65 years, undertake to give up agricultural work, and be employed on farms on which the farmer is in receipt of an annuity or a premium. They must also be covered by the social security system.

Reimbursement by FEOGA is normally limited to 25 per cent of the eligible expenditure by Member States. The only exceptions to the normal reimbursement rate are on expenditure in all regions of Ireland and in the majority of regions of Italy (eighteen out of twenty—the two excluded being Liguria and Lombardia).[48] In these cases the reimbursement rate is 65 per cent. A condition of all reimbursement is that the land freed has been reallocated for the purposes laid down in Art. 5 *with the exception* of those cases where the land has passed to a non-development farm. In the latter circumstance no refund from Community sources is possible.

In its second report on the application of the structural Directives [29] the Commission clearly indicates its disappointment at the lack of impact of Directive 72/160, and its dissatisfaction can be seen in the proposals which it made at the end of 1977 and in 1979 for revisions to the Directive [28 and 43a]. In COM (79) 122 the Commission proposed that the premium which Member States may pay over and above the annuity to make retirement more attractive should cease to be optional and should be made eligible for FEOGA reimbursement within an upper limit per hectare of utilised agricultural area released. The minimum level of the premium would also be stipulated for the first time and the granting of a premium could be made conditional on the release of land for the purposes set out in Art. 5.1 and 3. It was further proposed that the requirement under Art. 5 that 85 per cent of the land of a retiring farmer must be released should be reduced to 66 per cent.

The Commission also suggested the introduction of what it called a 'single anticipatory premium' for full-time farmers aged 50–55 who undertake to retire within five years. The premium would be on a sliding scale, the highest payment being available to farmers who apply in their fiftieth year. FEOGA reimbursement of the cost of the premium would be available up to a maximum per hectare of utilised agricultural area and would also be based on a sliding scale depending on the age of the farmer when applying for the premium.

In less-favoured regions of the Community (i.e. those regions in which simultaneously the percentage of the population engaged in agriculture is above the Community average, the GAP per person employed is below the Community average, and the total percentage unemployed is higher than the Community average) the Commission proposed that the annuity for farmers and farm workers aged 55–65 should qualify for assistance providing that the area released is used to enlarge a full-time farm but without the requirement that such a farm is the subject of a development plan under Directive 72/159. It was further proposed that in these less-favoured regions full-time farmers aged sixty years and over should receive a succession allowance, providing they legally transfer the running of the farm to a family heir up to the third degree of succession and providing that the heir has been employed for more than five years on the farm. FEOGA would reimburse the costs involved up to an annual maximum for a period of not more than ten years.

SOCIO-ECONOMIC ADVICE AND TRAINING

The last of the 1972 structural Directives is Directive 72/161/EEC *concerning the provision of socio-economic guidance for and the acquisition of occupational skills by persons engaged in agriculture* (Sp. OJ 1972(II)). Community structural policy is based on the maintenance of viability on currently viable farms and on assisting farmers with potential to become viable. To this end, it is thought important to provide a system whereby farmers and their families can receive guidance on the income opportunities facing them both within agriculture and elsewhere, and to help them achieve higher skill levels whether they remain in farming or not.

The system whereby such a guidance service is made available is set up under the first Title of Directive 72/161. The second and third Titles are concerned with (a) the provision of vocational training to assist farmers and others in agriculture to obtain the skills necessary for developing their enterprises and achieving greater specialisation, and (b) (temporarily) the provision of income aids to those who are pursuing retraining courses for occupations outside agriculture. This third Title however, has been superseded by the reform of the European Social Fund which is now responsible for such training. Proposals were made in COM (79) 122 to substitute a new scheme under Title III and this is outlined below.

Taking the provision of socio-economic guidance first, Art. 1.1 lays down that Member States must set up schemes designed to provide farmers, hired and family workers with a greater degree of information. The service provided can be set up either as a separate entity or integrated into existing services. The Member States are required to bear the cost of training the necessary socio-economic counsellors, except in so far as is provided under Art. 12. This latter stipulates that FEOGA will reimburse 25 per cent of the expenditure actually incurred in the training of counsellors subject to an upper limit per counsellor, and it will also reimburse 25 per cent of a standard amount per new counsellor placed in post. This refund applies to the initial appointment only; any subsequent replacement of that counsellor by another is not eligible.

Title II of Directive 72/161 is concerned with the acquisition of skills within agriculture. Under Art. 5.1 Member States are to set up schemes to help those in farming aged eighteen years or over to acquire new agricultural skills or to improve existing skills, but the schemes concerned must not be part of the normal agricultural courses of study at second or third level education. The new schemes can be of a general, technical or economic nature and can be conducted either at training centres or be on an in-service basis. They can be either at a basic or advanced vocational level. Subject to an upper limit, FEOGA reimburses 25 per cent of the expenditure actually incurred in respect of each farmer or farm worker who completes a course of basic or advanced vocational training.

In COM (79) 122 the Commission proposed that the FEOGA reimbursement of the allowance made to farmers and workers attending training courses should be raised to 50 per cent normally and in priority regions under the European Social Fund to 55 per cent. The Commission also put forward a proposal for a new scheme under Title III of this Directive. This new measure would cover the training and advanced training of managers and other staff working in producer groups and in enterprises undertaking the processing and marketing of agricultural products. FEOGA would reimburse 50 per cent of the expenditure involved up to a maximum per person completing a specialised course.

AIDS IN DISADVANTAGED AREAS

The origin of Directive 75/268 *on mountain and hill farming and farming in certain less-favoured areas* (OJ L128, 19 May 1975) lies partly in the Declaration on hill farming [52] appended to the Treaty of Accession, which recognised the special conditions prevailing in some regions of the Community which hindered the preservation of reasonable incomes for farmers, and partly to an admission that Directive 72/159 makes inadequate provision for assistance to investment in such regions.

The purposes of the disadvantaged areas Directive are manifold and include the desire to ensure the continued conservation of the countryside in mountainous and other less-favoured areas, and to counteract the large-scale de-population caused by declining agricultural incomes and poor working conditions. If these circumstances were allowed to continue, it would lead eventually to the abandonment of land previously farmed, which in turn would threaten the viability of regions which are predominantly agricultural.

Article 3 sets out the types of region which can be deemed to be less-favoured. They include, firstly, mountain areas in which farming is necessary to protect the countryside, especially in order to guard against erosion and to meet leisure needs. Secondly, those parts of the Community in which the maintenance of a minimum population or the conservation of the countryside are not assured. Thirdly, besides these two major categories, other smaller pockets with specific handicaps can qualify as less-favoured if the continuation of farming is necessary to conserve the countryside and to preserve the tourist potential of the areas concerned, or in order to protect the coastline. However, the total extent of such pockets may not exceed 2.5 per cent of the area of any Member State.

The actual regions within each country which are designated as less-favoured according to all the above criteria are set out in a series of Directives (one for each Member State) numbered 75/269/EEC/–/75/276/EEC (OJ L128, 19 May 1975).[49]

Four types of assistance are available under Directive 75/268. They comprise a compensatory allowance based on permanent natural handicap; improved rates of aid to farms suitable for development under Directive 72/159; aids for joint investment projects for fodder production and grazing land; and national aids for farms that cannot attain the comparable earned income standard.

The compensatory allowance is available to farmers with at least three hectares of utilised agricultural land who undertake to remain in farming for at least five years. Where the allowance is made in respect of cattle, sheep and goats it is based on the number of livestock units on the farm, with an upper limit on the number of units of account per livestock unit and per hectare of total forage area on the farm. In less-favoured areas, other than mountainous ones, restrictions are placed on the assistance which can be given in respect of cows whose milk is intended for marketing.

Expenditure by Member States on the compensatory allowances is eligible for reimbursement by FEOGA on the usual 25 per cent terms, except in the case of Italy and Ireland. In these two countries under an amendment to the Directive passed in 1976, (Directive 76/400/EEC, OJ L108, 26 April 1976) expenditure on the compensatory allowances is reimbursed at the level of 35 per cent.

The manner in which farmers in less-favoured areas can benefit from more advantageous treatment under the modernisation Directive 72/159 is set out in Arts. 9 and 10 of Directive 75/268. Firstly, the interest rate payable by the beneficiary of a development loan under Art. 8 of 72/159 is reduced and the interest rate subsidy (or equivalent capital grant) correspondingly increased. Secondly, with regard to the guidance premium payable under Art. 10 of 72/159 to those farmers who intend to concentrate on the production of beef, veal, mutton or lamb within a development plan, provision is made whereby it may be made more generous. However, the increased rate of assistance would apply only to those farms with more than 0.5 livestock units per hectare of forage area. FEOGA reimbursement of the eligible expenditure on the increased interest rate subsidy and the more generous guidance premium is at the usual 25 per cent rate, except in Ireland and Italy where reimbursement of the premium is at 35 per cent.

Thirdly, the compensatory allowance outlined above can be included by the farmer in calculating the level of earned income to be attained on the completion of the development plan submitted under Directive 72/159. This provision clearly makes it easier for a farmer to reach comparable income status and therefore benefit from the most favourable levels of assistance available under 72/159. Fourthly, whereas normally under Directive 72/159, when calculating the comparable earned income for one man-work unit, the proportion of earned income derived from non-agricultural activities cannot exceed 20 per cent, under Directive 75/268 this is raised to 50 per cent.

Fifthly, in mountainous less-favoured areas the requirement under 72/159 that, on the completion of a development plan, earned income from agriculture must equal the comparable earned income in non-agricultural activities in the same region is reduced to a level of 70 per cent. Finally, in less-favoured farming areas which are suitable for tourist or craft industry development, the interest rate subsidy can be applied to investment on the farm for tourist or craft industry purposes. An upper limit is placed on the amount of aid available per farm.

As to the aids for joint investment schemes for fodder production, and for the improvement and equipping of jointly farmed hill grazing and pasture land, the Community contributes towards the cost of such schemes up to a maximum amount per scheme or per hectare of land improved and equipped.

The fourth and last measure available is by way of a derogation from some of the requirements for aid laid down in Directive 72/159. Member States are free to grant investment aids to farms which are not capable of achieving the comparable earned income level required under Art. 4 of 72/159, but any such aid must not be on a basis that is more favourable than that available to farmers who are operating a development plan within the framework of the modernisation Directive.

Late in 1977 the Commission proposed amendments to Directive 75/268 [28] which were the subject of minor modifications in COM (79) 122 [43a]. The first proposal relates to the minimum size of holding on which a compensatory allowance may be paid. The proposal is that in the Mezzogiorno (i.e. southern Italy) and the Italian islands, and in the French overseas departments, (DOM),[50] the minimum should be lowered to two hectares of utilised agricultural area. The Commission also suggested that the restrictions imposed on the provision of compensatory allowances when assessed on the basis of dairy cows should be modified in respect of certain parts of Italy. These would be hill areas in danger of depopulation or certain small areas suffering from specific handicaps. The Commission further proposed that eligible expenditure on the compensatory allowance in Italy and Ireland should be reimbursed at the rate of 50 per cent.

Another suggested modification is that in the Mezzogiorno and the Italian islands and in the west of Ireland the rate of reimbursement for eligible expenditure on the interest rate subsidy and the guidance premium coming within the framework of Directive 72/159, and on the extra interest rate subsidy under Directive 75/268 should be raised to 50 per cent. Also, in the Mezzogiorno and Italian islands it is proposed that the rate of reimbursement for fodder and grassland improvement projects should be raised to 50 per cent of eligible expenditure, but that the upper limits in cash terms on each joint investment scheme or per hectare of land improved or equipped should be continued.

PROPOSAL ON YOUNG FARMERS

Late in 1974 the Commission proposed a special aid for young farmers (defined in the draft Directive as aged forty and under), who have been farming for less than five years and are implementing a development plan [14]. The rationale behind the proposal is that young farmers are at a considerable financial disadvantage during the first few years of farming, possibly having to compensate co-heirs while trying to build up stock and equipment on the farm. They are short of capital and under great pressure to raise productivity.

The aid envisaged would be for no more than five years and degressive in nature. It would only be paid providing the investments under the development plan were above a certain level. The FEOGA reimbursement would be at the usual rate of 25 per cent of eligible expenditure.

Specific sectors

Over the years the Community has taken action to improve the production situation which exists in various sectors. The difficulties which have been experienced are of two kinds: a chronic excess of output in total or the production of varieties within a commodity group for which there is a limited demand. Sometimes both these types of problems are combined.

CITRUS

Since the late 1960s Community growers have experienced considerable difficulties in disposing of oranges and mandarins, largely because of the unsuitable varieties on offer. In 1969 the Council adopted Regulation (EEC) No 2511/69 *laying down special measures for improving the production and marketing of Community citrus fruit* (Sp. OJ 1969 (II)), which was intended to help rectify the matter.

The aids offered are of two kinds: infrastructural assistance of benefit to the whole industry, and temporary compensation to small growers for loss of income. The infrastructural measures were to be carried out before the end of 1976 and were to include the replanting of orange and mandarin groves with more suitable citrus fruits; and the establishment, improvement or enlargement of centres to grade, pack, store and process fruit. The Guidance Section of FEOGA was charged with refunding 50 per cent of the total eligible expenditure involved.

The second measure–the income aid–is available to growers of oranges and mandarins who undertake to replant their groves. The specific conditions under which this aid is given were set out in Art. 4 but this was amended in 1977[51] as it had been found to be unduly restrictive. The amended Article limits the aid to those growers for whom oranges and mandarins are the main crop, providing the income from their holding does not exceed the income derived from four hectares of orange and mandarin trees; that at least 40 per cent of the groves are replanted at one time; and that the replanted area covers at least 0.2 hectares. The premium takes the form of a flat-rate payment per hectare replanted, payment being made in five annual instalments. FEOGA refunds 50 per cent of the expenditure incurred by the Member States.

WINE

In recent years the table-wine sector has been subject to surplus production conditions which are clearly structural rather than cyclical. The situation on the wine market bears a strong resemblance to the adverse circumstances of the citrus sector: namely, the difficulty of disposing of a low quality product, in this case wine made from inferior varieties of grapes.

In 1976 the Council passed two measures aimed at tackling this problem from different angles. Firstly, under Regulation (EEC) No. 1162/76 *on measures designed to adjust wine-growing potential to market requirements* (OJ L135, 24 May 1976) steps were taken to curb the growth of production by prohibiting new plantings of wine grape varieties. Secondly, under Regulation (EEC) No. 1163/76 *on the granting of a conversion premium in the wine sector* (OJ L135, 24 May 1976) encouragement was given to change to different varieties of grapes.

With regard to the first of these Regulations (1162/76) new plantings were banned up to the end of November 1978 except for three specific cases. No FEOGA expenditure was involved. In contrast to this, Reg. 1163/76 involves the granting of grubbing-up premiums for unsuitable varieties and is intended to help towards not only the cost of grubbing, but also to make up at least some of the growers' resultant loss of income.

In order to qualify for the premium, a grower must guarantee that since the Regulation came into force any vine planting on his holding has been offset by the prior grubbing up of an equivalent area under vines. The grower must also give a guarantee to grub up by a set date the vines for which a premium is being paid and to refrain until early

1982 from planting the grubbed area with the named varieties of fruit trees for which grubbing premiums were available under Reg. 794/76. Another condition is that the grower is not allowed to increase the total area under vines on his holding for a period of six years, and finally, he must make an annual declaration of the area under vines which is productive and the area not yet productive.

The premium takes the form of a payment per hectare and varies according to the quality of the vine. It is also degressive in nature, being at its highest in the 1976/77 wine-growing year, declining in the two subsequent seasons. FEOGA reimburses 50 per cent of eligible expenditure within the limits per hectare set out in Art. 4.

Article 5 allows Member States to grant a premium higher than the one laid down in Art. 4 if they so wish in two sets of circumstances, namely, when the entire vineyard on a holding is grubbed up, or when the vines grubbed are of very high productivity. This extra premium is not eligible for FEOGA reimbursement.

This conversion premium was introduced to cover three wine-growing years only, 1976/77–1978/79, but already in 1978 the Commission had proposed a number of new measures for the wine sector, and among them is a new conversion premium scheme. If it is adopted it will replace Reg. 1163/76.

Proposal for conversion and permanent abandonment: in effect this proposed Regulation *on granting conversion and permanent abandonment premiums in respect of certain areas of vines* (OJC209, 2 September 1978) would continue the work of Reg. 1163/76 in a more elaborate form. The belief is that greater efforts must be made to reduce the wine-growing potential of the Community and to this end the proposal is made to grant premiums to convert existing vineyards or to abandon wine growing altogether. The aim is to reduce the quantities of poor quality wine on the market and for this reason the proposed measures would be confined to Category II and Category III wine-growing regions (these classifications being established under another proposed Regulation).

The intention is that the conversion premiums would be available in each wine-growing year from 1978/79 to 1984/85 and that the abandonment premium would be available during the eight years following that in which the conversion premium was granted, i.e. the last year would be 1992/93. The conditions which the grower would have to meet in order to obtain a conversion premium are the same as under Reg. 1163/76.

The amount of the conversion premium would depend on the quality of vines being grubbed, there being four classifications. The abandonment premium would be a fixed amount per hectare per year except that it would start to decline per hectare in each year from the fourth onwards. The Guidance Section of FEOGA would reimburse half the eligible expenditure incurred on both premiums. Wine growers receiving a conversion premium under Directive 78/627 outlined below would not be eligible for the abandonment premium.

Proposal on vine root stock: parallel with the proposal on converting and abandoning vineyards is one for a Regulation *for the conversion and permanent abandonment of certain areas producing vine vegetative propagation material* (OJ C232, 30 September 1978). Growers of root-stock would be eligible for a premium for the conversion of their nurseries to other purposes and to a premium for abandoning wine growing. As with the proposal already described, the conversion premium would be available in each wine-growing year, 1978/79–1984/85, and the abandonment premium for the eight marketing years following that in which the conversion premium was granted. The conversion premium would be a once for all flat-rate payment per hectare grubbed; the abandonment premium would be a flat-rate payment per hectare paid annually, with a decline in amount in each year from the fourth onward. FEOGA Guidance would reimburse half the eligible expenditure.

Proposal for renouncing rights to replant: growers who would have grubbed an area of vineyard intended for table wine production prior to the coming into force of these new measures would in the ordinary course of events have been entitled to replant the grubbed area with new vines. This proposal for a *premium for renouncing the right to replant vines on certain areas* (OJ C232, 30 September 1978) is intended to encourage them not to go ahead with replanting. The renunciation premium would be available during the wine years 1978/79–1984/85. The premium would be a lump sum per hectare, declining in amount from the fourth year following the entry into force of the Regulation. FEOGA would reimburse half the eligible expenditure. Growers who received the renunciation premium would not be entitled to receive the premium available under another proposed Regulation on collective restructuring of vineyards outlined below.

Proposal for the retirement of wine-growers: The proposed Regulation *establishing a system of premiums for the cessation of wine-growing in France and Italy* (OJ C209, 2 September 1978) is intended to be complementary to Directive 72/160 on retirement. The idea is to encourage elderly wine-growers to retire without suffering any great financial loss by granting them an extra premium over and above what they would obtain under Directive 72/160. This extra premium would be available annually until the retired farmer reached the end of his sixty-fifth year. It would be calculated on the basis of the area used for wine-growing, with the proviso that the area under vines was at least 20 per cent of the total utilised agricultural area. In order to qualify, the grower would have to grub and permanently abandon his vineyard, and cease farming by the end of 1985. The premium would be in the form of a payment per hectare of vines withdrawn from use and FEOGA would refund 50 per cent of eligible expenditure incurred by the Member States.

Vineyards in the South of France
Reference has been made already to the package of measures intended to improve the structure of Mediterranean agriculture. Among this group is Directive 78/627/EEC on the programme to accelerate the restructuring and conversion of vineyards in certain Mediterranean regions of France (OJ L206, 29 July 1978). The intention behind this scheme is twofold: to improve those areas which are capable of producing good quality wine; and to encourage growers in other areas to change the use of their land. One means of helping them to do this is through the provision of more irrigation. The Directive covers the region of Languedoc-Roussillon and the departments of Ardèche, Bouches-du-Rhône, Var and Vaucluse.

FEOGA reimburses expenditure on (a) re-structuring of areas of vines at a flat rate per hectare re-structured with an upper limit of 66,000 hectares, of which 44,000 hectares must be in Languedoc-Roussillon; b) new public hydraulic works, up to a maximum of 33,000 hectares, including 22,000 hectares in Languedoc-Roussillon; (c) conversion grants with a ceiling per converted hectare, the aid being degressive from the third year onwards. The rate of reimbursement is 35 per cent of the cost of re-structuring and hydraulic works, and 50 per cent of the cost of the conversion aid. The scheme is available for five years starting in 1978.

Conversion in the Charentes

The problems of wine-growing in Languedoc-Roussillon are well known and many of the structural measures in force or proposed have them in mind. However, this present Directive No. 79/359/EEC *on the programme to speed up the conversion of certain areas under vines in the Charentes departments* (OJ L85, 5 March 1979) is intended to cater specifically for another area in difficulties.

The French authorities must draw up a programme designed to convert some of the vineyards in the Charentes to other uses. The scheme is to last for three years, and FEOGA will reimburse 50 per cent of eligible expenditure up to a maximum of 7500 hectares. Part of the aid available is in the form of a special conversion premium and this is subject to a maximum of 4000 UA/hectare of land converted.

Proposal on collective restructuring: the proposed Regulation *on collective projects for the restructuring of vineyards* (OJ C232, 30 September 1978) is rather different from the other wine measures already outlined. The purpose behind this proposal is to assist growers collectively in regions which have a viable future as producers of quality wines produced in specific regions (psr) and table wines to rationalise their operations.

Collective restructuring projects would have to contribute to a lasting improvement of working conditions, thereby improving the return to labour; they would need to guarantee an improvement in the quality of the wine; and offer sufficient guarantee of economic effectiveness. Projects for restructuring of table wine areas would have to relate to a total area of at least 100 hectares under vines, made up of unbroken wine-growing areas of not less than five hectares each. The aids proposed are, firstly, a restructuring premium, the actual amount varying within limits according to the type of work undertaken; and secondly, a replanting premium which could not exceed an upper limit per hectare. The Guidance Section of FEOGA would reimburse 35 per cent of eligible expenditure and the measure would last for seven years.

DAIRYING

The Community has had a number of schemes the intention of which has been to curb the growth of the chronic milk surplus. The efforts have been aimed at reducing dairy cow numbers, encouraging the non-delivery of milk and stimulating beef production. The most recent Regulation in this family is EEC No. 1078/77 *introducing a system of premiums for the non-marketing of milk and milk products and for the conversion of dairy herds* (OJ L131, 26 May 1977), as amended by Reg. 1041/78 (OJ L134, 22 May 1978). This measure is intended to assist farmers either to give up milk production altogether or to refrain from marketing milk and milk products. The means employed are the granting of premiums intended to compensate the farmer in part at least for the loss of income involved in participating in the scheme.

The non-marketing premium is calculated on the basis of the quantity of milk (or its equivalent in milk products) delivered by the producer during the preceding year. The premium varies in an inverse relationship with the quantity of milk delivered: thus, the lower the quantity of milk delivered, the higher the unit payment per kilogram. Half the premium is paid during the first three months of the non-marketing period and the remainder is paid in two equal instalments in the third and fifth years.

In order to obtain the conversion premium a producer has to prove that he delivered at least 50,000 kilograms of milk (or the equivalent milk products) during the previous year and that he still has the appropriate number of dairy cows, or he must prove that he has at least fifteen dairy cows (including in-calf heifers) on his holding. As with the non-marketing premium, the producer must agree not to dispose of milk either by sale or free of charge for a period of five years. In addition, he must undertake to keep on his holding during the four-year conversion period an average number of cattle or sheep equal to or greater than the number on the holding at a reference date. If the producer retains his cows during the conversion period, he must be able to show that he is converting his herd to a predominantly beef type.

The conversion premium is calculated on the basis of the quantity of milk delivered in the previous year, with a lower rate of payment per 100 kilograms for quantities in excess of 120,000 kilograms. Sixty per cent of the premium is paid in the first three months of the conversion period; the remainder is paid in two equal instalments in the third and fourth years. If a producer takes part in the programme to eradicate certain diseases in cattle (outlined below), he is still entitled to receive the non-marketing and conversion premiums.

This non-delivery and conversion scheme is unusual in that both the Guarantee and Guidance Sections of FEOGA participate in its financing. The Guarantee Section provides 60 per cent of the refunds on eligible expenditure and the Guidance Section 40 per cent.

THE ERADICATION OF CERTAIN DISEASES

In 1977 the Council passed Directive 77/391/EEC *introducing Community measures for the eradication of brucellosis, tuberculosis and leucosis in cattle* (OJ L145, 13 June 1977).[52] There are a number of reasons why this measure was adopted. Firstly, the Community is interested in a general way in improving livestock health. This is because good health makes livestock breeding more profitable and because it protects the human population from certain diseases which can be communicated by animals. Secondly, the existence of certain livestock diseases hinders inter-Community trade in fresh meat and live animals because all Member States operate veterinary controls on imports.

The eradication schemes are to run for three years, and Member States are eligible to receive assistance from the Guidance Section in the form of a headage grant per beast slaughtered. The payment is twice as high for cows as for other cattle.

PROPOSAL ON BEEF AND SHEEP IN ITALY

At the same time as the Commission put forward revised proposals on the structural Directives (already oulined in this chapter) it made a number of proposals for completely new measures the first of which is a draft Regulation on the development of beef cattle and sheep production in Italy [43a].[53] The aim is to assist cattle and sheep production in the mountainous areas of northern Italy, in the centre and in the Mezzogiorno. The Italian government would be required to draw up a programme for the development of the beef cattle and sheep industry and within this framework aids would be made available for the improvement of animal housing, the purchase of machinery for forage production, the improvement of meadows and pasture; and the retention of calves of beef breeds on the farm of origin for at least twelve months. FEOGA would reimburse 50 per cent of eligible expenditure up to a stipulated maximum in units of account and the proposed measure would have a life of ten years with an examination of its progress after five years.

PROPOSAL ON SHEEP FARMING IN GREENLAND

The possibilities for farming are very limited in Greenland but one of the few activities with potential is sheep rearing in the south. With this in mind the Commission put forward a draft Regulation for the development of sheep farming in Greenland [43a]. The Danish government would be required to draw up a development programme and within this FEOGA assistance would be available for the reclamation and development of additional forage areas; the improvement of the agricultural infrastructure by the provision of roads and a harbour; the provision of winter shelter for sheep and equipment for hay making, transporting and drying; the improvement of farm buildings; the purchase of additional breeding stock; the provision of an advisory and veterinary service; and the extension of slaughtering facilities. FEOGA would reimburse half the eligible expenditure (within a maximum allowed) on all the items listed except roads and the harbour for which its contribution would be 40 per cent. The proposed measure would have a life of ten years.

Notes to Chapter 11

46. On the assumption that no Member State is providing illicit support to a particular commodity—an assumption which is not always well founded.
47. The details of this guidance premium are not set out in Directive 72/159 but appear in a supplementary Directive No. 73/131/EEC *on the guidance premium provided for in Article 10 of the Directive*

of 17 April 1972 on the modernisation of farms (OJ L153, 9 June 1973). This Directive was amended in 1978 under Directive 78/1017/EEC (OJ L349, 13 December 1978).

48. Decision 74/517/EEC *regarding the list of agricultural regions where unfavourable conditions exist within the meaning of Directive No. 72/160/EEC, situated in Italy;* and Decision 74/518/EEC *regarding the list of agricultural regions . . . situated in Ireland,* OJ L290, 29 October 1974.

49. Directive 75/269/EEC *concerning the Community list of less-favoured farming areas within the meaning of Directive No. 75/268/EEC* (Belgium); 75/270/EEC (Germany); 75/271/EEC (France); 75/272/EEC (Ireland); 75/273/EEC (Italy); 75/274/EEC (Luxembourg); 75/275/EEC (the Netherlands); 75/276/EEC (United Kingdom). No areas have been designated as less-favoured in Denmark. In a number of cases the lists were subsequently revised.

50. DOM became entitled to receive aid from the Guidance Section of FEOGA as a result of the passing of Regulation (EEC) No. 1795/76 *concerning the application of Article 40 (4) of the Treaty to the French overseas departments* (OJ L201, 27 July 1976).

51. Under Regulation (EEC) No. 340/77 (OJ L48, 19 February 1977).

52. As amended by Directive 79/9/EEC (OJ L6, 10 January 1979).

53. As amended by COM (79) 122 final/2, 2 April 1979.

CHAPTER 12

Off-farm structural and social policy measures

We have already met Reg. 17/64 in connection with the setting up of FEOGA discussed in chapter 5. We meet it here again in another important guise, namely, as a provider of assistance in improving the structure of the agricultural sector.

GUIDANCE SECTION AIDS UNDER REG. 17/64

Article 11 of Reg. 17/64 sets out the types of actions for which funds were to be made available under the Guidance Section of FEOGA. They included projects for the adaptation and improvement of the production conditions in agriculture, and the marketing of agricultural products; the adaptation and guidance of agricultural production; and the development of outlets for farm commodities.

According to Art. 14 a project could only qualify for aid if it met three criteria simultaneously: it had to come within the framework of a Community Programme: it had to be for a purpose necessitated by the economic consequences of the implementation of the CAP or it had to meet the requirements of that policy; and it had to offer an adequate guarantee of the lasting economic effects of the improvement to be made in the structure of agriculture.

Article 14 permitted a derogation from the first of these three criteria so that individual projects were able to receive aid for a period of up to two years from the entry into force of the Regulation even though no Community Programme covered the action concerned.

In point of fact, it was not until 1967 that the Commission presented draft proposals on Community Programmes to the Council in COM(67)194 [9]. They were never implemented and individual projects continued to receive aid under Reg. 17/64. In 1970 under Reg. 729/70 it was laid down that these individual projects would continue to receive aid until such time as the annual amount of money spent on common measures under the Guidance Section reached 285 million UA (later revised upwards to 325 million UA on the Enlargement of the Community and now 325 million EUA). By 1978 this ceiling had been reached, and while money will continue to be paid out for many years to come on projects sanctioned in earlier years, no new projects are being considered under Reg. 17/64. There is one small exception to this: under Regulation (EEC) No. 2992/78 *on the granting of aid from the Guidance Section ... in 1978 and 1979, pursuant to Regulation No. 17/64/EEC* (OJ L357, 21 December 1978), 70 million EUA were allocated for some remaining projects in Benelux.

The popularity of Reg. 17/64 as a source of aid was unquestionable: far more projects were submitted each year than were ultimately aided. Half of the assistance went on projects to improve the structure of production–land improvements, drainage and irrigation, afforestation for example; about 43 per cent of the funds went on schemes to improve market structures, in particular milk and meat marketing; and the remaining 7 per cent was used to assist mixed production/marketing projects.

One of the striking features of the aids granted under Reg. 17/64 is that the assistance tended to go to the better farming regions. In some respects this is hardly surprising as so often it is in the better regions that people are most alive to the availability of aids, and have the capital to invest in improving existing structures or in the launching of new ventures.

Although new aids are no longer being sanctioned under Reg. 17/64, it remains important for a number of reasons. Firstly, it was for many years the only source of structural aid of any significance at Community level. Secondly, due to the fact that payments are made in arrears, it will continue to appear in FEOGA accounts for many years to come; and thirdly, it was the forerunner of a new measure which has replaced it in part, and to which we now turn.

AGRICULTURAL PROCESSING AND MARKETING

As far back as 1973 the Commission announced its intentions in the *Improvement* [13] to submit proposals to the Council for common measures on marketing and processing. These were intended to improve and rationalise these two sectors by making aid available to projects falling within action programmes for specific products. A draft

Regulation was submitted to the Council in 1975 and early in 1977 this draft, somewhat amended, was agreed by the Council and so became Regulation (EEC) No. 355/77 *on common measures to improve the conditions under which agricultural products are processed and marketed* (OJ L51, 23 February 1977). The granting of assistance under this Regulation commenced in 1978.

To qualify for aid projects must fulfil one or more of a number of criteria:

1. They must help to guide production in a direction sought by the CAP or involve the development of new outlets for agricultural production.
2. They are likely to lighten the burden on the intervention mechanisms.
3. They are in regions experiencing particular difficulty.
4. They help to shorten or improve marketing channels or to rationalise processing methods.
5. They contribute to the improvement of the quality, presentation and preparation of products or the better use of by-products.

If a project falls within one of these general groups, then it may be eligible for assistance providing it relates wholly or in part to buildings and/or equipment which help (a) to rationalise or develop storage, market preparation, preservation or other processing of agricultural products; (b) to improve marketing channels; or (c) to achieve a better standard of market intelligence.

Provision is made under Art. 12 for the financing of projects until the end of 1980 in sectors of the agricultural economy and geographic areas for which action programmes are not yet approved, but from the beginning of 1979 priority is given to projects within approved programmes. These programmes, which are being drawn up by the Member States, are intended 'to develop or rationalise the treatment, processing or marketing of one or more agricultural products in part or all of the Community' (Art. 2). In view of the impossibility of getting Community Programmes launched under Reg. 17/64, it will be interesting to see whether this latest effort at co-ordinated action is more successful.

In the first instance the Regulation is to operate for five years. Assistance from FEOGA is normally granted at the rate of not more than 25 per cent of the total investment, although in certain regions the percentage may be raised to 30. Normally the beneficiary must contribute at least half the cost of the investment and the relevant Member State at least 5 per cent. At the time of writing, no figures were yet available on the progress being made in implementing this Regulation.

As part of the Community effort to improve Mediterranean agriculture, amendments were made to Reg. 355/77 under Regulation (EEC) No. 1361/78 (OJ L166, 23 June 1978). These concern Articles 12 and 17 of Reg. 355/77. Under Art. 12.2 the date on which priority must be given to projects falling within approved programmes is put back to the beginning of 1980 in certain areas and circumstances. This derogation applies to all projects in the Mezzogiorno and Languedoc-Roussillon, and to projects concerning wine in the departments of Vaucluse, Bouches-du Rhône, Var, Ardèche and Drôme. The effect of the derogation is to permit individual projects in these areas to continue to receive aid even if the action programmes have not been drawn up by the Member States concerned.

As for Art. 17, the derogation here reduces the financial contribution of the beneficiary to 25 per cent in the Mezzogiorno, to 35 per cent in Languedoc-Roussillon and to 35 per cent for wine projects in the departments listed above. The proportion of the total cost reimbursed by FEOGA is raised to 50 per cent in the Mezzogiorno, to 35 per cent in Languedoc-Roussillon, and to 35 per cent for wine projects in the departments listed above.

Early in 1979 the Commission proposed an amendment to Reg. 355/77 in respect of the slaughtering of pigs and the processing of pigmeat in France and the United Kingdom [43a]. The intention is to give special assistance to the pigmeat sector in these two countries where facilities for processing and marketing are less well developed than in other Member States. The means by which this would be achieved would be by reserving certain funds allocated under the Regulation for the specific benefit of French and UK pigmeat projects during the three year period 1980–1982.

DRAINAGE IN THE WEST OF IRELAND

In 1978 the Council adopted Directive 78/628/EEC *on a programme to accelerate drainage operations in the less-favoured areas of the West of Ireland* (OJ L206, 29 July 1978). The intention is to assist in increasing yields and productivity in a part of the Community where agricultural incomes are low, a high proportion of the population is engaged in agriculture, and off-farm employment prospects limited.

As with a number of the measures concerning the Mediterranean area, this Directive covers both public works and work on farms so in a sense fits into neither the on-farm nor the off-farm structural measures categories. It is included here purely on grounds of convenience.

The Directive is confined to those less-favoured areas (as defined in Directive 75/272) in Ireland which come within the western region. The Irish government is required to draw up a comprehensive programme for submission to the Commission covering both public arterial drainage and field drainage. It receives a 50 per cent refund of eligible expenditure from FEOGA on the following: (a) public arterial drainage up to a maximum of 30,000 hectares in the catchment areas concerned; (b) field drainage work up to a maximum of 100,000 hectares drained but with an upper limit per hectare drained; and a maximum level of national aid of 70 per cent; (c) grants towards the purchase of drainage machinery by cooperatives during the first two years of the scheme.

This last form of aid is subject to a limit of no more than 5 per cent of the eligible expenditure on field drainage and no more than 25 per cent of the purchase price of the machinery. The programme is scheduled to run for five years.

DRAINAGE IN OTHER PARTS OF IRELAND

Early in 1979 the Council passed Directive 79/197/EEC *on a programme to promote drainage in catchment areas including land on both sides of the border between Ireland and Northern Ireland* (OJ L43, 20 February 1979). The intention is to help to increase agricultural income by improving the infrastructure through arterial drainage. The Irish and UK governments are required to draw up a joint programme for drainage covering the catchment area on both sides of the border. The measure is scheduled to last for five years from the date of approval of the programme (or mid-1981 at the latest).

FEOGA will reimburse 50 per cent of the eligible expenditure of both governments.

PROPOSAL ON AGRICULTURAL DEVELOPMENT IN THE WEST OF IRELAND

Hard on the heels of the enactment of the two measures on drainage in Ireland outlined above came a proposal for a Regulation for the stimulation of agricultural development in the less-favoured areas of the west of Ireland [43a]. This is an extremely wide-ranging proposal, many features of which are reminiscent of the measures enacted for the benefit of the Mezzogiorno and southern France which are outlined below.

The Irish government would be required to draw up an outline plan and within this assistance would be available from FEOGA to help finance projects involving the improvement of the physical and educational infrastructure; the orientation of farm production towards more intensive beef and sheep rearing; the improvement of processing and marketing facilities; forestry; and the provision of training facilities and specialised support services for advisers. FEOGA would contribute 40 per cent of the total cost of infrastructural measures to improve electricity, water and roads within a maximum amount laid down, and 50 per cent of the actual cost of the remaining measures other than aids for processing and marketing. This last would be aided by extending to the west of Ireland the special arrangements already enacted for the Mezzogiorno and Languedoc-Roussillon under Reg. 355/77 (as amended by Reg. 1361/78). The proposed Regulation would have a life of ten years.

PROPOSAL ON FORESTRY

In February 1974 the Commission submitted a draft Directive on forestry [14] to the Council. This was subsequently revised and re-submitted the following year [15]. The Commission sees many advantages in encouraging forestry: it facilitates the better use of labour and other factors of production; it improves the ecosystems; it reduces the Community's dependence on imported timber, while increasing the beauty of the landscape and conserving the soil, fauna and flora, and water systems; it adds to the productivity of adjacent agricultural land by providing shelter and improves the quality of air and water.

The aids proposed under the draft Directive would take the form of grants or fiscal incentives or interest-rate subsidies or any combination of these for any of the following measures:

afforestation of marginal agricultural land and of uncultivated land suitable for forestry;

by means of restocking, the conversion of unproductive or low-productive woodland into productive woodland;

the establishment and improvement of shelter belts;

the construction and improvement of forest roads;

the creation of recreation facilities.

Community reimbursement of eligible expenditure was proposed at 25 per cent or for certain of the measures at a maximum amount per hectare.

Mediterranean measures

Reference has already been made to the problems of Mediterranean agriculture and the subject will have to be taken up again in chapter 13 in the context of Enlargement to the South. However, it might be useful at this point to explain briefly what is meant by the term 'Mediterranean'. In fact there is more than one definition.

The narrowest definition admits only the Italian Mezzogiorno (including the islands of Sardinia and Sicily), and the French region of Languedoc-Roussillon. But Mediterranean-type regions have also been defined much more broadly to include all regions in which the share of Mediterranean products in total agricultural production is at least 40 per cent [23]. This definition covers a much wider area and includes most of Italy, the regions of France bordering the Mediterranean as well as Aquitaine on the Atlantic Coast (!) and many inland areas in both France and Italy such as Ardèche, Rhône, Vercelli, Novara and Trento. In practice, as far as legislation and proposed legislation are concerned, the definition of the area is dependent on the measure involved and the definition of the exact area is always given in each Regulation, Directive or draft proposal. We have already seen this in the outline given above of the amendments to Reg. 355/77 contained in Reg. 1361/78.

IRRIGATION IN THE MEZZOGIORNO

One of the many handicaps of the Mezzogiorno is the inadequate rainfall during the growing season. The extension of the irrigation network would greatly alleviate this problem and produce a rapid and lasting improvement in the level of farm incomes. Regulation (EEC) No. 1362/78 *on the programme for the acceleration and guidance of collective irrigation works in the Mezzogiorno* (OJ L166, 23 June 1978) is intended to assist in the provision of an enlarged irrigation network which will make better use of the existing capacity of reservoirs and main irrigation channels. It should help to reorientate agricultural production in the areas concerned and to increase farmer response to the aids available under Directive 72/159. To this end it also provides funds to assist in the appointment of advisory officers in such areas.

The estimated time required to carry out the measures receiving aid under the Directive is five years. Aid from FEOGA is in the form of capital grants. Public hydraulic works carried out under special programmes are assisted by a FEOGA reimbursement of 50 per cent of the cost up to a maximum of 200,000 irrigable hectares and subject to a ceiling payment per hectare irrigated. FEOGA reimbursement of 50 per cent of the cost of the remuneration and expenses of newly appointed advisory officers is also available, subject to a maximum per advisory officer.

IRRIGATION IN CORSICA

Like that of the Mezzogiorno, Corsican agriculture suffers from inadequate rainfall during the growing season and also, as in Italy, the capacity of its reservoirs and main irrigation channels is greater than the use being made of them by the irrigation network. Because of this, the Council has adopted Directive 79/131/EEC (OJ L38, 14 February 1979) *on the acceleration and guidance of irrigation works in Corsica,* which bears a strong resemblance to Reg. 1362/78 on irrigation in the Mezzogiorno just outlined, although without the aid for the provision of advisory officers. FEOGA will reimburse 50 per cent of eligible expenditure on irrigation works for a maximum of 15,000 hectares, and within a ceiling limit per hectare irrigated.

PUBLIC AMENITIES

As we saw earlier in this chapter, when Reg. 17/64 came to an end it was replaced in part by Reg. 355/77. This latter Regulation takes care of assistance to marketing and processing projects but no single Regulation has been enacted to cover the infrastructural activities which fell under Reg. 17/64. Specific measures such as Directive 78/628 on drainage in the west of Ireland and Reg. 1362/78 on irrigation in the Mezzogiorno are coping with certain aspects of infrastructure in certain regions. Regulation (EEC) No. 1760/78 *on a common measure to improve public amenities in certain rural areas* (OJ L204, 28 July 1978) takes care of yet other infrastructural matters but once again in a limited area of the Community.

Throughout the less-favoured agricultural regions of Italy and southern France there are many villages and farmsteads which are not yet connected to the public electricity and water supply systems, and where the rural road network is inadequate. Clearly these conditions add to the difficulties faced by people living in such areas, and structural change and agricultural reform cannot succeed unless these basic amenities are improved.

Article 1 sets out the areas to benefit from this measure and they are: (a) the less-favoured areas in Italy as set out in Directive 75/268; (b) the areas of the Mezzogiorno which are not regarded as less-favoured under Directive 75/268; and (c) in France the regions of Midi-Pyrénées, Languedoc-Roussillon, Provence-Côte d'Azur and Corsica, and the departments of Pyrénées-Atlantiques, Ardèche and Drôme.

Projects to receive aid must be concerned with the provision of electricity, potable water and better roads. They may not be in receipt of other aids coming under the Guidance Section nor of aids funded by the European Regional Development Fund. The aid is expected to be available for five years and the actual FEOGA assistance is in the form of capital subsidies. The total cost of the investment is to be shared out in the following way:

at least 10 per cent of the cost being met by the beneficiary;

at least 20 per cent of the cost being met by the Member State concerned;

a subsidy of 40 per cent of the cost granted by FEOGA.

ADVISORY SERVICES IN ITALY

The Commission is concerned with the serious structural deficiencies and the very low agricultural productivity which affect the greater part of Italy. One of the shortcomings facing the farming sector is the absence in many areas of an effective advisory service, but the economic and budgetary constraints faced by Italy preclude the government from establishing the necessary service. In order to help the Italians overcome these difficulties, a Regulation has been passed–(EEC) No. 270/79 *on the development of agricultural advisory services in Italy* (OJ L38, 14 February 1979). The Regulation hinges on two measures: the establishment of arrangements for the training of advisers, and the assignment of the majority of trained advisers to posts in the Mezzogiorno.

Unlike most structural measures which are given a life–in the first instance at least–of five years, this Regulation is given a life of twelve years. During the first two years FEOGA involvement is in the nature of assistance towards the cost of training teachers and contributing towards the running expenses of training centres. Over the following ten years FEOGA will assist with the running costs of the training centres and will provide course attendance allowances up to a maximum amount per student. FEOGA will also help to defray the cost to the Italian government of employing the advisers during (at most) the first six years of their appointment. The rate of reimbursement is 50 per cent for advisers in the Mezzogiorno and 40 per cent elsewhere.

FORESTRY IN MEDITERRANEAN ZONES

Among the many problems of the Mediterranean area is the damage which has been caused by intensive land clearance and overgrazing. This has resulted in soil deterioration, erosion and in some places the creation of desert conditions. In order to protect the soil from deterioration and to achieve a satisfactory water balance, the Council has adopted Regulation (EEC) No. 269/79 *establishing a common measure for forestry in certain Mediterranean zones of the Community* (OJ L38, 14 February 1979). This measure involves a forest programme to be carried out primarily in hill and mountain areas. It covers not only afforestation but also the improvement of deteriorated forests, the construction of forest roads, and the cost of research.

The areas to benefit from this measure include, in Italy, not only the Mezzogiorno but also the regions of Lazio, Toscana, Liguria, Umbria, Marche and Emilia–Romagna, as well as the provinces of Cuneo and Alessandria in Piemonte, and Pavia in Lombardia. In France, the areas include the regions of Languedoc-Roussillon, Provence-Côte d'Azur and Corsica, and the departments of Ardèche and Drôme.

FEOGA assistance takes the form of capital grants paid in one or more instalments to cover 50 per cent of the cost of (a) afforestation up to a maximum per hectare, and a total limit of 88,000 hectares; (b) improvement of deteriorated forests up to a maximum per hectare, and a total of 96,000 hectares; (c) associated works such as terracing up to a maximum per hectare, and a total of 80,000 hectares; (d) fire protection also with a maximum per hectare, and a total of 200,000 hectares; (e) forest roads with a maximum per kilometre, and a total limit of 2,400 kilometres; (f) preparatory work required in drawing up programmes of development up to a total cost of 6 million EUA over the five years or 5 per cent of the cost of each programme. The minimum national contribution must be 40 per cent of the cost of this measure and, usually, the owner of the land involved must contribute 5 per cent.

FLOOD PROTECTION IN HERAULT

All the measures concerning hydraulics in the Mediterranean area so far discussed have sought to provide at least some of the assistance needed to increase the number of hectares benefiting from irrigation. Directive 79/174/EEC *concerning the flood protection programme in the Herault valley* (OJ L38, 14 February 1979) is intended to aid a very different sort of area. Two separate difficulties can be identified. Firstly, the Herault valley is only partly suited to vineyards and so it would seem advisable to encourage farmers to convert their vineyards into other crops. But secondly, the area is subject to frequent flooding so alternative uses of land are limited. If this latter defect could be corrected, it would assist farmers by widening their choice of enterprise and in particular put them in a position to avail of the aids under Directive 72/159.

The Directive is intended to assist in the provision of a barrage and dams in the lower and middle valley. The French government is required to submit a programme to the Commission for approval. This must include information on the extent of the area affected by flooding, the location of the vineyards and the number of hectares of vines to be converted to other uses, the measures necessary for flood control and their cost. Expenditure incurred by the French authorities relating to the construction of a barrage and dams up to a total of 23 million EUA will be eligible for aid from FEOGA. Its contribution will equal 35 per cent of the eligible cost. The scheme is intended to last for seven years.

Producer groups

This section is very largely concerned with measures aimed at improving the performance of producers in the market place. It has long been felt that the bargaining power of producers and the discipline of the market are weak, and the Commission has always been keen to encourage the formation of producers' organisations which would give producers greater strength, particularly in the negotiation of commercial contracts. At the same time such organisations would improve the producers' response to the needs of the market in terms of regularity of supply and quality. The efforts made by the Commission to persuade the Council to pass legislation to encourage the formation of producer groups are many and stretch over more than a decade. The first attempt was made in the field of fruit and vegetables, and it is to this Regulation that we now turn.

PRODUCER GROUPS IN FRUIT AND VEGETABLES

Horticultural growers face particularly acute marketing difficulties which are inherent in the types of products themselves. There is strong seasonality of supply, a high degree of perishability, sharp fluctuations of yields and prices, and significant localisation of markets. All these conditions weaken the bargaining power of producers and accentuate the need for orderly marketing.

In 1966, under Reg. 159/66 provision was made for the granting of aids to facilitate the formation and operation of producers' organisations whose members were obliged to comply with certain rules regarding marketing. When the fruit and vegetables Regulations were consolidated under Reg. 1035/72, the launching aids for producers' organisations were continued.

These organisations (often referred to as producer groups) are established voluntarily by producers with the intention of furthering the following ends:

    (a) to help to concentrate supply and to stabilise producer prices;

    (b) to assist members in the presentation and marketing of produce;

    (c) unless the requirement is waived, to sell the members' total output of the product in respect of which they joined the group;

    (d) to apply rules intended to improve quality and to adapt supply to market requirements.

Under Art. 14.1 Member States are given the power to grant launching aids to producer groups in the three years following the date on which they are established. These aids must not exceed 3 per cent, 2 per cent and 1 per cent of the value of production marketed under the auspices of the group in the first, second and third years respectively of its operation. Fifty per cent of the amount of assistance granted is refunded by FEOGA.

Up to the end of 1977 launching aids had been granted to a total of 302 organisations distributed as follows: 157 in France, 78 in Federal Germany; 41 in Italy; 5 in the UK; 20 in Denmark; and 1 in Belgium [39]. No organisation in Luxembourg, Ireland or the Netherlands had received assistance.

As part of the extra aids being provided in Mediterranean areas an amendment to Reg. 1035/72 was passed, namely Regulation (EEC) No. 1154/78 (OJ L144, 31 May 1978), which is relevant to the present discussion. By way of derogation from Art. 14 of Reg. 1035/72, Member States are allowed to grant aid to producers' organisations which are established in the seven years starting October 1977. During the first five years of operation, aid can be made available equal to 5 per cent, 4 per cent, 3 per cent, 2 per cent and 1 per cent of the value of the production marketed, with an upper limit expressed in terms of the actual cost of forming and running the organisation concerned. Fifty per cent of this increased expenditure is reimbursed by FEOGA.

PRODUCER GROUPS IN FISHERY PRODUCTS

Under Reg. 2142/70 provision was made for launching aids to assist in the formation of producers' organisations. The intention was to encourage the creation of a mechanism which would further the two aims of adjusting 'supply to market requirements and to guarantee, as far as possible, a fair income to producers' (Reg. 2142/70 preamble). When the fisheries Regulations were consolidated under Reg. 100/76 launching aids were maintained as part of the regime.

Producer groups formed after the coming into force of the Regulation are eligible for launching aids. They are available during the first three years following official recognition of the group and they may not exceed 3 per cent, 2 per cent and 1 per cent of the value of products marketed under the auspices of the group in the first, second and third years respectively.

This assistance is subject to a restriction which does not apply in the case of fruit and vegetables, which is that the launching aids may not exceed 60 per cent, 40 per cent and 20 per cent of the group's administrative expenses in the three years in question. The level of FEOGA reimbursement is set at 50 per cent of the cost of the launching aids. By the end of 1977 a total of sixteen organisations had been assisted: seven in France; three in Federal Germany; one in Ireland and five in the UK [39].

PRODUCER GROUPS IN THE HOPS SECTOR

Hops are unusual in that while they are one of the lesser agricultural commodities, nevertheless production is highly localised in certain traditional and well defined areas of the Community and hops are a significant crop in such areas. They are also unusual in that a large proportion of output is marketed on contract. The Community, according to the preamble to Reg. 1696/71, takes the view that the centralisation of supply and the adaptation of the commodity to the requirements of the market should be encouraged. To this end, it wishes to promote producer groups and their unions.

Provision is made for the granting of launching aids by the Member States on exactly the same basis as is laid down in Reg. 2142/70 for fishery products (see above), but the FEOGA reimbursement level is set at only 25 per cent of eligible expenditure. By the end of 1977, five producer groups had received launching aids and 95 per cent of hops are marketed through producers' organisations.

PRODUCER GROUPS IN THE SILKWORM SECTOR

In 1975 the Council requested the Commission to submit a proposal for a Regulation under which recognition and launching aids could be given to producer groups in the silkworm sector. The aim of such a proposal was to assist breeders to overcome the economic difficulties which they were encountering. Later the same year the Commission complied with the Council's request and put forward a proposal in all essentials similar to the Regulations for fisheries and hops discussed above. Italy–effectively the only country concerned–rejected the proposal on the grounds that it did not meet the needs of the situation, which was the difficulty of marketing cocoons in competition with low-priced overseas supplies.

The Commission met the situation by amending its proposal so that while producer groups could become recognised in the ordinary way, they would not receive launching aids but rather their members would receive a special aid on the delivery of cocoons to the group. This would encourage breeders to join a recognised producer group, thereby assisting in the achievement of a more rational management of supply. This proposal was accepted and became Regulation (EEC) No. 707/76 *on the recognition of producer groups of silkworm rearers* (OJ L84, 31 March 1976). One producer group has received recognition and almost all Community production is marketed through this group.

PRODUCER GROUPS IN OTHER SELECTED COMMODITIES

Apart from proposing the measures in specific sectors outlined above, the Commission made a number of attempts to persuade the Council to adopt a general Regulation on producer groups and their unions. Such a Regulation would not have been limited to specific commodities but would have applied to the whole range of products listed in Annex II of the Rome Treaty.

The Commission presented its first general draft Regulation on producer groups to the Council in 1967. A revised draft formed part of the structural proposals put forward in 1970. A number of further revisions were made to the proposal in later years and it was not until 1978 that Regulation (EEC) No. 1360/78 *on producer groups and associations thereof* (OJ L166, 23 June 1978) was finally passed. It bears little resemblance to earlier drafts: most importantly it is neither general to the whole Community nor does it cover all products listed in Annex II.

Under Art. 2 the measure is limited geographically to (a) Italy; (b) the French regions of Languedoc-Roussillon, Provence-Côte d'Azur, Midi-Pyrénées and Corsica; the departments of Drôme and Ardèche; the French overseas departments; and (c) Belgium.

Article 3 limits the scope of the measure in terms of the products covered. Italy has the widest range as all products listed in Annex II are included, with the exception of fruit and vegetables, hops and silk worms. A group of processed agricultural products listed in the annex to the Regulation are also covered. In the case of the French areas, the coverage is narrower and yet more complex. Firstly, producer groups in table wines and grape must are included in the four regions referred to in Art. 2. Secondly, lavender and the plants used in perfumery are included in Provence-Côte d'Azur and in Drôme and Ardèche. Thirdly, table olives are covered in Languedoc-Roussillon, Provence-Côte d'Azur, Corsica and Drôme. Fourthly, tropical fruit, live cattle, beef and veal carcases or quarters are included in the French overseas departments. For Belgium, the Regulation applies to cereals, live cattle, piglets and lucerne.

In order to receive recognition, a producer group has not only to apply for recognition but it also must comply with a long list of conditions set out in Arts. 4, 5 and 6. Among the many requirements is one which stipulates that at least two-thirds of the members of a group must operate undertakings in the parts of the Community listed in Art.

2 and at least half of the produce marketed by the group must come from these areas also.

The aid available to a recognised group takes the form of a payment equal to a maximum of 3 per cent, 2 per cent and 1 per cent of the value of the products supplied by the members, and to which the recognition relates, and which are put on the market. However, the aid may not exceed 60 per cent, 40 per cent and 20 per cent of the actual expenses involved in forming and operating the group.

Aid to associations is equal to a maximum of 60 per cent, 40 per cent and 20 per cent of the actual formation and operating expenses for the first, second and third years respectively but it is subject to a maximum payment expressed in units of account. Under Art. 10.4 larger amounts may be provided for both groups and associations in respect of certain regions and products encountering particular difficulties.

The Regulation is to be in force for five years and the aids referred to above with the exception of those under Art. 10.4 are chargeable to the Fund. Normally, the Guidance Section refunds 25 per cent of chargeable expenditure, but the Council may decide to increase this up to a maximum of 50 per cent.

Fisheries

CONVERSION IN THE SALT-COD FISHING INDUSTRY

When Regulation (EEC) No. 2141/70 *laying down a common structural policy for the fishing industry* (Sp. OJ 1970 (III)) was adopted, provision was made under it for the future enactment of measures which would help to achieve the rational development of the fishing industry. The first such measure was enacted by the Council as Regulation (EEC) No. 2722/72 *on the financing by the EAGGF, Guidance Section, of conversion projects in the salt cod-fishing industry* (Sp. OJ 1972, (28–30 December)).

The need for a conversion scheme stemmed from the total lifting of duties on imports of salt cod coming into the Community from third countries—competition which the Community salt cod industry was ill-

equipped to meet. It was felt that it would be advantageous to encourage the fishermen involved to switch to other techniques—in
particular, deep-freezing on board—and to fish for other species,
especially tunny which is in short supply.

Projects receiving aid can cover the provision of equipment to further
any of the following:

deep-freezing on board;

increasing the market value of the catch *on board* by filleting or other
methods of preparation or processing in line with consumption
trends in Member States;

increasing the market value of fishing products by means of using the
drying-plants made redundant by the decline in the productive
capacity of the cod-fishing fleet.

In order to be eligible for aid, trawlers and tunny-fishing boats must
meet certain minimum technical requirements laid down in Art. 5.
Member States must approve the projects and must provide the
Commission with evidence that they are economically sound. The
Member States must also participate in the financing. Aid from the
Fund is in the form of capital subsidies. The FEOGA contribution must
not exceed 25 per cent of the total investment and the recipients of the
aid must contribute at least 50 per cent of the cost of the total
investment.

Under Art. 8 provision is made for allowances to be paid to
fishermen in the salt cod-fishing industry and to people working in
drying-plants made redundant by the lowering of the industry's
productive capacity to attend courses at vocational training centres.
FEOGA reimburses 25 per cent of the amount actually paid out by the
Member States within an upper limit set out in Art. 20 which restricts
the total amount payable per fisherman or per employee. This
Regulation was to run for five years.

RE-STRUCTURING THE INSHORE FISHING INDUSTRY

Many of the difficulties faced by the inshore fishing fleet bear a strong
resemblance to the types of problems to be observed among sections of
the farming population. Incomes in inshore fishing are low, thereby
preventing the small family enterprises from renewing vessels and

equipment in line with current technical and economic requirements. As in farming, fishermen need encouragement to change to new types of production–for instance to the cultivation of shell fish.

The Commission is undertaking an analysis of the production potential of inshore fishing. While waiting for this to be completed, the Council has adopted Regulation (EEC) No. 1852/78 *on an interim common measure for restructuring the inshore fishing industry* (OJ L211, 1 August 1978), as amended by Regulation (EEC) No. 592/79 (OJ L78, 30 March 1979). FEOGA is participating, through the provision of capital subsidies, in the financing of investment projects connected with the construction or purchase of fishing vessels, and the construction, equipping or modernisation of fish farms.

As a general rule, the beneficiary must finance at least half the total investment and the Member State at least 5 per cent. The subsidy from FEOGA cannot exceed 25 per cent except in special circumstances. These latter cover Greenland, Ireland, Northern Ireland, the Mezzogiorno and the French overseas departments, where the beneficiary has to find at least 25 per cent of the cost, the Member State at least 5 per cent, and the FEOGA contribution can be up to half the cost of the total investment.

PROPOSALS FOR INTEGRATED DEVELOPMENT PROGRAMMES

Included among the measures put forward in COM (79) 122 [43a] were three concerned with integrated development in the Western Isles of Scotland, the department of Lozère in France, and the province of Luxembourg in Belgium (this should not be confused with the Grand Duchy of Luxembourg which is an independent state). The intention is to facilitate overall development in the regions concerned by the drawing up of integrated development programmes which would cover not only the needs of agriculture but also the infrastructural requirements, tourism, crafts, industry and any other complementary activities vital for the improvement of the socio-economic situation of the regions concerned. FEOGA would assist the achievement of this integrated development by supporting projects related to agriculture.

The Western Isles of Scotland: the proposed Regulation would help to improve farming; processing and marketing of agricultural products;

afforestation of marginal land; infrastructure; and fishing. The UK government would be required to draw up an integrated development programme and within this FEOGA would reimburse 40 per cent of eligible expenditure on agricultural infrastructure and 50 per cent of eligible expenditure on the remaining measures, and on the actual cost of planning and administering the development programme up to a maximum amount. The Regulation would have a life of ten years but its progress would be reviewed before the end of the first five years.

The department of Lozère: under the proposed Regulation the French government would be required to draw up an integrated development programme and within its framework FEOGA would provide aid for the development and improvement of cattle and sheep pastures; wintering facilities; the construction of windbreaks; and the renewal of chestnut cultivation. The rate of reimbursement would be 50 per cent of eligible expenditure on these measures and also of the actual cost of drawing up and administering the programme up to a maximum allowed. The Regulation would have a life of ten years with a review before the end of the first five years.

The province of Luxembourg: as with the other regions, under the proposed Regulation the Belgian government would be required to draw up an integrated development programme within which FEOGA would contribute to the financing of measures designed to reparcel fragmented farms; to improve roads; to create experimental centres for new agricultural products, production techniques and management methods. This proposal differs from the others in that aid from FEOGA would be in the form of capital grants and would equal at most 35 per cent of the investment made, and the Commission would decide whether or not to grant aid for the projects concerned in accordance with various requirements laid down in the Regulation. The whole tenor of this proposal is reminiscent of the method of funding individual projects under Reg. 17/64. It would have a life of five years.

CHAPTER 13

Enlargement of the Community

This chapter is concerned with the implications for the CAP and for the existing Member States of the possible Enlargement of the Community by the accession of Greece, Portugal and Spain during the 1980s. In agricultural terms such an Enlargement would be of considerable significance—far more so than the 1973 Enlargement. It would mean, for instance, an increase of 55 per cent in the number of persons working in agriculture; a 49 per cent expansion of the agricultural area; a rise of 57 per cent in the number of farms; and a 24 per cent increase in total production [36].

But first we ought to ask what countries can apply for membership and what is the procedure for joining? The answers are to be found in Art. 237 of the Rome Treaty[54] which states:

> Any European State may apply to become a member of the Community. It shall address its application to the Council, which shall act unanimously after obtaining the opinion of the Commission.
>
> The conditions of admission and the adjustments to this Treaty necessitated thereby shall be the subject of an agreement between the Member States and the applicant State. This agreement shall be submitted for ratification by all the Contracting States in accordance with their respective constitutional requirements.

These two paragraphs need some elaboration. Firstly, it has become accepted within the European Community that applications for membership will only be considered if they come from countries which operate under a democratic system of government. Secondly, applicants must be capable of meeting the economic and social requirements of membership. This means that membership should not prove to be too great a strain on their economy nor should it be a burden on existing Member States.

As to the conditions for accession: these are thrashed out during negotiations between the applicants and the Community. While special arrangements can be made during a traditional phase to ease new members into the system, applicants must be willing to accept the corpus of legislation already in force in the Community, as this is not negotiable.

Enlargement involves adjustments of many kinds: obviously the new Member State has to adapt its legislation to take account of its new commitments, but also changes must occur within the Community. It will be recalled that in chapter 2 mention was made of the possible increases in size of the European Parliament and the ESC if Greece, Portugal and Spain join; the need to reconsider the question of official languages; and the number of Commissioners from each Member State.

More judges would have to be appointed to the Court of Justice; more board members for the EIB; new staff would need to be integrated into the Commission and other Institutions. Greater thought would need to be given to the vexed question of majority voting in the Council of Ministers.

All these and other technical matters would have to be attended to, as well as considering issues involving Community policies over the whole range of economic and social activities.

At its meeting in December 1978, the European Council took up the suggestion of the French that a small group of eminent and knowledgeable people should be asked to examine the whole question of the organisation and functioning of the various Community Institutions in the light of their current tasks and the prospect of moving towards European Union. The Council emphasised the need for specific proposals 'which may be implemented swiftly and which take into account experience to date and the prospective enlargement to twelve' [1]. The Committee which was set up as a result of this agreement has three members and is known as the 'Committee of Wise Men'. It is to report back to the European Council in October 1979.

In some respects new members become full members from the first day of accession– for instance, in the appointment of Commissioners or judges. In other respects both the existing Community and the new members are given time to adjust through the phasing of changes such as tariff levels or the application of the price and market aspects of the CAP. When the Community was enlarged in 1973 valuable experience was gained in coping with the difficulties which can emerge in such an exercise. Hopefully, as a result, any further Enlargement during the 1980s will proceed more smoothly.

The first enlargement came about as a result of the negotiations which started in mid-1970 between the Community and Denmark, Ireland, Norway and the UK. These resulted in the Treaty of Accession signed in January 1972. The following September the Norwegians withdrew from the Treaty as a result of the negative vote recorded in a national referendum on accession. Thus on 1 January 1973 only three new Member States joined. In 1975 Greece applied for membership and she was followed in 1977 by applications from Portugal and Spain. Negotiations with Greece began in 1976 and were completed early in 1979. Negotiations with Portugal began late in 1978 and those with Spain in 1979.

Economic characteristics of the applicants

Discussion on the possibility of adding these three countries is characterised by a far greater amount of public analysis than was the 1973 Enlargement. In many respects the problems involved are more serious and, in addition, it should not be forgotten that if the present negotiations are successful the Community will, as a result, contain double the original number of Member States. The absorption of three new Member States in 1973 revealed certain shortcomings in the structure of the Community and further Enlargement could strain the framework even more.

The Commission has issued a number of documents on various aspects of the proposed Enlargement to the South. The first was its opinion on the Greek application for membership [21] issued in 1976. This was followed in 1978 by a spate of documents starting with a general paper on the Commission's view of Enlargement (often referred to as the Fresco) [30]. Two further papers took up issues raised in the Fresco in more detail: one concentrated on the institutional problems [35], the other analysed in considerable detail the economic and sectoral issues involved [36]. Finally, there were the Commission's opinion on the Portuguese application [31] and its opinion on the Spanish application [40].

The clear message from all this activity is that, while Enlargement may be desirable from many points of view, it does entail considerable difficulties. While the three applicant countries have many features which distinguish them one from another and, so far as agriculture is concerned, some of these are outlined below, nevertheless they also have certain attributes in common which must be recognised. These common features complicate rather than simplify future Enlargement. In its analysis of the economic and sectoral issues [36] the Commission summarises these attributes as follows:

1. A level of general economic development which is well below the Community average: for instance, in 1975 while GDP per head in the Community ranged from US $ 3945 in France to US $ 2512 in Ireland—the level in all three applicants is below the Irish figure, the Portuguese figure being only 60 per cent of that in Ireland [37].

2. The applicants suffer from large-scale and growing regional disequilibria, population and economic activity being concentrated in a few regions and stagnation or depopulation characterising large areas of their territories.

3. Broadly similar structures which makes them competitors in a number of problem industries already causing concern in the Community.

4. Very marked orientation of international trade towards the Community, both in terms of imports and exports.

5. They have all experienced high levels of investment since the mid-1960s, but there has been a tendency to less buoyant investment in recent years and they have considerable problems of under-employment.

6. They have in the past provided very large numbers of workers for the existing Community.

7. They share the lack of a good infrastructure and public expenditure represents a low proportion of GDP.

8. Food purchases still remain a very large item in domestic expenditure.

9. They are all Mediterranean countries producing much the same range of agricultural commodities, and ones which are in competition with products from the existing Community.

This last point might not matter very much except that the

Community is experiencing production and marketing difficulties with many of these commodities. The addition of three new Member States will only add to the problems already faced unless the existing Community can adjust its own Mediterranean production pattern between now and the mid-to-late 1980s when, if negotiations are successful, the three new Members could be expected to be fully integrated into the Community.

The problems of the Mediterranean regions

Before outlining the characteristics of the agriculture of the three applicants, it would be as well to consider the difficulties faced by the Community's existing Mediterranean regions. Interest in this area has intensified in the Institutions of the Community in recent years: for instance, in 1977 the Commission issued two reports on Mediterranean problems [26 and 27]. These were followed by a series of proposals for measures to help alleviate the shortcomings of the farming sector. As we have seen in chapters 11 and 12 these proposals were accepted (with modifications) and became Community law in 1978 and early in 1979.

Agriculture in the Mediterranean regions is depressed: an above average proportion of the population is still engaged in this sector and productivity is low. This can be seen from the fact that 30 per cent of the Community's agricultural workforce is situated there–but only 18 per cent of the final agricultural output comes from the area. The agricultural sector suffers from hidden underemployment, little change is taking place in the structure of production, and marketing and processing facilities are poor.

If agriculture were the only problem sector in the Mediterranean region, one could suggest that people should move off the land into other occupations, but employment opportunities are limited and many of the manufacturing industries are also depressed. Growth is slow: for instance, the per capita GNP in the Community as a whole is two-and-a-half times higher than that in the Mezzogiorno. Economic activity in the Mediterranean area is characterised by a concentration on sectors with low or declining levels of productivity. The situation is not helped by the large numbers of young people coming onto the labour market for whom there are not enough jobs, and migration to other parts of

Italy or abroad offers far fewer possibilities than some years ago.

If, then, the non-farm sectors can offer only limited assistance in solving some of the problems which afflict agriculture, solutions must be found wherever possible within the agricultural sector itself. But whatever steps are taken, it is important that they do not run counter to the attempts being made to reduce structural surpluses, nor should they entail increases in protection, as this would run counter to the Community's external policies and be contrary to the interests of Community consumers.

The difficulties of the farming sector are compounded by the nature of the price and market regimes for a large proportion of the commodities produced in the Mediterranean region. It will be remembered that in chapter 7 the regimes were divided according to the degree of support which they afford to the various products. The market organisations for durum wheat, rice, olive oil and tobacco are fairly effective in terms of support, but the regimes for commodities such as wine, citrus, dessert grapes, pears, peaches and tomatoes are much more modest. For the remaining fruit and vegetables, fresh and processed, the only support available is the CCT set against third countries at a fairly low level. These last two groups of commodities, for which only medium to light regimes exist, account for well over half the total end-product of Mediterranean farming.

Because the price and market regimes offer so little assistance, the recent Community approach to the Mediterranean problem has been very largely concentrated on structural improvements. As we saw in chapters 11 and 12 the measures adopted have been mostly concerned with aids to improve processing and marketing, irrigation, forestry, with a lowering of the dependence on wine and encouragement to switch to other crops. The Community is also anxious to see greater use being made of existing measures such as the modernisation and retirement Directives (72/159 and 72/160) and Reg. 355/77 on aids to processing. It is also hoped that the Regional and Social Funds can assist in the general improvement of the Mediterranean region.

It is too early to know to what extent Community efforts in the various structural fields are likely to be successful but time is short–at most ten years which in terms of structural change is very little indeed. If the Community does not succeed in setting its own house in order before Enlargement, it could well face acute difficulties in absorbing three new Member States.

Agriculture in the applicant countries

Table 11 shows the composition of final agricultural production in the present Community and in the three applicants. It indicates quite well the differences which exist. Livestock products are very much more important in the Nine than in the Three: Italy for obvious reasons comes closest to the applicants' position. With regard to crops, the importance of fruit and vegetables in Portugal and Spain is particularly notable. The size of the 'other crop' category in Greece is largely caused by the importance of tobacco and cotton.

Greece: according to OECD [62], 'The most serious problem of Greek agriculture is structural: firstly, the small size of farms, aggravated by considerable fragmentation, and at national level, the wide disparities between one region and another.' Greece suffers not only from a poor agricultural structure, but also from difficult farming conditions. The irregularity of rainfall leads to soil erosion and the need for irrigation. Only 30 per cent of the total agricultural area is cultivated, and 40 per cent of the agricultural area is situated in mountainous and hilly regions where the possibilities for improvement are limited.

Despite this, agriculture remains an important sector employing (in 1975) some 35 per cent of the labour force and producing 15 per cent of the GDP (in constant 1970 prices). Agricultural produce accounts for a third of total exports. Greece is a net exporter of farm commodities, exports covering 125 per cent of imports. Fruit and vegetables are extremely important, accounting for 30 per cent of the cultivated area and 58 per cent of agricultural exports. Raw tobacco is the second most important agricultural export, accounting for 21 per cent. Other major crops are wine, raisins and olive oil. The main agricultural import is maize, which accounts for 26 per cent of total agricultural imports. This is followed by live animals and meat (15 per cent), sugar (12 per cent), milk products (11 per cent), and vegetable proteins (8 per cent).

Although Greek farming is subject to some major difficulties, and although certain commodities–particularly some of the fruits and vegetables–could cause problems on the Community markets, Greece

TABLE 11
Composition of final agricultural output, 1975
(%)

	FR Germany	France	Italy	Nether-lands	Belgium	Luxem-bourg	UK	Ireland	Denmark	The '9'	Spain	Greece(a)	Portugal
Crop production	**29.6**	**43.6**	**60.0**	**33.3**	**31.6**	**20.4**	**35.4**	**15.7**	**23.9**	**40.3**	**58.8**	**68.5**	**65.1**
Cereals	7.8	15.1	12.0	2.1	4.0	3.9	12.2	6.4	13.0	10.8	10.6	13.3	12.2
Fresh veg.	2.0	6.8	12.7	8.9	11.1	1.6	7.4	3.1	2.0	7.1	13.9	7.7	9.7
Fruit	4.0	3.4	6.9	2.0	3.3	3.0	2.0	0.4	0.8	3.8	11.7	6.3	12.3
Wine	3.0	8.3	8.2	—	—	9.0	0.0	—	—	4.6	4.9	6.1	10.5
Olive oil	—	0.0	6.6	—	—	—	—	—	—	1.4	4.3	8.3	5.6
Other	12.8	10.0	10.7	20.3	13.2	2.9	13.8	5.8	8.1	8.0	10.2	25.0	14.8
Livestock products	**70.1**	**54.9**	**39.5**	**66.7**	**62.8**	**80.6**	**64.6**	**84.3**	**76.1**	**58.9**	**41.2**	**30.9**	**34.9**
Meat	41.7	35.4	25.9	36.5	43.2	38.7	35.9	53.0	48.7	34.9	27.0	18.2	23.4
Milk	22.9	16.9	10.0	26.8	15.6	37.2	22.1	27.9	25.9	18.7	9.6	8.5	8.4
Eggs	5.3	2.5	3.5	2.8	4.0	4.2	6.0	1.9	1.4	3.8	4.3	2.7	2.7
Other	0.2	0.1	0.1	0.6	—	0.5	0.6	1.5	0.1	1.5	0.3	1.5	0.4
Total	100	100	100	100	100	100	100	100	100	100	100	100	100

(a) 1976. *Source:* [37]

is nevertheless a small country and a small agricultural producer and so, by itself, it could be absorbed without too much dislocation. However, everyone involved in the negotiations with Greece was acutely aware that behind it stood Portugal and Spain—countries with similar commodities to sell and similar structural shortcomings to be surmounted.

The negotiations with Greece were virtually completed in December 1978, the agricultural package being one of the last items on which agreement was reached. According to *Agence Europe* [2], the main elements of this package are that there will be a five-year transition period, except for fresh and processed tomatoes, and fresh and canned peaches for which the transition period will be seven years. Transition compensatory amounts will be applied to certain Greek exports to the Community so long as Greek prices are not harmonised with those of the Community. This procedure (which was also used during the earlier Enlargement of the Community) is to prevent Greek exports undercutting produce from other Community countries. The Community has agreed to include cotton under the CAP with the possibility of production aids both to fibre and seed output. The Community also agreed to consider production aids for dried figs and grapes. The production quota for sugar will be set at around the quantities produced during a recent period.

If the planned timetable is adhered to, the Act of Accession with Greece will be signed in the summer of 1979. The parliamentary ratification of the Treaty by the Member States and by Greece should be completed within the following eighteen months, which would mean that Greece would be a member of the Community by the beginning of 1981.

Portugal: Agriculture in Portugal still employed 28 per cent of the working population in 1975 and produced 12 per cent of the GDP (at constant 1970 prices). The country is a net importer of agricultural products—exports in 1973–75 covered only 45 per cent of imports. As table 12 shows self-sufficiency levels are low for many commodities notably cereals, rice, beef and butter. They are high for potatoes, fruit and vegetables and wine. Portugal's main agricultural exports are wine, preserved fish, tomato concentrate, fruit and vegetables.

Portuguese agriculture suffers from many structural defects: on

TABLE 12
Percentage levels of self-sufficiency for the main agricultural products:
The Three Applicants 1973–75

	Greece[(a)]	Portugal	Spain
Vegetable products			
wheat		68	96
rye		85	101
barley		87	96
oats		100	100
maize		34	34
rice (husked)		69	83
sugar (white)		n.a.	70
potatoes		95	113
vegetables (dried)		88	88
vegetables (fresh)		149	n.a.
fruit (stoned)		143	153
citrus		n.a.	245
other fresh fruit		97	105
dried fruit		122	122
table olives		112	188
olive oil		102	138
other oils		87	47
wine		123	81
Animal products			
all meats	86	92	97
beef	69	78	93
pork	99	94	96
mutton and goat	85	104	99
poultry	98	100	100
eggs	100	100	101
whole milk	100	91	97
butter	87	22	85
cheese	98	92	96
fish (fresh or frozen)	n.a.	92	98

(a) No self-sufficiency figures for vegetable products are available.
n.a. Not available.

Source: [37]

average, farms are small and fragmented, yields of crops are low, and incomes are low. Natural conditions are unfavourable: many parts of the country suffer from a shortage of rainfall and poor soil quality. According to OECD [63], the present cultivated area is too large in relation to soil potential and sooner or later a considerable area should be converted to forests or other uses. Portugal is already a significant producer of cork, timber, and pulp for papermaking, and since the early 1970s eucalyptus plantations have been introduced for the production of cellulose.

Portugal has a fairly sizeable fishing fleet but structural problems abound here also. Many of the boats are small and old, and fishermen are underemployed. As with agriculture, the absence of job opportunities in other sectors makes it very difficult to solve the structural problems of the sector.

Because Portugal, like Greece, is a small country and a small agricultural exporter, the Community could absorb it without too much dislocation in agriculture if Enlargement applied to it alone. However, small though Portuguese output is, it must be added to that of the other applicants and to the output of the Community's existing Mediterranean region. It is this combination which makes for difficulties. However, any problems which the Community has in accommodating Portuguese agriculture are minimal in comparison with the problems which membership will create for Portugal. The freeing of trade with the rest of the Community (particularly if Spain is also a Member) could easily exacerbate the current trade imbalance in agricultural products. It is very likely that a longer than usual transition period will have to be negotiated in order to give Portugal more time to adjust to the new trading circumstances.

Spain: Agriculture accounted for 22 per cent of the Spanish workforce in 1975 and produced 10 per cent of the GDP (at constant 1970 prices). Although Spain is a net importer of agricultural products (exports covering 73 per cent of imports in 1973–1975), self-sufficiency levels are high for most commodities as table 12 confirms. The only major products for which the levels fall below 90 per cent are maize, rice, sugar, dried vegetables, oils other than olive oil, wine and butter. For some commodities Spain has considerable exportable surpluses: for instance, stoned fruit, citrus, table olives, dried fruit and olive oil. The apparent deficit for wine in table 12 is misleading. Spain is the world's largest single producer and it certainly has an exportable surplus of *vin ordinaire*–regarded by many as being of better quality than the similar grades in Italy and France. It is precisely this type of wine which is in surplus in these countries and for which the Community has introduced its restructuring measures.

Like Greece and Portugal, Spain suffers from many natural disadvantages in terms of soil and climate. Much of the country is mountainous, irrigation is essential over wide areas and the quality of many soils is low. Added to this are the problems associated with a poor farm structure: many very small farms with a high degree of fragmentation, side-by-side with very large, extensively operated estates. Medium-sized, full-time family farms are a minority.

The Spanish fishing fleet is the third largest in the world and because of its size (together with the much smaller fleets of Greece and Portugal), Enlargement would double the size of the existing Community fleet. Although some of its boats are small, it has a core of large, modern vessels which make it very competitive. Spain has traditional interests in many parts of the existing Community's waters, and Enlargement would lead to an intensification of its activities in these waters.

From the Community's point of view, the inclusion of Spain poses serious problems for the farming sector. Although it is doubtful if its agriculture has the same potential as that of France, its sheer size cannot be ignored: the area of France is 547 thousand km^2–by far the largest country in the Community. Spain's area is almost as great: 505 thousand km^2. Probably the greatest single fear is that entry to the Community will result in a substantial production response on the part of Spanish farmers faced with higher end prices. At the moment, many Spanish prices are only 60–70 per cent of the relevant Community price. However, there is reason to believe that the dynamic impact of membership which such a gap suggests may be less than might be expected at first glance.

Firstly, certain input costs in Spanish agriculture will increase. For one, wage rates in farming are already rising and there is no reason to believe this trend will slow down. Spanish agriculture is very heavily dependent on hired labour (about one-third of the labour force is hired). Thus it is vulnerable to increases in labour costs. Another input which is bound to rise in price is feedingstuffs for the livestock sector. Currently Spain imports considerable quantities of US maize at low prices. Whether it continues to import US maize after entry or whether it switches to Community sources for some of its requirements is immaterial: in either event the costs will rise.

Secondly, while Spain has large exports of certain commodities and the potential for even more, one cannot overlook the fact that it is geographically remote from its main European markets. Its markets in the Mediterranean area are limited by production of a similar range of commodities in neighbouring countries and, even more important, the main population centres of the Community are in the highly industrialised regions of Germany, Benelux, northern France and southern Britain. Spanish produce has to travel considerable distances to reach these centres. Transport costs both by rail and road are high and marketing methods need improvement.

Thirdly, Spanish agriculture is extremely heterogeneous; some producers are dynamic and well informed about market conditions and they could certainly reap a rich benefit from Enlargement. Other producers are not so well placed: they face severe structural problems—small-scale enterprises, low levels of mechanisation and technical difficulties to increased mechanisation, high dependence on manual labour. For such farmers, the benefits of Enlargement are much more problematical. Many aspects of Spanish agriculture require considerable injections of capital, not all of which can be provided from within the sector.

Finally, some consideration must be given to the rising importance of the North African Mediterranean countries as competitors in all the traditional Mediterranean-type products. The Community has striven in recent years to develop a coherent and uniform policy towards the Mediterranean area and, as part of this policy, has negotiated trade agreements with North African and Middle Eastern countries. These are an encouragement to these countries to try to increase their foothold in Community markets. Their production costs—in particular in relation to labour—are lower than those in the applicant countries and also in the current Member States. Consequently, they will hardly be pleased at the implications of Enlargement, when they see competitors currently outside the Community benefiting from membership. It is surely very likely that the North African countries will press for renegotiation of their agreements with the Community to compensate them in part at least for the change in their circumstances.

Note to Chapter 13

54. Similar sentiments are expressed in the Treaty of Paris (ECSC) and Treaty of Rome (Euratom).

References

References are denoted by numerals in square brackets.
1. Agence Europe (1978), Thursday 7 December, p. 6.
2. Agence Europe (1978), Friday 22 December, p. 3.
3. Andrews, S. (1973), *Agriculture and the Common Market*, xiii + 183 pp. Ames: Iowa State University Press.
4. Brown, L. N. and Jacobs, F. G. (1977), *The Court of Justice of the European Communities*, xxiv + 254 pp. London: Sweet & Maxwell.
5. Camps, M. (1964), *Britain and the European Community 1955–1963*, x + 547 pp. Princeton: Princeton University Press.
6. Camps, M. (1967), *European Unification in the Sixties: from the veto to the crisis*, xii + 273 pp. London: OUP.
7. Comité Intergouvernemental créé par la Conférence de Messine (1956), *Rapport des chefs de délégation aux ministres des affaires étrangères*, 135 pp. Bruxelles: Secretariat du Comité.
8. Commission de la Communauté Economique Européenne (1962), *Recueil des travaux de la conférence consultative sur les aspects sociaux de la politique agricole commune*, Rome, du 29 septembre au 4 octobre 1961, 103 pp. Bruxelles (?): Services des Publications des Communautés Européennes.
9. Commission de la Communauté Economique Européenne (1967), *Programmes Communautaires pour la Section Orientation de Fonds Européen d'Orientation et de Garantie Agricole*, COM(67)194 final, various pageing, Bruxelles: La Commission.
10. Commission des Communautés Européennes (1968), *Memorandum sur la reform de l'agriculture dans la Communauté Economique Européenne*, COM(68)1000, Partie A et B, Bruxelles: La Commission.
11. Commission Européenne (1973), *Repertoire des organismes communs créés dans le cadre des Communautés européennes par les Associations industrielles, artisanales, commerciales et des*

services des six pays; associations des professions libérales; organisations syndicales de salariés et Groupements de Consommateurs, 4th ed. various pageing, Brussels: Service des publications des Communautés Européennes.

12. Commission of the EEC (1960), *Proposals for the working-out and putting into effect of the common agricultural policy in application of Article 43 of the Treaty, establishing the European Economic Community*, VI/COM(60)105, various pageing, Brussels: The Commission.

13. Commission of the European Communities (1973), *Improvement of the Common Agricultural Policy*, COM(73)1850 final, 37 pp. Brussels: The Commission.

14. Commission of the European Communities (1974), *Commission proposal to the Council on the fixing of prices for certain agricultural products and connected measures*, COM(74)2001 final, 187 pp. Brussels: The Commission.

15. Commission of the European Communities (1975), *Revised proposal for a Council Directive concerning forestry measures*, COM(75)88 final, ii + 15 pp. and annex, Brussels: The Commission.

16. Commission of the European Communities (1975), *Stocktaking of the Common Agricultural Policy*, COM(75)100, 58 pp. Brussels: The Commission.

17. Commission of the European Communities (1976), *Report on the application of the Council Directives on agricultural reform of 17 April 1972*, COM(76)87 final, various pageing, Brussels: The Commission.

18. Commission of the European Communities (1976), *Amended proposal for Council Regulation on the common organisation of the market in ethyl alcohol of agricultural origin and laying down additional provisions for certain products containing ethyl alcohol*, COM(76)274 final, 5 + 37 pp. + annexes, Brussels: The Commission.

19. Commission for the European Communities (1976), *Communication on longer-term measures in the field of Monetary Compensatory Amounts*, COM(76)600, Brussels: The Commission.

20. Commission of the European Communities (1976), *European Union: report by Mr Leo Tindemans to the European Council*, 36 pp. Bulletin of the European Communities, supplement 1/76, Luxembourg: Office for Official Publications of the European Communities.

21. Commission of the European Communities (1976), *Opinion on Greek application for membership*, Bulletin of the European Communities, Supplement 2/76, 42 pp. Luxembourg: Office for Official Publications of the European Communities.

22. Commission of the European Communities (1977), *Directory of non-governmental agricultural organisations set up at Community level*, 464 pp. Munich: Verlag Dokumentation.

23. Commission of the European Communities (1977), *Mediterranean Agricultural Problems*, COM(77)140 final, 8 pp. + annexes, Brussels: The Commission.

24. Commission of the European Communities (1977), *Report on the use of European Unit of Account in the Common Agricultural Policy*, COM(77)480 final, 13 pp. Brussels: The Commission.

25. Commission of the European Communities (1977), *Proposal for a Council Regulation relating to the fixing of representative conversion rates in agriculture*, COM(77)482, Brussels: The Commission.

26. Commission of the European Communities (1977), *Guidelines concerning the development of the Mediterranean regions of the Community, together with certain measures relating to agriculture*, COM(77)526 final, Vol I, 32 pp. Brussels: The Commission.

27. Commission of the European Communities (1977), *Guidelines concerning the development of the Mediterranean regions of the Community, together with certain measures relating to agriculture*, COM(77)526 final, Vol II, various pageing, Brussels: The Commission.

28. Commission of the European Communities (1977), *Proposal for a Council Directive amending Council Directive 72/159/EEC . . . on the modernisation of farms; Proposal for a Council Directive amending Council Directive 75/268/EEC . . . on mountain and hill farming and farming in certain less favoured areas; Proposal for a*

Council Directive amending Council Directive 72/160/EEC ...
concerning measures to encourage the cessation of farming ... ;
*Proposal for a Council Directive on the programme to accelerate
drainage operations in the less favoured areas of the West of
Ireland,* COM(77)550 final, various pageing, Brussels: The
Commission.

29. Commission of the European Communities (1977), *Second report
on the application of the Council Directives on agricultural reform
of 17 April 1972,* Part I, attached to COM(77)550,
51 pp. + appendices, Brussels: The Commission.

30. Commission of the European Communities (1978), *General
considerations on the problems of enlargement,* Bulletin of the
European Communities, Supplement 1/78, 17 pp. Luxembourg:
Office for Official Publications of the European Communities.

31. Commission of the European Communities (1978), *Opinion on
Portuguese application for membership,* Bulletin of the European
Communities, Supplement 5/78, 50 pp. Luxembourg: Office for
Official Publications of the European Communities.

32. Commissions of the European Communities (1978), *Economic
effects of the agri-monetary system,* COM(78)20 final, 19 pp.
+ annexes, Brussels: The Commission.

33. Commission of the European Communities (1978), *Global
appraisal of the budgetary problems of the Community,*
COM(78)64 final, ix + 25 pp. Brussels: The Commission.

34. Commission of the European Communities (1978), *Proposal for a
Council Regulation on the common organisation of the market in
sheepmeat,* COM(78)81 final, 42 pp. + annexes, Brussels: The
Commission.

35. Commission of the European Communities (1978), *The transitional period and the institutional implications of enlargement,* COM(78)190 final, 22 pp. Brussels: The Commission.

36. Commission of the European Communities (1978), *Economic and
sectoral aspects: Commission analyses supplementing its views
on Enlargement,* COM(78)200 final, 231 pp. Brussels: The
Commission.

37. Commission of the European Communities (1978), *Economic and
sectoral aspects: Statistical annexes relating to the general*

economic problems involved in Enlargement, COM(78)200 final, annexes, not numbered, Brussels: The Commission.

38. Commission of the European Communities (1978), *Proposal for Council Regulation (EEC) Amending Regulation (EEC) No. 729/70 concerning the amount allotted to the EAGGF, Guidance Section*, COM(78)473 final, Brussels: The Commission.

39. Commission of the European Communities (1978), *Seventh financial report on the European Agricultural Guidance and Guarantee Fund, 1977*, COM(78)594 final, iii + 46 pp. and annexes, Brussels: The Commission.

40. Commission of the European Communities (1978), *Opinion on Spanish application for membership*, COM(78)630 final and annex, 70 pp. + not numbered, Brussels: The Commission.

41. Council of the European Communities (1978), *Proposal for a Council Regulation on the common organisation of the market in potatoes*, S/1037/78(CSA 192), 38 pp. Brussels: The Council.

42. Commission of the European Communities (1979), *Commission proposals on the fixing of prices for certain agricultural products and on certain related measures*, COM(79)10 final, Volumes I and IV, 61 + 118 pp. Brussels: The Commission.

43. Commission of the European Communities (1979), *Proposal for Council Regulation on the progressive dismantling of monetary compensatory amounts and differèntial amounts applicable to certain agricultural products and processed products*, COM(79)10 final, Volume III, various pageing, Brussels: The Commission.

43a. Commission of the European Communities (1979), *Proposals on policy with regard to agricultural structures*, COM(79)122 final, various pageing, Brussels: The Commission.

44. Communautés Européennes (1959), *Recueil des documents de la conférence agricole des États membres de la CEE à Stresa du 3 au 12 juillet 1958*, 250 pp. Bruxelles (?): Service des publications des Communautés Européennes.

45. Coppock, J. O. (1963), *North Atlantic Policy–the agricultural gap*, xv + 270 pp. New York: Twentieth Century Fund.

46. ECE/FAO (1954), *European Agriculture: a Statement of problems*, vi + 83 pp. Geneva: ECE/FAO.

47. Economic and Social Committee (1977), *The right of initiative*

of the Economic and Social Committee, 123 pp. Brussels: ESC General Secretariat.

48. Eurostat (1975), *Yearbook of agricultural statistics,* xxxii + 247 pp. Luxembourg: Office for Official Publications of the European Communities.

49. Eurostat (1977), *National Accounts ESA,* 1970–1976, xxv + 431 pp. Luxembourg: Office for Official Publications of the European Communities.

50. Fearn, H. A. (1978), *The evolution and basic concepts of the green currency system,* Government Economic Service Working Paper No. 12, 10 pp. London: MAFF.

51. Harris, S. and Swinbank A. (1978), Price fixing under the CAP–proposition and decision, *Food Policy,* 3, 256–271.

52. HMSO (1972), *Treaty concerning the Accession of the Kingdom of Denmark, Ireland, the Kingdom of Norway and the United Kingdom of Great Britain and Northern Ireland to the European Economic Community and the European Atomic Energy Community,* Cmnd. 4862–1, vi + 144 pp. London: HMSO.

53. House of Commons Select Committee on European Legislation etc. (1978), *Common organisation of the market in sheepmeat,* Session 1977–78, 36th report, xii + 75 pp. London: HMSO.

54. House of Lords Select Committee on the European Communities (1977), *Green Money,* Session 1976–77, 18th report, xv + 46 pp. London: HMSO.

55. House of Lords Select Committee on the European Communities (1978), *Mutton and Lamb,* Session 1977–78, 36th report, xii + 58 pp. London: HMSO.

56. House of Lords Select Committee on the European Communities (1978), *Relations between the United Kingdom Parliament and the European Parliament after direct elections,* Vol I–Report, Session 1977–78, 44th report, 31 pp. London: HMSO.

57. Intervention Board for Agricultural Produce (1978), *Report for the Calendar Year 1977,* 54 pp. London: HMSO.

58. Irving, R. W. and Fearn, H. A. (1975), *Green Money and the Common Agricultural Policy,* Occasional Paper No. 2, 66 pp. Ashford: Centre for European Agricultural Studies.

59. Kapteyn, P. J. G. and Verloren van Themaat, P. (1973),

Introduction to the law of the European Communities, xx + 433 pp. London: Sweet & Maxwell.

60. Mansholt, S. (1962), On the threshold of a common agricultural policy, *Bulletin of the European Economic Community*, 3, 5–7.

61. Noël, E. (1973), The Commission's power of initiative, *Common Market Law Review*, 10, 123–136.

62. OECD (1973), *Agricultural Policy in Greece*, 53 pp. Paris: Organisation for Economic Co-operation and Development.

63. OECD (1975), *Agricultural Policy in Portugal*, 44 pp. Paris: Organisation for Economic Co-operation and Development.

64. Secretariat-General Council of the European Communities (1975), *ACP–EEC Convention of Lomé*, 357 pp. Luxembourg: Office for Official Publications of the European Communities.

65. Statistical Office of the European Communities (1961), *Basic Statistics for Fifteen European Countries*, 133 pp. Brussels: SOEC.

66. Swann, Dennis (1978), *The economics of the Common Market*, 4th ed., 332 pp. Harmondsworth: Penguin Books.

67. Sweet & Maxwell (1977), *European Community Treaties*, 3rd ed., xii + 355 pp. London: Sweet and Maxwell.

Index

The Author

Dr Rosemary Fennell is a lecturer at Oxford University, in the Institute of Agricultural Economics, and is a Fellow of Linacre College. After attending university in Ireland and the United States she was engaged in research into rural problems in Ireland for a number of years before moving to Britain where she joined the staff of the Ministry of Agriculture and worked on the UK entry negotiations to join the European Community. She subsequently moved to London University where she received her doctorate and was Research Fellow on European Agricultural Economics at Wye College prior to her present post. Dr Fennell has written many research papers and journal articles and has also written *The Common Agricultural Policy: A Synthesis of Opinion* which has been widely praised for the attractiveness and lucidity of style and presentation.

She first became acutely aware of the need for her new book in lecturing to students on various aspects of the CAP and giving talks to farmers' groups.